DEMOCRACY UNDER SIEGE

Recent Titles in
Contributions in Military Studies

DEMOCRACY UNDER SIEGE

New Military Power
in Latin America

Edited by
AUGUSTO VARAS

SPONSORED BY
THE JOINT COMMITTEE ON LATIN AMERICAN STUDIES
OF THE SOCIAL SCIENCE RESEARCH COUNCIL
AND THE
AMERICAN COUNCIL OF LEARNED SOCIETIES

Contributions in Military Studies, Number 84

GREENWOOD PRESS
New York • Westport, Connecticut • London

Library of Congress Cataloging-in-Publication Data

Democracy under siege : new military power in Latin America / edited by
  Augusto Varas ; sponsored by the Joint Committee on Latin American
  Studies of the Social Science Research Council and the American
  Council of Learned Societies.
      p.   cm. — (Contributions in military studies, ISSN 0883–6884
  ; no. 84)
  Bibliography: p.
  Includes index.
  ISBN 0–313–26034–6 (lib. bdg. : alk. paper)
      1. Latin America—Politics and government—1948–   2. Latin
  America—Armed Forces—Political activity—History—20th century.
  3. Civil-military relations—Latin America—History—20th century.
  4. Latin America—Armed Forces—History—20th century   I. Varas,
  Augusto.   II. Joint Committee on Latin American Studies.
  III. Series.
  F1414.2.C44   1989
  322′.5′098—dc19   88–25105

British Library Cataloguing in Publication Data is available.

Library of Congress Catalog Card Number: 88–25105
ISBN: 0–313–26034–6
ISSN: 0883–6884

First published in 1989

Greenwood Press, Inc.
88 Post Road West, Westport, Connecticut 06881

Printed in the United States of America

∞

The paper used in this book complies with the
Permanent Paper Standard issued by the National
Information Standards Organization (Z39.48–1984).

10   9   8   7   6   5   4   3   2   1

Ameerll

CONTENTS

PREFACE

Although the military has had an important political role in Latin American societies, few scholars have dedicated much effort to the study of this phenomenon. Little attention has been given to the complex set of civilian–military relations in each country. Few studies have focused on the specific ways in which military institutions become intertwined with the rest of the state apparatus, the economy, and society.

Almost all of the major studies to date on national armed forces in Latin America have been by foreign scholars, and usually they have been concerned with processes related to the institutional intrusion of the armed forces into local politics. Studies undertaken during periods of stability, focusing on the development of a wide and divided network of ideological, political, and economic linkages among the armed forces and the rest of society, are uncommon.

As a result, a group of Latin American scholars started a long-term research program comparing current linkages among the armed forces and local social and political structures and institutions. The individual studies within each nation all point to the increasing process of military autonomy vis-à-vis the state and society. The research shows that this very same institutional autonomy has allowed the military to develop as independent political actors within the different countries. This process seems to be common to all Latin American societies, although there are differences in intensity according to different local conditions. The research has demonstrated how the military diversify themselves when acquiring higher degrees of institutional autonomy.

The importance of this topic has been underscored by the increasing contradictions observed between the military and the democratic Latin American governments. Therefore, a group of scholars created a regional network—the Latin American Center for Defense and Disarmament (CLADDE)—to disseminate information, conduct research, and organize training programs for researchers. This volume stems from the first international seminar on civilian–military relations and democracy.

This first endogenous effort to produce fresh knowledge on military autonomy and democracy in Latin America was made possible through the support and advice of the Joint Committee on Latin American Studies of the Social Science Research Council and the American Council of Learned Societies with funds provided by the Andrew W. Mellon Foundation. Joan Dassin, the staff to this committee, offered friendly and wise guidance that was particularly helpful, and the committee provided additional financial support for the translation of the Spanish manuscript into English. The Berghof Stiftung and the International Social Science Council (ISSC) cofinanced the international seminar ''Military Autonomization and Democracy: Dynamics of Militarization and the Arms Race in Latin America'' in Santiago, Chile, in May 1985. The intellectual understanding of the importance of these issues exhibited by Dieter Senghaas of the Berghof and Luis Ramallo and Evelyne Blamont of the ISSC was decisive in this research project.

I would also like to thank the Latin American Faculty of Social Sciences (FLACSO) for institutional support which was crucial to this seminar. Significant international support was provided by the Chilean Peace Research Association (ACHIP), the Latin American Council of Social Sciences (CLACSO), the Institute for Ibero-American Cooperation (ICI) in Madrid, the Center for Research on Latin America and the Third World (CETRAL) in Paris, the Latin American Advanced Studies Institute at the University of Paris (VIII), and the Research Committee on Armed Forces and Conflict Resolution of the International Sociological Association (ISA).

Finally, but not least, the translation of the Spanish manuscript into English was done by Eduardo Silva, to whom I would like to express my personal gratitude.

On behalf of all my fellow colleagues, my sincere thanks to all of the institutions and scholars who made this academic effort possible.

DEMOCRACY UNDER SIEGE

1 MILITARY AUTONOMY AND DEMOCRACY IN LATIN AMERICA

Augusto Varas

In the 1980s, most Latin American authoritarian regimes experienced sustained political liberalization and democratization. Differences in form, nature, and speed notwithstanding, these processes recreated a regional political framework in which civilian participation in decision making once again dominates politics. No matter what else the future may hold, it seems clear that civilian democratic forces will play a much larger role in the coming decade than in the last. It is equally evident that in Latin America the armed forces, which were directly responsible for the destruction of some democratic regimes in the 1970s, will retain a considerable share of political power. Even with the advance of democratization, they will most likely not content themselves with the roles they played before becoming so deeply involved in politics.[1]

Politics will most likely become more democratic in a number of nations that experimented with a variety of military-sponsored socioeconomic models, such as Brazil's industrializing (1964), Peru's national-populism (1968), and the authoritarian coups d'etat in Chile and Uruguay (1973) and Argentina (1976). The military establishments of these nations, however, did not content themselves with a return to the status quo ante. On the contrary, instead of immersing themselves in purely professional matters, these armed forces retained significant political influence in the newly installed democratic regimes. Regardless of the constitutional arrangement, they continue with a high level of institutional prerogatives to exercise some kind of power over civilian political forces.[2]

This represents a new form of military intervention in Latin American politics. From the strongman on horseback of the 1920s–1950s, to the industrializing coups of the 1960s, to the labor-repressive institutional coups of the 1970s, the armed forces have steadily increased their relative independence from civilian political forces. Today, the Latin American military establishments have emerged as permanent and stable political actors within democratic regimes, wielding substantial negative power over many of the most important national political decisions.[3]

The level of institutional autonomy acquired by military establishments throughout the region will shape the politics of democratic transitions and consolidation. In other words, an independent military has emerged as a new variable that must be taken into account in analyses of Latin America's secular political crisis. In the past, whenever the state faced a crisis of hegemony, the military came to the aid of landowners, industrialists or the business community. In some cases they intervened to increase the space for political participation. In the future the armed forces will tend to act more independently of social forces. This should lead to the emergence of new state forms. As a result, the consolidation of democratic regimes in Latin America will increasingly depend on the ability of political forces to reestablish civil–military relations within novel institutional arrangements. This change in the armed forces' relationship to society demands further research. We must come to understand recent changes in their doctrine, ideology, and organizational form. Otherwise, the leaders of newly installed democratic regimes run the risk of developing inappropriate strategies for bringing the armed forces under civilian control.[4]

MILITARY AUTONOMY

A number of scholars perceived in their analysis of the Latin American military a potential political role in society. At first, some of them believed that the military was a modernizing force capable of undertaking state and nation-building tasks without succumbing to the temptation to participate in politics. They based this optimistic assessment on the assumption that there was an inherent contradiction between the armed forces' need to maintain their institutional integrity (professionalism) and the business of rule.[5] This perspective led the United States to develop a permanent and privileged relationship with Latin American armed forces. In the eyes of U.S. policy-makers, they embodied such cherished ideals as modernity, political independence, and the ability to maintain political order in the wake of the Cuban revolution.[6]

Military coups d'etat in Brazil (1964) and Peru (1968) shattered this image of the Latin American armed forces.[7] They led scholars to conclude that the military had developed a new professionalism, heavily influenced by U.S. counterinsurgency doctrine. This created those conditions that eventually led to the development of neoconservative economic policies and the rise of authoritarian military regimes in the 1970s.

Other analyses both gained and lost something in their appreciation of the military's role in Latin American politics when they abandoned the view that the military was simply a tool for containing the left and developed the idea that the military wanted to deepen dependent capitalism through the establishment of bureaucratic-authoritarian regimes.[8] Analysts recovered a historical dimension:

Table 1
Indicators of Militarization in Latin America: 1975 and 1985

	1975	1985
Military expenditures (billions, constant $)	4.7	12.9
Military expenditures as a % of GDP	1.6	1.8
Military expenditures as a % of GDP per capita	27	31
Armed forces (millions, men/women under arms)	1,297	1,814
Proportion of armed forces/1,000 inhabitants	4.1	4.5
Arms imports (millions, constant $)	585	1,780
Arms imports as a % of total imports	1.2	2.5
Arms exports as a % of total exports	0.2	0.1

Source: ACDA, World Military Expenditures and Arms Transfers
          (Washington, D.C.: Government Printing Office, 1987
          and 1988).

that Latin American armed forces tended to become increasingly autonomous from the upper classes over time. However, the analysts neglected to investigate the military's political and ideological links to dominant social forces.[9]

The emphasis on the new professionalism or on the emergence of bureaucratic-authoritarian regimes uncovered important dimensions of the military's changing political situation and role in Latin American society. They did not anticipate a new stage in civil–military relations—professional autonomy—that emerged with slow but steady redemocratization in the 1980s.

During the 1980s, the armed forces of Latin America gained greater autonomy from social forces and from the state in the management of their affairs. This has provided the military with new sources of political power which they exercise in both democratic and authoritarian forms of government. Moreover, this trend holds true regardless of the circumstances that led the military to modernize: that is, regardless of whether modernization was forced upon them due to confrontations with praetorian militias (Nicaragua, Guatemala, and El Salvador); whether it was the result of regional tensions (Argentina, Chile, Peru, Ecuador); related to new levels of economic development (Brazil); the product extra-regional arrangements (Cuba); or simply the logical outcome of military governments (Uruguay, Chile, Argentina, Bolivia, Brazil, and Panama). The Latin American armed forces developed their own corporate ideologies and doctrines, expanded their personnel, built arms industries, and started to experiment with nuclear technology. As a result, military expenditures rose sharply (see Table 1). The armed forces that reached this new stage in the 1980s had higher levels of institutionalization and corporateness. Meanwhile, civilian control over them weakened.

The Latin American military's growing autonomy resulted from three main types of factors. First, it arose from the armed forces' growing corporate aware-ness.[10] This process has been heavily influenced by a number of modernizing developments of a purely military nature, such as the import of new professional doctrines and modern warfare technologies. One ideological product of this new stage has been armed forces' national security doctrines providing them with a conceptual framework useful for their political positioning.[11] This "guide sys-tem" defines the armed forces as a crucial institution and locates the military and security in the center of national life.

Secondly, the military's enhanced autonomy has been a product of increased military social segregation from the rest of society. This factor is, in turn, produced by civilian political forces' growing inability to integrate the military into the state and society and to control their institutional development through sound military policies. Considering the organizational trend prevailing in Latin America to keep the military as a relatively closed institution, its values, notions of service, role commitments, appeals, reference groups, types of performance evaluation, bases of compensation, and social interaction separate it from the rest of social life. This set of cultural factors segregates the military (occupation, individuals, and families) from normal social interaction. While useful for the institutional esprit de corp, this has negative effects in domestic politics, creating a sense of political corporate awareness which makes it difficult for other social groups to keep the military under control.[12]

Thirdly, another set of factors related to the process of military segregation from society and the lack of control of the state over military institutions has been the organization of Latin American armed forces and the potential to perform national roles due to a non-professional and weak state apparatus.

Some systems of organization of the military are more or less compatible with liberal democracy. However, in Latin America the most common system is the cadre-conscript one, which is closely related to non-democratic governments.[13] In this case the training of conscripts creates a peculiar dynamic. On the one hand, there is a strong corporate sentiment among the permanent cadre. On the other, the draft strengthens internal authoritarianism, leaving the technical and professional training for cadres and mechanical operations for draftees, deepening corporate awareness among cadres. The ideological consequence of this cleavage between cadres and conscripts creates a "model" of social relations inside the military corporation characterized by authoritarianism. In this ideological ap-proach to society, order is defined and seen as total submission. In viewing the civilian world the military disregard its values as non-conducive to the achieve-ment of military goals. Regarding social change, for instance, the military rejects the politics of mobilization—typical in underdeveloped countries—equating it with anarchy, chaos and disorder.

The military responds to the states' inconsistencies and ambiguities. Its hi-erarchical corporate integration makes it able to perform some tasks that the Latin American states, in a permanent crisis, cannot organize. The idea of the military as the backbone of state and society is reinforced by the political crisis that effects the state apparatus in Latin America.

INTERNATIONAL MILITARY RELATIONS

From their very inception modern Latin American armed forces have been heavily influenced by their links to extra-regional military establishments. Every great power that has ever tried to penetrate the region has also attempted to influence the development of the local armed forces. For example, Germany, France, and Italy sent military missions to Latin America when they challenged Great Britain's world hegemony in the nineteenth century. Later, and especially after World War II, the United States complemented its growing economic influence over the region by establishing military missions in virtually every Latin American nation.[14] These institutional linkages—relatively independent of governments—have given local militaries access to the latest technologies and know-how, contributing to their corporate identity and sharpening their segregation from the rest of society.

U.S. policy toward Latin American military establishments—originally guided by concerns over the Nazi, and later, the Soviet threats—shifted to counter-insurgency doctrines after the Cuban revolution. Thus the initial Cold War arguments over hemispheric defense quickly degenerated into civic-action activities. In the 1960s, Latin American military men concluded that the latter did not address their professional interests. Peru, in 1969, was the first Latin American country to reduce its military dependence on the United States by buying French airplanes, and withdrew from the Panamerican security system in 1973. The U.S.—in particular, the Joint Chiefs of Staff—has concluded that its relations with Latin American military establishments are crucial for the prevention and possible containment of Soviet threats and the stabilization of democratic governance. According to General Fred W. Woerner (USSOUTHCOM), the Latin American military "will be a major player in the total life of those nations. It is important to have a relationship with that . . . [It has] stepped out from the role of arbiter or determinant of the political process and stepped into a very new role, that of guarantor."[15]

The United States' emphasis on internal political roles for the Latin American military generated a gap between the technical training that it imparted and its restrictive arms transfer policy to the region. Shortages of weapon supplies and the emphasis on ideological training induced Latin American military to seek out new sources of technology. As a result, by the end of the 1970s, the character of Latin America's relations with extrahemispheric military establishments changed dramatically.[16] At present, Latin American nations receive their military hardware from at least eleven foreign suppliers, most notably, the Soviet Union, France, Great Britain, Spain, West Germany and Canada, and to some extent the United States.[17] This diversification reflects the change in the international system from a tight bipolar post–World War II system to a more multipolar one in the 1980s.[18]

In short, supplier diversification gives Latin American states a broader range of policy alternatives. New suppliers include the U.S.S.R. for Peru, Cuba, and to a lesser degree, Nicaragua. The Israeli armed forces have penetrated Central America, Ecuador, Chile and Argentina.[19] Moreover, France has emerged as a major purveyor of aircraft and armor; while Italy, Sweden, and Germany (submarines), as well as that old stalwart England, are now important naval suppliers.[20]

Over the last few decades, technological breakthroughs are structuring a new worldwide productive system. Inventions and innovations applied to production are characterizing the new industrial mode of production.[21] There have been important inputs that change military science and make it possible for small military establishments to perform new and heretofore unimagined political-military functions. These same factors also permit small contingents of irregular forces to confront professional armies. This results in a growing use of military force in domestic politics. Advances in military technology have played a key role in developing the Latin American armed forces' growing corporate awareness. Latin American militaries became acutely aware of the advantages of technological improvements and diversification during the South Atlantic war and realized that it was urgent to establish alternative sources of supply.

The diffusion of military technology and arms industries created a global arms market in which all of the Great Powers, and some lesser powers, compete to maintain their economic, political, and strategic positions in Latin America. The most important consequence of this diversification of international military relations and technological diffusion has been the Latin American military's ability to increase their autonomy from society and the state.

MILITARY CORPORATENESS AND CIVILIAN CONTROL

A number of factors have contributed to difficulties in the maintenance of civilian control over Latin American military establishments. These include the armed forces' new political-military roles, their acquisition of more sophisticated technology, and the new framework of international military relations. Moreover, in cases where these factors may not be very relevant, the fact that the armed forces have acquired greater autonomy in managing their own purely professional functions has made their control by civilian forces more precarious.

Consequently, the difficulties civilian governments are experiencing in controlling ''their'' militaries largely derive from institutional changes within the armed forces themselves. These changes have generated strong demands within the military to impose their definition of the national interest on both civilian rulers and the other armed forces of the region. This rather volatile conception of the national interest (and pressure to impose it) has led to an increasing militarization of Latin American societies (with the corresponding political instability) and a heightening of interstate tension.

As a result, the armed forces of Latin America have tended to favor geopolitical approaches to problem solving. Narrow nationalism combined with a labor-repressive outlook (Chile 1973) or opposition to the organized left (Peru 1968) characterized the typical ideologies of the 1970s. Those of the 1980s, however, place more significance on geopolitical variables in the interpretation and management of international conflict. This perspective overemphasizes military solutions to the detriment of negotiated settlements or flexible alliances. All of these factors reinforce tendencies towards militarization.

The Latin American military's preference for geopolitics also has a second effect: it generates an unstable system of political-military alliances. Shifting intra-regional alliances lead to military processes that often contradict government policy. Moreover, modernizing military establishments frequently define and resolve problems that arise from rapid change independent of government mediation.

Consequently, the scope and importance of government mediation, which tends to moderate militarism, has been reduced. Latin American armed forces are now able to establish international connections without much governmental supervision. These transnational links become transmission belts for the transfer of arms, ideologies, and economic and strategic interests from a diverse range of extra-regional military establishments. As a result, Latin American armed forces are exposed to multiple external influences, making it even more difficult for civilian governments to establish effective control over their militaries.

These processes tend to reinforce the privileged position of the Latin American armed forces in their societies, which heightens their corporate awareness and functional independence. These factors, in turn, encourage the military to press their governments for a larger share of scarce fiscal resources at the expense of civilian applications. This often has a negative effect on economic growth, and in the more extreme cases leads to sharp increases in foreign debt even during financial recessions.

Paradoxically, these military processes tend to atomize the national interest. To the degree that the armed forces become more autonomous they lose the ability to articulate diverse societal interests and to carry out consensual policies. The military's desire to secure the national interest by protecting and developing their own institutional processes ultimately reveals the ideological character of such pretensions and unmasks the purely corporate interests that guide them.

In order to fully understand the armed forces' growing autonomy we must place it in the context of Latin America's permanent political crisis—the crisis of the state. On the one hand, the region has always found it difficult to establish legitimate political order. Attempts at social change in Peru, Chile, Argentina, Uruguay, and Brazil foundered because the governing coalition of these countries could not convince the armed forces of the legitimacy of their policies. On the other hand, the structural changes that Cuba and Nicaragua seek require—largely for external reasons—the existence of effective military forces capable of defending national decisions. Even in these countries, however, the special relationship between the armed forces and civilians is not without its contradictions.

In general, these contradictions appear at two levels. First, Latin American governments have difficulty striking a balance between military and civilian spending. The divide between "guns" and "butter" has dramatic consequences for underdeveloped countries with high debt burdens. In countries where the general population does not have its basic needs satisfied military spending harms the masses; in cases where the government provides basic needs, increased military spending leads to cuts in redistributive programs. In short, the debate over military and civilian spending is a crucial political issue.[22] Second, spending levels tend to reflect the interests and capabilities of diverse pressure groups. Thus, when military spending is high it generally reflects the dominance of the armed forces over civilian groups. The armed forces' dominance may be due to a number of factors, such as direct control of the government, the weakness of a civilian government in crisis, or the exigencies of external threats. The military's growing autonomy, fed by multiple sources, makes it increasingly difficult for civilian governments to establish control over the development and budgetary requirements of their armed forces. These difficulties are compounded by the military's growing corporate awareness—the result of rapid modernization—which has led the armed forces to segregate themselves from the rest of society.

We must not, however, lose sight of the inherent difficulties that civilians face in their quest to dominate the military. After all, the capacity of civilians to control the military probably also depends on the coherence of the state. In other words, civilians will be able to dominate the armed forces to the degree that political groups and social classes establish hegemony over the state. In order for civilians to control the military, broad social coalitions espousing coherent policies will have to take charge of complex, corporate, Latin American states. Otherwise the military will retain varying measures of autonomy.

In sum, a Latin American military establishment's level of autonomy depends on two major factors: the state's capacity to establish effective control over military institutions (their ideological and material development) and budget; and the extent to which the military has developed its corporate awareness—the product of professional modernization and segregation from society.

MILITARY AUTONOMY IN LATIN AMERICA

Given these characteristics four major types of military autonomy can be established (see Table 2). Although the cases within each box manifest certain differences, they are sufficiently similar in the crucial variables to place them in the same category. Since the following chapter provides a deeper analysis of each of these cases, they will be only briefly described here.

Table 2
Institutional Autonomy of the Latin American Armed Forces

Strong	Weak
Conditioned Corporateness	Professional Autonomy
Colombia	Brazil
Argentina	Chile
Ecuador	Panama
Venezuela	Peru
	Uruguay
Integrated Corporateness	Unprofessional Autonomy
Cuba	Bolivia
Mexico	El Salvador
Nicaragua	Guatemala
	Honduras

CONDITIONED CORPORATENESS

The cases are characterized by a high degree of corporateness—highly modernized institutions segregated from society—with some kind of civilian control over them.[23] The Argentine, Colombian, Ecuadorean and Venezuelan cases belong in this category. In this category democratic governments still have the capacity to direct the military's main institutional processes, even though—as some chapters in this book show—civilian-military relations sometimes face serious crises.

In Argentina, this is a relatively recent development and the ultimate success of the Argentine government's attempt to control the military remains uncertain. Nevertheless, the Argentine case shows a remarkable achievement: for the first time in decades a democratically elected government characterizes its administration. The governmental policy of eliminating the post of commander in chief and reserving that position for the president of the republic, creating the post of chairman of the Joint Chiefs of Staff, cutting military spending, and removing officers from top managerial positions in military industries represents an earnest effort to reestablish civilian control over the military. Nevertheless, the lack of a governmental military policy able to project into the coming decades has been the main deficit of the administration.

The Colombian armed forces, to be sure, retain great financial independence. Moreover, there is a certain amount of tension between them and the executive branch, especially with regard to the government's counterinsurgency policy. In general, however, civilians still exercise strong control over the Colombian military.

The Ecuadorean case is similar to Colombia's in that its armed forces have tended to escape government control regarding the border dispute with Peru in

Amazonia. Nevertheless, civilians still basically dominate the military in
Ecuador.

Civilian control over the military appears most clear-cut in the Venezuelan
case. After the dictatorship of Pérez Jiménez, Venezuela's civilian political forces
imposed strong controls over their armed forces. Nevertheless, the Venezuelan
military have managed to acquire new power resources: officers occupy top
managerial positions in a series of important state enterprises, such as oil companies, the Corporación para el Desarrollo de la Guyana, and the Consejo de
Precios, as well as in the steel and aluminum industries.

The military in these four countries also exhibit relatively high degrees of
corporateness. In Argentina, Colombia, and Venezuela this manifests itself in
the high level of technical and professional training of its personnel. Meanwhile,
the Ecuadorean armed forces have developed a corporatist ideology modeled on
national security and geopolitical doctrines. The Venezuelan military has done
much the same, although less intensively.

Professional Autonomy

The cases in this category exhibit high degrees of corporateness and weak
governmental control over their activities. However, the conditions that led to
this outcome in Brazil, Chile, Panama, Peru, and Uruguay may be quite disparate,
ranging from early institutional and ideological development in Brazil and Chile
to political-ideological independence in Panama and Peru.

The Brazilian armed forces represent the purest case of professionalized autonomy. They were the only ones who simultaneously formulated a transnational
economic development model and used it to build an arms industry (beginning
in 1969) which now earns up to three billion dollars a year in exports. Moreover,
the Brazilian arms industry is also exploring nuclear technology. The central
position that the military occupy in bureaucratic policy networks—which include
local capitalists, foreign businessmen, and government personnel—is a clear
expression of their autonomy.[24]

The Chilean case is equally illustrative, although the military did not support
industrialization to the extent that the Brazilians did. And, although the Chilean
armed forces are not as directly involved now in ruling the nation as they were
in the early years of the regime, they intend to control any political transition
and most likely aspire to retain a tutelary role over any future government. At
present, the Chilean armed forces play an important part in government through
their participation in the Junta and in the future in the National Security Council.
This gives them great negative (veto) power over political decisions. The Chilean
military establishment's autonomy will be the most important constitutional issue
to be confronted by the new democratically elected government.

The Panamanian case, although not as dramatic as the previous ones, is
important because of the function its military serves in the defense of the Canal
Zone as well as the role the military plays in internal politics, as the Noriega

case has shown. This political-military role has allowed the armed forces to become permanent political actors, and they have maintained their political prominence despite the death of General Torrijos, their undisputed political-military leader. He had managed to recover sovereignty over the Canal Zone for Panama with a clever nonaligned strategy.

Peru constitutes yet another solid case of military autonomy, beginning in 1968 with the government of General Velasco Alvarado. He did not develop an anticapitalist set of policies, but he did advance more anti-American and populist policies. The Peruvian armed forces' independence from the left and the right, based on a clear ideology developed by its Center for Advanced Military Studies, permitted them to break the United States' near-monopoly over arms transfers and to retain a tradition of independence and functional autonomy. Evidence of the latter is that the commander in chief of the army took a different position during the South Atlantic conflict from that of President Belaúnde. This functional independence has also allowed the Peruvian armed forces to maintain military relations with the Soviet Union. Finally, the Peruvian high command has pressed for rapid modernization of their equipment as a result of geopolitical analysis that emphasizes threats to their northern and southern borders.

Integrated Corporateness

This type is characterized by strong civilian and governmental control over the military, even though in these cases one can find a hypertrophic military establishment. The military have achieved a prominent position in Cuba and Nicaragua as a result of two factors: their rise to power through armed struggle and negative U.S. response to the processes of social change that they sought to advance. In both cases the armed forces are the primary defenders of the regime. Nevertheless, in these two cases segregation from society has not accompanied modernization. This is largely due to the typical "armed peoples" type of relationship between civilians and the military.

The Mexican armed forces, due to their proximity to the United States and their being under civilian control after the revolution, have only recently begun to modernize. This modernization has taken the form of an ambitious program to develop military industries and the establishment of military-related research and development projects. Yet modernization has neither weakened civilian control of the military nor led to the military's segregation from society.

Unprofessional Autonomy

This type consists of cases with weak civilian control over the military and low corporate awareness, such as Bolivia, El Salvador, Guatemala, and Honduras. The military establishments of these countries have not modernized significantly, nor have they become highly segregated from society. In Bolivia, drug traffickers have seized control of the military's national development funds and have corrupted the officer corps. The praetorian character of the military in three Central American cases has had disastrous effects on the professional development of their officer corps. The armed forces in El Salvador control 25 autonomous state agencies, and in Guatemala they manage a commercial bank.

CONCLUSIONS

The cases of professional autonomy, conditioned corporateness, and unprofessional autonomy represent a continuum. In effect, unprofessional autonomy tends to end with a return of the military to the barracks, and their submission to civilian control. In the ensuing period, a number of changes at the ideological, professional, and technical levels transform such military establishments from a condition of unprofessional autonomy toward conditioned corporateness. As a result, when a breakdown of consensus among civilian political forces once again opens the door for the military to become directly involved in politics they tend to develop into an autonomous and highly professional military force.

In other words, the military's involvement in politics during the 1970s did not lead to a decline in their professionalism, nor did their involvement in repression produce such an effect. Moreover, it did not simply represent another phase of the familiar professionalization-politization-professionalization cycle.[25] On the contrary, the distinctive feature of their intervention was their ability to sustain increasing political autonomy without sacrificing rapid modernization or professional standards. If this tendency among Latin American military establishments continues unchecked, redemocratization should lead to the emergence of new state forms, different from traditional western democratic ones.

By the same token, those cases characterized by integrated corporateness also risk a shift toward professional autonomy. In order to avoid such an outcome the Cuban, Nicaraguan, and Mexican states must undertake a profound reform of both their institutions and civil-military relations. This underscores the value of correctly interpreting changes in Latin American civil–military relations: our ability to diagnose future political trends and institutional forms in the region depends on it.

NOTES

1. On the differences between demilitarization of government and the state, see Alain Rouquié, ''Demilitarization and the Institutionalization of Military-dominated Polities in Latin America,'' in Guillermo O'Donnell, Philippe Schmitter and Laurence Whitehead, *Transition from Authoritarian Rule: Comparative Perspectives* (Baltimore: Johns Hopkins University Press, 1986), 133.

2. A comparative analysis of military in transition can be found in Karen Remmer, ''Military Rule in South America: State Institutions and Political Outcomes,'' paper presented at the Fourteenth World Congress of the International Political Science Association, Washington, D.C., August 28–September 1, 1988. For the Argentinian case,

see Andrés Fontana, "Notas sobre las relaciones cívico-militares y el proceso de consolidación democrática en la Argentina" (Buenos Aires: Fundación Simón Rodriguez— Editorial Biblos, 1987); and Carlos H. Waisman, "The Consolidation of Democracy in Argentina: Constraints and Opportunities," paper presented at the American Political Science Association Convention, Washington, D.C., September 1-4, 1988, p. 12. For the Brazilian case, see Eliezer Rizzo de Oliveira, "O aparelho militar: papel tutelar na Nova República," in João Quartim de Moraes, Wilma Peres Costa and Eliézer Rizzo de Oliveira, *A Tutela Militar* (Sao Paulo: Vértice, Editora Revista dos Tribunais, 1987), p. 77; and Alfred Stepan, *Rethinking Military Politics: Brazil and the Southern Cone* (New Jersey: Princeton University Press, 1988), pp. 103–127. For the Uruguayan case, see María del Huerto Amarillo, "La estrategia 'democrática' de seguridad nacional," *Fuerzas Armadas y Sociedad: Defensa y desarme en América Latina y el Caribe*. Vol. 3, no. 1–2, January-July, 1988, pp. 1–6; and Juan Rial, "Las relaciones cívico-militares en el Uruguay tras la restauración de la democracia, 1985–1988," paper presented at the Seventeenth Congress of the Latin American Sociological Association, Montevideo, Uruguay, December 2–6, 1988, p. 31. For the Paraguayan case, see Diego Abante, "The Military in Paraguay and the Prospects for Democratization," paper presented at the American Political Science Association Convention, Washington, D.C., September 1– 4, 1988, p. 36. For the Guatemalan case, see Jennifer G. Schimer, "Rule of Law or Law of Rule? Guatemalan Military Attitudes Toward Law, National Security and Human Rights," paper presented at the New England Council on Latin American Studies Conference (NECLAS), Wellesley College, October 22, 1988, p. 17.

3. This is a worldwide tendency which could be observed in other Third World regions. In this respect, see Anton Bebler, "Contemporary Civilian-Dominated versus Military-Dominated Political Systems in the World" (Ljubljana, Yugoslavia: Edvard Kardelj University, 1987); Asha Gupta, "Types of Military Regimes in the Third World," paper presented at the Fourteenth World Congress of the International Political Science Association, Washington, D.C., August 28–September 1, 1988; and Carolina G. Hernandez, "Civil-Military Relations in Transition Regimes: The Case of the Philippines under the Aquino Government," paper presented at the Fourteenth World Congress of the International Political Science Association, Washington, D.C., August 28–September 1, 1988.

4. Some elements for a new framework for civilian-military relations are in J. Samuel Fitch, "The Armed Forces and Democracy in Latin America: Toward a New Relationship" (Boulder: Center for Public Policy Research, University of Colorado, December 1988); and Augusto Varas, "Las relaciones cívico-militares en un marco democrático: elementos para un re-equilibrio de los vínculos fuerzas armadas-estado-sociedad," *Documento de Trabajo*, no. 376 (Santiago: FLACSO, June 1988).

5. The most salient work in this respect is Samuel Huntington, *The Soldier and the State* (New York: Vintage Books, 1964).

6. U.S. Ambassador to the United Nations, Jeane Kirkpatrick, revived these themes in the 1980s.

7. Alfred Stepan, "The New Professionalism of Internal Warfare and Military Role Expansion," in Alfred Stephan, ed., *Authoritarian Brazil* (New Haven: Yale University Press, 1973).

8. The best example of this school of thinking is: Guillermo O'Donnell, "Tensions in the Bureaucratic Authoritarian State and the Question of Democracy," in David Collier, ed., *The New Authoritarianism in Latin America* (New Jersey: Princeton University Press, 1979).

9. See Fernando Henrique Cardoso, "The Characterization of Authoritarian Re-

gimes," in David Collier, ed., *The New Authoritarianism*, especially the section where he defines bureaucratic-authoritarianism as a form of regime rather than a form of state. This distinction links these regimes to national or international business groups without assuming that the military simply do their bidding.

10. I define corporateness or corporate awareness as collective self-consciousness, identity and solidarity of the military corporation around homogeneous institutional-political interests. I base this definition on Antonio Gramsci, "La Science politique et le prince moderne," in Antonio Gramsci, *Oeuvres choisies* (Paris: Editions Sociales, 1959), pp. 240–241. For an operationalization of variables close to this definition in the institutional model of military social organization, see Charles C. Moskos, "Institutional and Occupational Trends in Armed Forces," in Charles C. Moskos and Frank R. Wood, *The Military: More Than a Job?* (London: Pergamon-Brassey's International Defense Publishers, 1988), p. 16.

11. See Augusto Varas, *Militarization and the International Arms Race in Latin America* (Boulder: Westview Press, 1985). pp. 16–24.

12. Since in Latin America the transformation of the military from institution to occupation will be a long-term process, the way to counterbalance this institutional trend is for democratic governments to provide the military with a professional and institutional policy that could be synthesized under the label of a defense policy. This would ameliorate the segregational trend.

13. See Samuel Huntington, "Tocqueville's Armies and Ours," remarks delivered to the seminar "Democracy in America Today: A Tocquevillian Perspective," John M. Olin Center for the Inquiry into the Theory and Practice of Democracy, University of Chicago, February 15, 1984, p. 11.

14. Alain Rouquié, *El estado militar en América Latina* (Buenos Aires: Emecé Editores, 1984), pp. 90–97; and Jack Child, *Unequal Alliance: The Inter–American Military System, 1938–1978* (Boulder: Westview Press, 1980), pp. 27–167.

15. See the report on General Fred W. Woerner's requirement of resources for the USSOUTHCOM in *The New York Times*, April 3, 1988. Also, Joint Chiefs of Staff, *U.S. Military Postures*, volumes published between 1980 and 1984.

16. For an analysis of the inter-American military system, see Augusto Varas, "Las relaciones militares internacionales de América Latina: evolución y perspectivas," in Gustavo Lagos, ed., *Las relaciones entre América Latina, Estados Unidos y Europa Occidental* (Santiago: Editorial Universitaria, 1980), pp. 117–148.

17. To shore up its declining position the U.S. government now encourages business relationships between the U.S. and local arms manufacturers, exemplified by a recent proposal for a joint venture between Northrop and Embraer to produce F-5E fighter-bombers for export to Third World countries. See Fernando Bustamante, "La transferencia de technología militar desde Estados Unidos al Brasil," *Documento de Trabajo*, no. 335 (Santiago: FLACSO, April 1987).

18. Although, the U.S. has not lost military control over the hemisphere, it is having increasing difficulty defining the terms of a regional military balance.

19. See Bishara Bahbah, *Israel and Latin America: The Military Connection* (New York: St. Martin Press, 1986).

20. For an analysis of the international military relations of Latin American countries, see Isaac Caro, *Las relaciones militares internacionales de América Latina* (Santiago: FLACSO, 1987). An analysis of the region's relations with arms suppliers is in Augusto Varas, "La transferencia de tecnología militar hacia América Latina," paper presented

at the Experts Meeting on Strengthening of Political Cooperation in Latin America, United Nations Regional Center for Disarmament, Lima, December 6–9, 1988.

21. Carlota Perez, "Las nuevas tecnologías: una visión de conjunto," in Carlos Ominami, ed., *La Tercera Revolución Industrial: Aspectos Internacionales del Actual Viraje Tecnológico* (Buenos Aires: Grupo Editor Latinomericano, 1987), pp. 43–89.

22. Regarding this issue, see Augusto Varas, ed., *Paz, desarme y desarrollo en América Latina* (Buenos Aires: Grupo Editor Latinomericano, 1987).

23. In our definition the armed forces consist of the army, the navy, and the air force. We have excluded militarized police forces, but have included the Panamanian National Guard.

24. See Cardoso, "The Characterization of Authoritarian Regimes."

25. See Guillermo O'Donnell, "Modernization and Military Coups: Theory, Comparisons, and the Argentine Case," in Abraham Lowenthal, ed., *Armies and Politics in Latin America* (New York: Holmes and Meier, 1976).

2 THE ARMED FORCES OF COLOMBIA AND ECUADOR IN COMPARATIVE PERSPECTIVE

Fernando Bustamante

The following pages describe the development of the Ecuadorean and Colombian armed forces over the last fifteen years. Their history is organized around a number of elements that characterize the evolution of their institutions, as well as their armaments policies.

THE COLOMBIAN CASE

Colombia's military spending (calculated as a percentage of gross domestic product—GDP) is one of the lowest in Latin America. The country's defense policies were designed to develop a relatively small, low-cost military system. Since the 1950s, however, Colombia has also been the second largest recipient of U.S. military aid in the region—$253.2 million by 1980. U.S. largesse had two sources. Some of the aid was related to Colombia's participation in the Korean War. Early on, however, the Pentagon also placed Colombia on its priority list for counterinsurgency assistance; as a result, Colombia became a laboratory for the development of the hemisphere's counterinsurgency doctrine and praxis. It is clear, then, that the Colombian state and its armed forces have had many resources at their disposition which were not extracted from the national economy. In other words, the "lightness" of the Colombian armed forces is a function of their relatively modest size, their emphasis on weaponry suitable for waging internal war, *and* their access to significant external financing. U.S. military assistance has allowed Colombia to field an army without having to militarize its economy and society.

The Colombian armed forces' participation in various U.S. military assistance programs highlights their subsidized nature. In Latin America, Colombia ranked only seventh in the United States' foreign military sales program ($39.59 million between 1950–1980), which offers material at reduced prices. It occupied the same position with regard to strictly commercial purchases at market prices ($17.7 million between 1950–1980). In short, the bulk of U.S. military assistance took the form of donations and loans, not sales. Until 1970, the Colombian armed forces depended heavily on the Pentagon. This allowed them to carry out their professionalization without experiencing debilitating conflicts with social groups over the allocation of the nation's economic resources. To a certain extent, then, U.S. military aid liberated the Colombian state and armed forces from potentially restrictive struggles for scarce resources. That aid also induced them to be highly receptive to U.S. policies; for example, the Colombian military were among the earliest and most enthusiastic supporters of the Alliance for Progress and the "civic action" doctrines of the Kennedy administration. In any case, in material terms, Colombia's civil war (La Violencia) and the subsequent fight against leftist guerrillas came relatively cheap. Moreover, the Colombian state and political forces managed to keep the issue of repression separate and distinct from other national political issues. In this manner, Colombia was able to join a civilian form of government and a nonmilitarized economy with a sustained and relatively successful counterinsurgency campaign.

Military appropriations provide useful indicators for analyzing the development of the Colombian armed forces. Until the 1960s, salaries and benefits constituted a significant proportion of the military budget—even in comparison to other Latin American countries. Weapons and equipment were relatively simple and inexpensive. As of 1970, expenditures for larger and more sophisticated items consumed a bigger share of the budget. The principal beneficiaries, however, were the air force and the navy; the army, by contrast, continued to buy light arms, better suited for keeping internal order. These systems, in general, were not well-suited for conventional defense against external forces.[1]

The figures presented by the U.S. Arms Control and Disarmament Agency and the International Institute for Strategic Studies reveal that Colombian military spending doubled between 1972 and 1980.[2] In constant dollars, however, such spending has actually increased very little, if at all. For the most part, in 1981 dollars, Colombia has spent about $300 million on the military annually. Nevertheless, some years evince a marked jump in the military budget. Such a jump occurred between 1975 and 1976 when the air force acquired the Mirage fighters. A second sharp increase occurred between 1978 and 1980, but a contraction from 1980 to 1982 compensates for it. The same cycle repeats itself with a rise in 1983 and a drop in 1984. It seems, then, that increases in the military budget were followed by proportional decreases, which was why the mean budget (in constant dollars) remained more or less unchanged over time.

The Colombian armed forces also place relatively slight demands on the nation's human capital. In proportion to the overall population, Colombia maintains one of the smallest military establishments in the region.[3] Nevertheless, over the last ten years, the armed forces have grown both in absolute and relative terms. Since overall military spending remains constant, more manpower did not result in increased outlays per soldier.

We can bring this tendency into sharper focus by looking at military spending as a percentage of the state's overall budget, on a per capita and per soldier basis, and as a percentage of the gross domestic product.[4] Although there has been a slight increase in per soldier expenditure, the Colombian armed forces have reduced their share of overall government spending and GDP. Moreover, per capita spending for defense has remained stable.

These figures, however, may present a distorted picture. For the most part, they exclude expenditures related to the armed forces' growing internal security functions, which began in earnest in the 1970s. It is precisely this component of military spending that seems to have increased the most during the 1970s. If this is true, the assertions of the previous paragraph need to be qualified. Establishing the human and budgetary impact of the Colombian military's new "nontraditional" activities, however, must await further research.

Colombia's international military relations have evolved much like those of most other South American countries. The available data suggest that during the 1980s Colombia has spent less on military imports and has diversified suppliers. Until the 1960s the United States provided most of Colombia's military hardware. As of 1972, however, Colombia began to buy from medium and small nations instead of the traditional great powers. Brazil and Israel becme the largest alternative arms suppliers for the infantry, military vehicles, light aircraft, electronic equipment, and the like.

Between 1972 and 1982 Colombia imported $100 million (1984 dollars) in arms from lesser powers. All other purchases were made from West Germany, France, and the United States: Germany played a fundamental role in the navy's refitting and modernization; France resupplied the air force; and the United States provided counterinsurgency, logistical, police, and liaison support.[5]

The public record suggests that Colombia has maintained a stable and modest level of military imports. These data reaffirm the impression that the Colombians are implementing an austere and conservative modernization program.[6]

The Gradual, "Associated" Institutionalization of the Military's Political Role

The creation of the National Front marked the beginning of the most recent period in the institutionalization of the Colombian armed forces' political role.[7] The National Front was a political pact between the Liberal and Conservative parties that laid the ground rules for political competition after the ouster of dictator Rojas Pinilla. It also led to a fundamental redefinition of the military establishment's role in Colombian politics. The National Front recognized that Colombia would have to reorganize its internal security and defense forces in order to overcome the rural violence and state of emergency that had gripped the country since 1948.

To build the National Front, the political parties and the military agreed on a series of mutual guarantees. The armed forces had to give up political power and refrain from meddling in party politics. That meant that the officer corps had to sever its strong ties to the Conservative party, especially the Ospinista faction.[8] Moreover, the military had to subordinate themselves to civilian political forces—meaning the two major political parties. In short, the military became the guarantors of the political rules of the game as defined by the National Front, thus assuring the dominance of the Liberal and Conservative parties.[9]

For their part, the political parties agreed to support a process of military professionalization in which the armed forces would retain a modicum of autonomy. The professionalization process also entailed an institutionalization of civil–military relations in which the state, rather than traditional strongmen, mediated relations between the military and the political parties.[10] In this manner, the armed forces participated directly in the foundational pact, whereas in the past they had only done so as the clients of civilian "notables."

This arrangement changed gradually over the following decades. In a succession of incremental steps the military took over a number of public and internal security functions. Meanwhile, the civilian government became increasingly dependent on the armed forces to maintain the political system. This dependency had its roots in a succession of military and political challenges, such as leftist insurgency, generalized banditry, and General Rojas Pinilla's ANAPO movement.

The National Front's troubles began in the 1960s. Some officers proposed that the armed forces should develop their own sociopolitical doctrine. In their eyes, this represented the most feasible path for overcoming the limitations that the coalition government placed on their efforts to pacify the countryside and restore order.[11] Although civilian presidents supressed these proposals, the military persisted in developing their own doctrine well into the 1970s. This prompted civilian authorities to force the retirement of Generals Valencia Tobar (1975), Matallana (1977), and Landazábal (1982). However, the content of the proposed doctrines changed from the 1960s to the 1970s. In the 1960s these doctrines took the tone of a "leftist" critique to the civilian regime, and they prompted many officers to support General (retired) Rojas Pinilla's ANAPO during the 1970 elections. Moreover, on that occasion a few officers were even tempted to stage a coup d'etat because they believed that the former dictator had been the victim of electoral fraud.[12]

After the heated election of 1970 the Colombian military apparently embraced the Doctrine of National Security. It had a much greater influence on military thought than General Ruiz Noboa's developmentalist ideas. In 1978, President López Michelsen gave in to several years' worth of military lobbying and promulgated the National Security Statute.

During the 1970s the military greatly strengthened their police and internal security functions.[13] This led the armed forces to stress their repressive role and to abandon their previous emphasis on socioeconomic development. Many people had believed in the 1960s that the military played a mediating and peacemaking role in political party conflict. In the 1970s, however, the military used force against guerrillas, drug traffickers, and delinquents with increasing frequency. The armed forces viewed these social ills as an internal enemy which they had to defeat, and likened their efforts to a crusade.

Civilian pressure also influenced the Colombian armed forces' decision to abandon developmentalist policies. The traditional parties harbored a strong aversion to both "reformist developmentalism" and the populism of Rojas Pinilla. This led them to purge the military of doctrines and practices that seemed to question the political bargain struck in 1958. Projects such as General Pinzón Caicedo's "Andes Plan," which was designed to weaken the great landowners, made both Liberals and Conservatives uneasy. As a result, starting with the Pastrana Borrero administration the civilian political leadership began to promote a narrower conception of professionalism among the military. But when the civilians expunged political reformism from the armed forces they left a vacuum that was filled by militarist doctrines.

As a result, the armed forces gradually began to replace civilian institutions in tasks that involved maintaining sociopolitical control in various parts of the country. This led to a progressive militarization at the local level, because the central government appointed more and more military men to governorships and mayoralties in regions that were wracked by conflict. The central government also instructed the nation's department heads to consult with local military commanders on all internal security and public order issues.[14] This led to the militarization of local government and public administration, which has in turn generated a number of problems, such as competition for control of these areas, jurisdictional disputes, and a lack of coordination between military and civilian authorities. The virtually permanent state of siege also contributed to the military's hubris, by giving them the means to impose their views with increasing frequency over local civilian government. In this struggle, the central government almost invariably supported the armed forces. Consequently, the militarization of local government did not appear as an erosion of the national government's authority. On the contrary, the national political leadership used the armed forces to weaken the power of local strongmen. Therefore, in spite of their greater autonomy, the military remained subordinate to the political order established by the Liberal and Conservative parties.

The military's influence in the administration of justice also grew as a result of this increase in areas governed by military law. Moreover, the judicial power granted military tribunals a significant degree of independence. This included ceding the administration of the penal system to the armed forces.

The deepening of the military's presence in Colombian society and politics extended beyond matters of public safety. They also acquired a significant measure of control over the teaching of civics and the delivery of public services.

For example, the army created a "civil defense" corps organized along the lines of a paramilitary reserve force. The functions of the civil defense corps by far exceeded the usual support role for public emegencies. The army also expected these units to take part in counterinsurgency maneuvers—to act as a fifth column capable of joining military units and the civilian population.

Based on their experience with the civil defense corps the high command initiated additional programs designed to project the armed forces' presence in civil society. It is from this perspective that we should interpret their introduction of national security courses for business executives. These courses suggest that the armed forces sought to create an "old boy" network of businessmen socialized into military thought. In 1977, for much the same reason, the armed forces established a special program by which executives could obtain military rank. They also sought to establish a Military University. To that end the armed forces made an effort to improve the quality of their institutions of higher learning and invited civilians to enroll in them. The military, then, clearly sought to influence the thought and allegiances of strategic social actors.

The armed forces complemented their effort to create a civil-military elite steeped in national security doctrines with attempts to increase their role in the education of Colombia's youth. Although the introduction of military service for students did not generate much enthusiasm, the so-called military academies fared better. The latter were secondary schools modeled after Colombian military schools and under the direction of the Defense Ministry.

Like its counterparts in the rest of Latin America, the Colombian military has changed the orientation of its doctrine from one of hemispheric defense to a more nationalist conception of the nation's defense requirements. The Superior War College was the locus of this change, and Brazilian and Argentine military advisors heavily influenced new directions in Colombian military doctrine. This doctrinal shift also marked a diminution of heretofore relatively close ties with the United States, especially within the air force and the navy.[15]

The shift in military doctrine also induced the Colombian armed forces to pressure the government to impose a "national security regime." Decree 1,573 of 1974 organized public administration around a system of five "fronts" coordinated by the National Defense Superior Council and horizontally linked to the Economic, Political, and Social Council (EPSC). The Superior Council was responsible for defining long-term "national objectives," while the EPSC drew up plans and strategies. This sytem was similar to the one established by General Onganía in Argentina in 1966 and to the one that Ecuador implemented in 1976. It represented another step in the establishment of military criteria for the conduct of state affairs.

Although Decree 1,573 outlined mechanisms for coordinating action, it lacked substantive content. As a result, toward the end of the 1970s the military, led by General Landazábal Reyes, once again put pressure on the government. This time they wanted government to turn over the formulation of development programs directly to the National Defense Superior Council. Now the armed forces were attempting to take over control of the entire public administration system, or at least to make it conform to the standards of military thought.

During this period, the armed forces also attempted to reformulate their own doctrine, and their thinking converged around the core concepts of the National Security Doctrine. Indications that such a process was occurring surfaced in 1975. A conflict erupted between a group of officers led by the commander of the armed forces, General Valencia Tobar, and the López Michelsen administration. Under Valencia Tobar, military thought displayed considerable independence from the civilian government. This was largely due to the general's links with "reformist" intellectuals and the legacy of General Ruiz Noboa. The government purged these officers and turned over command to officers such as Generals Varón Valencia, Camacho Leyva, Landazábal, and Matallana, among others. Some of these new commanding officers favored more strictly professional stances for the armed forces, while others admired the thinking of their Brazilian and Argentine colleagues.

The ouster of General Valencia Tobar did not end the friction between the government and the armed forces, however. His successor, General Matallana, was a hard-line veteran of numerous counterinsurgency campaigns that had won him a reputation for severity. General Matallana did not approve of many of the functions the government wanted the military to perform, such as fighting drug traffickers and crime. He believed that these functions tended to deprofessionalize the armed forces and adversely affected their morale, and when he became commander in chief General Matallana sought to limit the military's participation in such tasks. Moreover, his interpretation of military professionalism led him to adopt anti-American views which strained the traditional close relationship between the armed forces of Colombia and the United States. This about-face expressed itself in the Colombian military's support for the campaign to expel the Protestant North American missionaries of the Summer Linguistics Institute from the Colombian Amazon. The civilian authorities forced General Matallana into retirement in 1977 as a consequence of his conflictual behavior.

General Matallana's successor, General Camacho Leyva, wanted to develop a military cogovernment. As early as 1977 the high command demanded that the government approve a proposed Security Statute that would give the military a tutelary role over Colombian political life. Their efforts succeeded in 1978, when the recently inaugurated Turbay administration promulgated Decree 1,923. This degree sealed the Colombian military's autonomous integration in the Liberal/Conservative state. Nevertheless, there were still frictions and contradictions between the armed forces and the government. Between 1980 and 1982, and later under President Belisario Betancur, the military opposed and sabotaged the government's efforts to pacify the countryside through the use of amnesty programs and truces with Colombian guerrillas—mainly the Armed Forces of the Colombian Revolution and M-19. Moreover, the military gained increasing autonomy from civilian political authorities in the conduct of counterinsurgency campaigns both at the national and at the local level. The military's actions led to a series of confrontations with civilian authorities. In 1982 this situation led President Betancur to retire the commander in chief of the army because he opposed negotiations with insurgents. The military, however, ignored their civilian commanders and continued with their counterinsurgency campaigns. They organized or tolerated "white guards" and forced guerrillas who had abided by the terms of the cease-fire to take up arms in self-defense.

Let us now turn briefly to the question of ideological tendencies within the Colombian armed forces. According to Gonzalo Bermúdez Rossi, the Colombian armed forces have five important ideological tendencies.[16] The first is the developmentalist current. According to this line, the military should help the disadvantaged sectors of Colombian society to modernize and gain economic security. Officers in this current, such as Generals Ruiz Noboa and Valencia Tobar, support civic action, state paternalism, and "colonization."[17]

The second tendency, the so-called nationalist or Peruvian current, enjoyed its greatest influence in the 1970s. It expresses anti-American, anti-oligarchic, and antitraditional political party sentiments. Most of the officers still on active duty who supported Rojas Pinilla adopt this position. They believe that the military has a national duty to oversee Colombia's development. Unlike the developmentalists, the nationalists argue that the military should work to change the nation's political and institutional structures rather than merely lend technical support to development projects.

The third ideological tendency, known as the "golden star" current, represents the political left within the Colombian armed forces. It opposes human rights violations in counterinsurgency warfare, corruption, and the excessive independence of intelligence and security forces. This ideological tendency received its name from the bulletin "Golden Star," in which its adherents expressed their views. General Camacho Leyva and his successors effectively purged this faction from the military and with it its influence on military thought.

The fourth tendency, National Security, takes its inspiration from the authoritarian models of the Southern Cone (Argentina, Brazil, Chile, and Uruguay) and seeks to impose a national security state.

The fifth tendency is variously known as the "barracks," "trooper," "Chilean," or "Prussian" current. Its adherents espouse a strict military professionalism, meaning that they oppose involving the military in national politics. They believe that the military should remain subordinate to civilian authorities as long as the latter meet two conditions: civilians should confine their political activity to the limits imposed by the National Front; and they should not jeopardize Colombia's external or internal security.

THE ECUADOREAN CASE

Ecuador ranks fifth with respect to military spending as a percentage of GDP in Latin America. Nevertheless, Cuba excepted, in 1978 Ecuador ranked first in the region with respect to military spending as a percentage of government expenditures. Meanwhile, Ecuador's military budget for that year ranked sixth in terms of per capita spending, placing it ahead of such nations as Mexico and Brazil.

U.S. military aid to Ecuador between 1950 and 1979 totaled $112.5 million, or less than half of the aid that Colombia received in the same period. In terms of U.S. aid to the region, Ecuador ranks ninth in the hemisphere. Ecuador obtained $91.5 million through U.S. commercial sales programs (sixth place in the region), roughly three times the assistance provided to Colombia by these same programs. Regular commercial sales totaled $21.55 million (fifth place in the region), which was also more than what Colombia spent in the same category.

Ecuador possesses a "heavy" military establishment, that is, one that places a heavy burden on the state's fiscal capabilities as well as, to a lesser extent, the economy as a whole. Ecuador has received relatively little military aid. Moreover, the aid that it has received has been on less generous terms than that which the United States has extended to Colombia. Thus, the cost of Ecuador's defense establishment has been high not only in relative terms but also in terms of the direct burdens it places on the taxpayer. That is because the development of the Ecuadorean armed forces has depended more on the state's capacity to extract revenue from its own economy. Since the Ecuadorean state exhibits a relatively weak taxing ability, the military budget consumes a larger share of fiscal expenditures.

From 1972 to 1978, the last year of the military regime, military spending increased sharply. In 1978 it even surpassed that of Colombia. Military expenditures remained at high levels during the subsequent civilian government until 1982 when the drop in oil prices undermined the state's finances.[18] Ecuador's armed forces enjoyed a vigorous expansion during the military regime. The fact that this expansion continued during the first years of the civilian government suggests an at least tacit agreement between the military and civilian politicians to retain that growth. The government's fiscal problems after 1982 upset the pact. This suggests that Ecuador's oil bonanza may explain the armed forces' expansion better than the effect of the military as an autonomous interest group strategically situated in the political system.

The available data allow us to distinguish between two periods.[19] During the government of Rodríguez Lara (1972–1975), per capita military spending increased gradually, while troop levels as a proportion of the total population remained stable. Military spending as a percentage of GDP also increased moderately. However, 1976 marked the beginning of a strong expansion in troop strength and per capita spending which peaked in 1978, the last year of the military regime. Between 1978 and 1982 the government stabilized military spending, albeit at higher levels than in 1972. During the military regime, the Rodríguez Lara administration favored modernizing the armed forces and deepening their professionalism. Admiral Poveda's administration emphasized their quantitative expansion.[20]

Throughout this period Ecuadorean troop strength was about half that of

Colombia's. As a proportion of total population, however, Ecuador's troop levels were much higher than Colombia's and that difference increased throughout the 1970s; as a result, Ecuador's population is increasingly more militarized than Colombia's. Ecuador's per capita military expenditures in 1972 were twice those of Colombia, and by 1982 Ecuador's per capita spending was three times as high. Moreover, in 1972 Ecuadorean military spending represented 2.4 percent of its GDP while Colombia spent only 1.3 percent of its GDP on its armed forces. The two countries maintained approximately the same ratio in 1982: 1.8 percent and 0.8 percent. In terms of their share in total fiscal spending, Ecuadorean and Colombian military spending reached 15.6 percent and 9.2 percent of total revenues, respectively, in 1972. In 1982 those proportions were 11 percent and 7.8 percent respectively. Finally, in 1972 Ecuador spent $2,150 per soldier, while Colombia spent $1,714 per soldier; ten years later, Ecuador was spending $1,000 more per soldier than Colombia.

Ecuador significantly increased its purchases of arms and equipment after 1972, buying $725 million worth of new materiel to Colombia's $170 million.[21] As a percentage of total imports in selected years Ecuadorean arms purchases increased twenty times faster than any other import item in 1982. Military imports increased significantly on two occasions: during the transition to political democracy, and after the armed confrontation with Peru in the Paquisha region.

Like Colombia, Ecuador also changed and diversified its military suppliers. France became Ecuador's principal source for sophisticated weapons systems, and other purchases were parceled out to a number of suppliers, such as Canada, Switzerland, and Israel. While the United Kingdom retained its position as the third largest purveyor of armaments, the United States slipped to fourth place, and West Germany and Italy occupied fifth and sixth place respectively.

The Defensive Corporate Retreat of the Ecuadorean Military

Since 1948 the Ecuadorean military had repeatedly attempted to develop a professional style that would enable it to become the guarantors of the state, while at the same time establishing civil–military relations that would protect the armed forces from the personalism and clientelism of national politics.[22] Toward 1961 a profound change took place in the political ethos of the officer corps: most officers began to adopt a modernizing bureaucratic corporate identity. Thus, the coup d'etat against President Arosemena was the first time that the military acted politically as an institution. In the past, coups had always been led by individual military strongmen. The military government of 1963 collapsed due to the strong opposition of Ecuador's traditional civilian political forces. The armed forces' inability to consolidate their government resulted in the reestablishment of personalized rule by cliques of notables. This political style clashed strongly with the beliefs and operating procedures of a military that had managed to wrest a measure of independence from civilian forces. Continual conflict erupted as civilian rulers attempted to "reclientelize" the armed forces.

Extreme turbulence in civil–military relations characterized the fifth government of Velasco Ibarra. Since 1970, Velasco had governed as a virtual civilian
dictator, and although his administration retained the support of the armed forces,
his relationship with them was not an easy one. Velasco's efforts to control the
officer corps through his nephew, Defense Minister Jaime Acosta Velasco, constituted the major irritant. Defense Minister Acosta attempted to make the military
his and the president's personal instrument. These maneuvers prompted a group
of officers to mutiny, which forced the defense minister's resignation in 1971.
The 1971 movement sought to resolve a situation that encroached on the military's
professionalism and threatened to turn them into the political booty of factional
struggles among politicians. This incident increased the officers corps' awareness
of the growing incompatability between their professional development and the
nature of the current political regime. The volatility and anomie characteristic
of politics among strongmen and notables weakened the efficacy of the state,
national integration, and the armed forces' capacity to defend the nation. Consequently, the Ecuadorean military became deeply concerned about the outcome
of a possible conflict with Peru and about integrating the Amazon frontier into
the rest of the nation—one of their principal projects.

The officer corps believed that the ad hoc and nepotistic style of Ecuadorean
politics undermined the armed forces. It stunted their corporate development,
proved itself incapable of addressing the problems of modernization, and demonstrated an inability to integrate marginal and popular urban social groups into
mainstream society. The political system's deficiencies threatened to provoke a
hegemonic crisis of the state that might well culminate with the unraveling of
civic life and a descent into barbarism. Thus the military believed in 1972 that
they were the only force capable of establishing new legitimizing principles for
the state. They sought to base the state's legitimacy on technical values and
universalistic standards in order to eliminate nepotistic clientelism.

In the Ecuadorean case, classical "strategic" thinking informed military
thought to a larger degree than in Colombia. Securing Amazonia, rather than
internal warfare, was their central concern. Planning revolved around either a
defense against Peruvian aggression or the recovery of territories lost to Peru in
1941. Officers were highly sensitive to the state's capacity to integrate and
mobilize the nation in order to secure those goals. But Ecuador, like Peru and
Bolivia, is not well integrated along ethnic, cultural, and regional dimensions.
This situation, along with the political system, weakened the state as a national
unitary actor and undermined the capacity of the armed forces to fulfill their
goals.

In every respect, the problems that the Ecuadorean armed forces faced in 1972
were different from those confronting the Colombian military. In Colombia the
resolution of a hegemonic conflict between the two traditional political parties
shaped the development of a modern, bureaucratized military profession. The
struggle against bandits, drug traffickers, and guerrillas represented the reaction
of political society against groups external to it. By contrast, in Ecuador the

armed forces had to resolve the problem of building an institutional order that would allow them to develop professionally. They had to create a framework that would make it possible for them to carry out their project. In short, the armed forces felt that they had to reorganize Ecuadorean political life in order to strengthen the state.

The military government established the following priorities: (1) to lay the foundations for the development of needs and interests based on national, statist, and universal-institutional characteristics; (2) to establish the foundations for a more self-sufficient, diversified economy than the agro-export economy; (3) to create the basis for incorporating marginal social groups such as Quechua peasants and urban migrant groups; (4) to develop the state's organizational and operational capacities, rid the state of partisan cliques, and imbue the state with norms designed to wring out clientelism; (5) to support the development of intellectuals, entrepreneurs, and technocrats centered on the state; (6) to increase the state's ability to extract revenue from the economy in order to finance state-building, and hence the expansion of the military (this contributed to the emergence of a heavy military establishment, in relation to Ecuador's size, because it led the armed forces to purchase high-technology conventional weapons systems[23]); (7) to give the state the capacity to design and carry out national development planning.

Consequently, a statist orientation and state-building activism characterized the Ecuadorean armed forces during the 1970s. Unlike their government in 1963, however, this time the military realized that they would have to reorganize the civilian political system—that is, the mechanisms and styles of political representation. To this end, they promoted the development of new civilian political actors. The armed forces believed that these new groups shared the military's interest in promoting rational, universalistic, and technocratic values.

Although the military had to abandon political power in 1979, their government nevertheless partially succeeded in achieving its goals. New intellectual groups not linked to traditional clientelism appeared, as did new political organizations sympathetic to the armed forces' project. These groups cooperated with the military to reduce the power of the strongmen's cabal and to broaden new channels of political action as well as formal and substantive democratization. These new groups wrote the 1978 Constitution and supported the civilian governments of Jaime Roldós (1979–1981) and Osvaldo Hurtado (1981–1984).

Despite these advances, starting in 1975 traditional politicians seeking to renew their influence within the armed forces began to undermine the military's project. Tension built up among military men who supported reform, officers connected to conspiratorial cliques of civilian notables, and commanders influenced by national security doctrines. Under these circumstances the political scenario grew increasingly complex. Old clientelistic political parties and populist strongmen coexisted with new entrepreneurial groups who favored neoconservative free-market policies, as well as with groups who depended on protectionism and state support for internal markets, and relatively autonomous technocratic groups.

These social groups pressured the military with contradictory demands, leading to growing factionalism within the officer corps. We may distinguish the following tendencies in the military: authoritarian and pro-business "hard-liners," best represented by General González Alvear, who attempted a coup d'etat in 1975; the "professionalists," who favored a rapid return to the barracks in order to preserve the military's unity; the "progressives," who allied with new center-left political parties in order to institutionalize and preserve the legacy of revolutionary nationalism (Generals Levover and Vargas Pazos best represent this current); and a number of traditional clientelistic, civil–military cliques.[24] The latter revealed the persistence within the military of officers who had not internalized the new corporate-bureaucratic ethos. Overall, however, most officers believed that the exercise of political power damaged the military's unity, and they supported restoring civilian rule within the bounds of a political system that contained built-in safeguards against the divisiveness of clientelism and factionalism.

Military Professionalism versus Political Cabals

The conditions under which the military returned to the barracks actually constituted a partial victory for them. The 1978 Constitution, approved by a national referendum, granted a number of concessions to the armed forces. (1) Defense ministers would be senior general officers. (2) The president would have less influence than before in the promotion and posting of officers. In the military's eyes, this clause shielded them from two of the worst characteristics of Ecuadorean civilian politics: presidential *caudillismo* and clientelism. (3) The constitution included a number of reforms designed to change Ecuadorean political style and statecraft; for example, it sanctioned the creation of a number of public and semi-public agencies to promote rigid, centralized macroeconomic planning on the basis of "technical" criteria. (4) Additional clauses strengthened public administration in general and placed a number of strategic bureaus under military control. (5) Ecuador's new charter also sought to develop a modern party system, to stimulate public opinion, and to increase mass political participation. To achieve these goals, the 1978 Constitution contained a universal franchise rule (including illiterates), and a political party law designed to limit the number of parties and to make them programmatic. (6) Additional clauses, aimed at improving the state's technical competence, redefined the functions of the vice-presidency, giving it control over national socioeconomic planning. All of these changes favored the growth of both "center-left" tendencies and currents of public opinion opposed to traditional-style *caudillismo* and clientelism.

Since 1979, the Ecuadorean armed forces have experienced three ongoing processes: they have adapted to a new civilian political order and abandoned their governmental functions; they have adjusted their conventional war-fighting strategies to new equipment and technology acquired during the oil boom; since 1980 they have also striven to increase troop strength in order to deter Peruvian aggression. The Ecuadorean armed forces also became more introverted, retreating into professionalism by dedicating themselves to classical military functions. The barriers they had erected to civilian military influence, however, began to erode after 1986 during the presidency of Febres Cordero, who revived the practice of presidential *caudillismo*.

During this period, Ecuador's political forces divided into two blocs, the populist and traditional political parties on one side, and on the other the so-called Progressive bloc—a coalition of Christian Democrats, Social Democrats, Roldoists, and, more loosely, the Marxist left. The first bloc attempted to reestablish clientelistic and clan-based politics in alliance with important free-market-oriented business groups. The Progressive bloc supported the state's universal-relationalist project in its diverse manifestations (Catholic corporatist, laic, and statist among others).

Two phases characterized civil–military relations between 1979 and 1984. The governments of Roldós and Hurtado strove to project the armed forces from oppositionist political cabals and scrupulously respected the provisions of the 1978 Constitution. In sharp contrast to the political style that dominated until 1972, these administrations refrained from establishing personalistic control over the military. Instead, they cultivated a legalistic and impersonal relationship between the state and the armed forces. This guaranteed the military autonomy and freedom to pursue their professional goals. The government's military policies during this period allowed the armed forces to mend internal ruptures—the legacy of the past. The 1981 border clash with Peru proved the wisdom of this course of action, given the need to place military considerations before domestic politics. The Paquisha incident tightened the armed forces and reinforced their conviction that they had to guarantee internal stability. It also deepened their commitment to republican institutions and helped to shield the officer corps from politicization.

Military studies for staff officers flourished beginning in the Rodríguez Lara administration and incorporated civilian subject matter. The armed forces also demonstrated an interest in educating civilians in the Doctrine of National Security. Although the authoritarian version of this doctrine has failed to dominate military thought in Ecuador, "total-war" conceptions of national defense that seek closer links between the armed forces and civilians have gained ground. The main institutions elaborating these ideas are the Institute for Advanced Military Studies, the War Academy, the Military Geographic Institute, and Army Polytechnical School. To a certain extent, these educational establishments have managed to influence civilian elites in administrative areas characterized by a substantial military presence. The armed forces have not gained much ground with private sector elites and independent professionals. Instead, they have penetrated technocratic civilian elites in state enterprises and state-dependent clienteles born of the protectionist policies of the 1970s. These were the civilians who entered office in 1978–1979. They shared the military's statist political philosophy and waged a campaign against personalistic governing styles.

In the second, or post–1984 phase, the center-left lost its hold on power and with it the ability to mediate struggles between the state, the military, and civilian political forces. Instead, Febres Cordero's administration attempted to reintroduce traditional personalistic controls over the armed forces. These actions threatened the military's integrity and tended to weaken their loyalty to democratic institutions.

From the very start, Febres Cordero sought to make the officer corps dependent on him and openly interfered in promotions to achieve his goal. This provoked a defensive reaction from the armed forces, culminating in an uprising staged by General Frank Vargas Passos and his followers. Although General Vargas Passos invoked the cause of professionalism and institutional integrity to justify his action, the mutiny nevertheless represented a return to strongmanship within the armed forces. The general tended to emphasize loyalty to his person rather than to his position. In a bid for mass support, he also added a populist twist to his *caudillismo* by fulminating against civilian notables active in Ecuadorean politics. Consequently, the military saw their efforts to strengthen their professionalism attacked from outside by the president, as well as from inside by their would-be defenders. The latter, in the name of recovering their professional principles, embraced the personalist-charismatic leadership style of General Vargas Passos.[25]

CONCLUSIONS

Two tendencies characterize the political development of the Colombian armed forces over the last decade and a half. First, they reaffirmed their loyalty toward the Liberal–Conservative state and acknowledged the dominant political parties' capacity to exercise social control. Second, the Colombian military increased their capacity to defend the political system from internal threats based on their own independently generated doctrines.

Colombian officers remain loyal to the civilian regime, but not on a traditional clientelistic basis. Their present loyalty derives from an impersonal conception of the common good and national interest. This allows the military to be their own judge of what strengthens or weakens the nation's security regardless of whether civilian political elites share their judgments. Consequently, their loyalty to democracy is contingent, not automatic. Military men will only uphold it to the degree that it serves their increasingly peremptory demands. In other words, they no longer value democracy for itself; they only value it to the extent that it fulfills their expectations regarding national security, order, and state capacity.

The Colombian military emphasizes internal security. As a result, they increasingly stress and broaden their repressive, educational, organizational, and integrative functions. Moreover, they seek to strengthen the central government's capacity to control a highly dislocated society.

For their part, the Ecuadorean armed forces have concentrated on resolving two problems: to reform the state on the basis of a centralizing-rationalist project;

and to strengthen its defensive capabilities in order to deter Peruvian aggression. Ecuadorean officers have also dedicated themselves to creating conditions capable of sustaining modern political forms compatible with their professional development. Traditional elites and other bearers of backward political cultures have opposed them. This conflict has generated tensions within the military that induced them to return to the barracks and to reserve for themselves the management of strategic government bureaus in order to depoliticize them and to run them with technocratic-efficiency criteria.

The Ecuadorean military, however, have not managed to neutralize those who oppose their project. On the contrary, the clientelistic opposition has gained strength with the election of Febres Cordero in 1984, a fact which has led to uprisings on the part of the air force. These events raise serious questions about the governability of Ecuador's fledgling democracy within the framework devised by a center-left, civil-military technocracy. A resurgence of populist, "bossist," and patrimonial sectors has weakened political forms installed by the revolutionary-nationalist movement of the 1970s. These traditionalist forces also threaten to disintegrate the system of civil–military relations based on professional and bureaucratic-legal values established by that same movement.

NOTES

1. Stockholm International Peace Research Institute (SIPRI), *World Armaments and Disarmaments* (London: Lord and Taylor, 1986).

2. U.S. Arms Control and Disarmament Agency, *World Military Expenditures* (Washington, D.C.: Government Printing Office, 1986); and International Institute for Strategic Studies (IISS), *The Military Balance 1984–1985* (London, 1986).

3. Ibid.; and Stockholm International Peace Research Institute, *World Armaments and Disarmaments*.

4. Ibid.

5. Ibid.

6. See Paul Oquist, *Violencia, Conflicto y Política en Colombia* (Bogotá: Instituto de Estudios Colombianos, 1978); John Martz, *Colombia: A Contemporary Political Survey* (Chapel Hill: University of North Carolina Press, 1962).

7. See John Martz, *Colombia*; Albert Berry, Robert Hellman, and Mauricio Solaún, *Politics of Compromise: Coalition Government in Colombia* (New Brunswick, N.J.: Transaction Books, 1980).

8. The faction was named after President Mariano Ospina (1946–1950). He headed a moderate faction of the Conservative party that sought to preserve a consociational form of government with the Liberal party. Ospina always strove to establish the basis upon which to assure a consensual style of government committed to a moderate and flexible program. He staunchly opposed the extremist factions of Laureano Gómez and Alzate Avendano.

9. Gustavo Gallón Giraldo, *La República de las Armas: Relaciones entre las Fuerzas Armadas y Estado en Colombia, 1960–1980* (Bogotá: Centro de Investigación y Educación Popular, 1983).

10. See Russell Ramsey, "Internal Defense in the '80s: The Colombian Model,"

Comparative Strategy, no. 4 (1984); Russell Ramsey, *Civil–Military Relations in Co-lombia* (Gainesville, Fla.: Regent Publishing Co., 1978); General Alberto Ruiz Noboa, *La Misión del Ejército* (Bogotá: Imprenta de las Fuerzas Armadas, 1960); General Alberto Ruiz Noboa, *El Gran Desafío* (Bogotá: Ediciones Tercer Mundo, 1965); General Fernando Landazábal Reyes, *Factores de Violencia* (Bogotá: Ediciones Tercer Mundo, 1975).

11. Gonzalo Bermúdez Rossi, *El Poder Militar en Colombia* (Bogotá: Ediciones Expre-sion, 1982).

12. For civil–military relations in Colombia, see Alain Rouquié, *L'Etat Militaire dans L'Amérique Latine* (Paris: Editions du Seuil, 1982); Lyle McAlyster, Antony Maignot, and Robert Potash, *The Military in Latin American Socio-Political Evolution: Four Case Studies* (Washington, D.C.: Center for Research in Social Systems, 1970); James Icen-hour, "The Military in Colombian Politics" (Ph.D. diss., George Washington University, 1975); Richard Maullin, *Soldiers, Guerrillas, and Politics in Colombia* (Santa Monica, Calif.: The Rand Corporation, 1980); Lee Simpson, *The Role of the Military in Colombian Politics, 1946–1953* (Bogotá: Universidad de Los Andes, 1969); Mark Ruhl, "Civil–Military Relations in Colombia: A Societal Explanation," *Journal of Interamerican and World Affairs* 23, no. 2 (1981).

13. Gallón Giraldo, *La República de las Armas.*

14. See Stockholm International Peace Research Institute, *World Armaments and Dis-armaments;* U.S. Arms Control and Disarmament Agency, *World Military Expenditures.* The Colombian navy's modernization programs are increasingly shaped by the need to respond to threats from neighboring countries. For example, Colombia has a standing dispute with Venezuela over borders in the Maracaibo Gulf, and with Nicaragua over the island of San Andrés. By the same token, the Colombian air force has matched Venezuela's purchase of supersonic fighters.

15. Bermúdez Rossi, *El Poder Militar en Colombia.*

16. Ibid.

17. Gen. Ruiz Noboa, *La Misión del Ejército,* and *El Gran Desafío;* Gen. Landazábal Reyes, *Factores de Violencia,* and *La Subversión y el Conflicto Social* (Bogotá: Ediciones Tercer Mundo, 1980); General Alvaro Valencia Tobar, *Soldados y Guerrilleros* (Bogotá: Ediciones Tercer Mundo, 1981).

18. Stockholm International Peace Research Institute, *World Armaments and Disarmament.*

19. Ibid., and U.S. Arms Control and Disarmament Agency, *World Military Ex-penditures;* International Institute for Strategic Studies, *The Military Balance 1984–1985.*

20. Ibid.

21. U.S. Arms Control and Disarmament Agency, *World Military Expenditures.*

22. John Samuel Fitch, *The Military Coup d'Etat as a Political Process* (Baltimore: Johns Hopkins University Press, 1977).

23. With respect to the introduction of new technologies this instills a much more positive attitude among officers than among civilian elites who are still steeped in legalistic humanism and political Aristotelianism.

24. Augusto Varas and Fernando Bustamante, *Fuerzas Armadas y Política en el Ec-uador* (Quito: Ediciones Latinoamérica, 1978); Osvaldo Hurtado, *Political Power in Ecuador* (Albuquerque: University of New Mexico Press, 1980).

25. Fitch, *The Military Coup d'Etat;* Fernando Bustamante, "Problemas y Dinámica de la Política Ecuatoriana Actual," *Documento de Trabajo,* no. 331 (Santiago: *Facultad Latinoamericana de Ciencias Sociales* (FLACSO), 1987).

3 THE ARMED FORCES IN PERUVIAN POLITICS

Marcial Rubio Correa

This chapter analyzes the role of the armed forces in the Peruvian political process from 1959 on, focusing on their formal relationship to the state, their capabilities, and the core concepts of their doctrine. In this context, the term armed forces refers exclusively to the army, navy, and air force. Peru's three national police organizations—the civil guard, the republican guard, and the investigations police—will not be taken into account for two reasons: first, their main function is to protect life and property and they rarely collaborate with the military; second, politically they respond to the Interior Ministry instead of the Defense Ministry, although they are under the immediate control of the Joint Chiefs of Staff.[1]

MANUEL PRADO'S ADMINISTRATION: 1956–1962

Shortly after the founding of the Centro de Altos Estudios Militares (CAEM) in 1954, the armed forces demonstrated their desire to turn the concept "participant professionalism" into reality.[2] Officers believed in the legitimacy and necessity of their involvement in the politics of national development. They felt that it was their right and duty to become involved in the policy-making process and to fight for the implementation of development programs that they favored, because they were certain that these would increase the nation's security. In other words, the military's security doctrine justified their political interventions under the banner of "participatory professionalism." There is no doubt that the Peruvian military envision a political role for themselves that goes far beyond counterinsurgency strategies, such as civic action, designed by the Pentagon.[3] In 1959, CAEM presented its first official development program, regarding the central jungle region, to President Prado. The plan revealed the military's preoccupation, as expressed in their doctrine, with turning potential strength into actual power. But President Prado resented the unsolicited advice, and declared that he would rather resign than bow to pressure from the military. He also undertook a series of largely ineffectual measures to limit CAEM to the study of military strategy proper.

The year 1959 was also marked by national outrage over the behavior of the International Petroleum Company (IPC), which rocked the Prado administration. A vigorous public debate over the firm's future followed. The Joint Chiefs of Staff joined the debate with a nationalist position on the subject of expropriation.

THE MILITARY JUNTA OF 1962

In 1962, for the first time in Peru's history, the military qua institution took over the reins of government. A brief discussion of the circumstances that led to the coup d'etat follows. These events reveal the main political cleavages and conflicts in Peruvian society.

APRA won a plurality in the 1962 presidential elections, but did not obtain enough votes to win the election outright. Under these circumstances, the choosing of the president fell to Congress. It soon became general knowledge that APRA would not fight for its candidate. Instead, the party instructed its Congressmen to vote for General Odría, who had come in third as the candidate of the National Odrist Union. The Odría–APRA coalition represented a continuation of APRA's turn to the right, which had begun in 1956 when it backed Manuel Prado—a representative of the Peruvian oligarchy.

Meanwhile, Fernando Belaúnde Terry had come in second. In those days, he represented a rising, modernizing middle class borne of Peru's belated efforts at import substitution industrialization. This middle class was fighting for political space in a largely agrarian society dominated by an oligarchy whose power rested on traditional, noncapitalist systems of land tenure and production. Needless to say, modernization threatened the foundations of the oligarchy's social power.

The military intervened, claiming electoral fraud. Regardless of whether that was actually the case, the junta's actions from 1962 to 1963 leave no doubt that they had well-defined goals. First, they clearly wanted Belaúnde to be president. After the coup, Belaúnde's supporters danced in the streets for joy and the junta turned the presidency over to him after new elections in 1963. Second, the armed forces continued to deny APRA the opportunity to become the ruling party.

The military also introduced a series of reforms which may seem mild in comparison to what happened in 1968, but which were quite significant at the time. For example, a national planning administration was established that has essentially remained unchanged. The armed forces also came out with an agrarian reform law and implemented a pilot project in the Convención valley, which had been the scene of strong union-based mobilization led by Hugo Blanco. Moreover, the junta approved additional progressive measures, such as a more flexible labor code and enforcement of minimum wage laws that had been on the books since 1933.

This represented a substantial amount of legislation given the junta's one-year tenure. The military's actions reflected their security doctrine and breathed new life into the nation's recent modernizing surge. But most important, the armed forces stayed in government only long enough to revamp Peru's electoral process. They updated the electoral register and passed a new electoral law that the military elaborated in close collaboration with a number of political parties. The generals also made sure that they left the government in the hands of a reformist politician who seemed committed to progressive positions on hydrocarbon development, agrarian reform, and industrialization.

THE COUNTERINSURGENCY CAMPAIGN, 1965

Peruvian leftists began Cuban-style guerrilla warfare throughout the country in 1965. At first, the government treated the disturbances as the result of conflicts between ranchers and cattle rustlers. But the authorities soon had to face up to the unpleasant reality and entrust a counterinsurgency campaign to the military. Ironically, while the armed forces developed their own security doctrine, they did not do the same with regard to counterinsurgency. Thus, they employed all of the standard strategies and tactics of the time.

Although the military defeated the guerrillas, the experience had rather paradoxical results. It awakened anti-imperialist and reformist sentiments among the officer corps. Two factors contributed to this state of affairs. To begin with, the armed forces became aware of their technological dependence on the United States when the Pentagon denied them a request for napalm bombs. The military realized that they could not rely on the United States to provide them with the material they wanted. That could prove disastrous in a conflict of a different nature, such as a war with one of their neighboring states. In short, the armed forces saw that they had to diversify their sources of military hardware—which they did during the government of General Velasco.

But the military also became acutely aware of the consequences of underdevelopment for internal security, in particular with regard to the most backward region—the highlands. Their prescription: the country needed an extensive development program oriented toward improving the living standards of the impoverished masses. This also became a central concern of General Velasco's government.

THE VELASCO ADMINISTRATION

These changes in the military's outlook also had their roots in the general transformation of Peruvian society, and were thus shared by other institutions, such as the Catholic church. But the executive branch of the government did not follow suit. Little by little, President Belaúnde abandoned his initially re-

formist positions. Conservative opposition in Congress—the Odría–APRA coalition—greatly contributed to Belaúnde's change of heart.

The critical period for Belaúnde's presidency turned out to be the months
between July and October of 1968. Peru was wracked by a prolonged economic
crisis which had led to a 40 percent devaluation of the sol in the previous year,
after nine years of stable exchange rates. Peru's balance-of-payments problems
brought the nation's 50-year-long confrontation with the International Petroleum
Company to a head. During his electoral campaign, Belaúnde had promised to
resolve the issue within 90 days. Most people, including military men, believed
that Belaúnde had some form of state expropriation in mind and approved of
such action.

But five years had passed and the situation remained unchanged. Then, on
July 28, 1968, Belaúnde announced that a solution to the IPC conflict was
immanent. When he made the details of his administration's settlement with IPC
public in August, Peruvian nationalists reacted with sharp disappointment. In
their eyes Belaúnde had given in to foreign corporate interests. The president
of Peru's state-run oil company contributed to the public outcry when he revealed
that one of the contract's pages was missing, which meant that the government
was hiding something. In the midst of this fracas, a split in the ruling party,
mass demonstrations, and a scandal over government officials implicated in
contraband schemes rocked the government. This state of affairs prompted General Velasco and a small group of army colonels to stage a coup d'etat on October
3, 1968. The coup marked the beginning of the most sweeping reforms that Peru
had experienced in the twentieth century. Although a number of works have
analyzed this period, some of the main transformations bear repeating.[4]

The virtual elimination of the oligarchy's political power and the emergence
of a modern state in Peru constituted the most significant change that occurred
in this period. At the time, there was much speculation about whether Velasco
was building a socialist state. Today, of course, it is clear that Velasco was
dedicated to modernizing Peru within a capitalist framework. Nevertheless, for
its time and place, that represented a long overdue undertaking.

The military implemented a number of drastic reforms in order to bring about
those structural reforms: they nationalized a number of strategic industries and
much of the financial system; they strengthened the state via a thorough administrative reorganization and by expanding the public sector; they regulated strategic economic sectors, encouraged worker participation in the management of
firms, and increased the state's role in providing start-up capital for new enterprises. Of course, two measures stand head and shoulders above the rest: the
nationalization of IPC and agrarian reform; which thoroughly transformed Peruvian land tenure systems.

Throughout this period a constant nationalist and anti-imperialist rhetoric had
a significant and lasting impact on the political consciousness of the people. In
some instances the government's oratory, concomitant with the political elimination of the oligarchy and the implementation of social reforms, produced

wholly unintended consequences. For example, it contributed to raising the self-esteem of the popular sectors and their penetration by the left. Suddenly, peasants, workers and shantytown dwellers recognized that they too had rights and began to fight for them. This new consciousness and combative spirit, in turn, made them more receptive to the Peruvian left. True, the Peruvian left had always had a political presence among these social groups, but it bordered on insignificance. The left's strong roots in these sectors today owes much to the policies of Velasco's government. Velasco himself, however, judging by his statements at the time, seemed dismayed over this development.

Velasco's tenure also had profound consequences for the armed forces themselves. Several transformations led to significant increases in their institutionalization, which gave rise to a largely autonomous military organization. First, his administration diversified the military's sources for weapons. From virtually total dependence on the United States, Peru began to acquire military hardware from a number of countries: from France and the Soviet Union for the air force, Italy for the navy, and again the Soviet Union for the army. The Peruvian armed forces' relationship with these nations continues to this day.

Second, the military diversified the types of combat units that it fields, and they now count on a number of highly specialized combat units. Moreover, combat units are manned mainly by enlisted personnel, who presumably have a greater commitment to the military than conscripts. This does not mean, however, that Peru has eliminated conscription.

Third, the armed forces developed their capacity to train personnel in highly specialized technical fields, including electronics—a field in which the military has taken the lead in Peru. As the military's capacity to manage firms and conduct basic research and development has increased, so has its budget, expressed as a share of gross domestic product.

In summary, it seems that General Velasco's administration remained true to Peruvian military doctrine both in terms of defense and national development policies. Adopting a reformist position on social issues, it also implemented a number of measures designed to strengthen the institutions of the armed forces. A belief that these actions were the direct responsibility of the military constituted a central characteristic of his government; otherwise, he may not have so vigorously resisted pressures to build a personal political movement.

GENERAL MORALES BERMÚDEZ'S ADMINISTRATION

Unfavorable international conditions and the Velasco government's fiscal policies produced a new economic crisis. Meeting the crisis within the boundaries of the military regime's original goals to transform the structure of Peruvian society required implementing more radical policies. At first, it seemed that General Morales Bermúdez might adopt such a course. But U.S. pressure steered him in a different direction: the military abandoned its reformist posture, thereby isolating itself; it lost popular support and proved unable to gain that of conservatives. A national general strike on July 19, 1977, highlighted the junta's isolation, and represented civil society's repudiation of the military regime. The generals realized that the time had come to leave government. Thus, in order to pave the way for a return to civilian government, in 1978 the junta set up a constituent assembly and an electoral timetable. General Morales Bermúdez stepped down on July 28, 1978, and Belaúnde Terry took his place.

The military's exit from government happened in a very orderly fashion. No one violated the timetable set by them. Moreover, during its last few months in office the junta established new legislation, much of it pertaining to the rights and privileges of the military, which Belaúnde did not attempt to alter. In fact, he gave them the force of law by ratifying them with new legislation, thus institutionalizing the role of the armed forces in the present democratic regime.

THE MILITARY IN CONTEMPORARY PERU

The Peruvian Constitution, article 278, stipulates that where politics are concerned the armed forces are nondeliberant institutions subordinated to constitutional rule of law. But "nondeliberant" is an ambiguous concept. For example, according to the *Real Academia de la Lengua Española,* it refers to the duly debated and voted-on executive decisions of associations regarding society-wide issues. Peruvians, however, define the term somewhat differently. Alberto Thorndike, a retired air force officer and assemblyman for the Popular Christian Party, defined it this way: "The active duty personnel of the armed forces and the police may not belong to political parties, nor may they engage in political activities. Moreover, they must obey the constitutionally established authorities, otherwise they would be eroding discipline, one of the very fundaments of their institution."[5] Moreover, Alan García Pérez, an APRA Congressman and current president of Peru, quoted the party's founder Haya de la Torre as saying: "The armed forces are democratic institutions charged with guarding the nation's security and should categorically refrain from all political activity."[6]

Jurists have also helped to define the role of the armed forces in Peruvian society. Dr. Jose Pareja Paz Soldan has written: "The high command of the armed forces are perfectly aware that their essential function is to defend both the constitution and the democratically elected political authorities. The military's institutional interest and sense of duty combine to reinforce this position. The problems of the nation are too formidable and complex for them to solve on their own, hence the military must refrain from political activity. To say that they are nondeliberant is to recognize that they are subordinate to the constitution."[7]

Unfortunately, Peruvian academics have historically tended to shy away from the unpleasant reality of the military's involvement in politics. According to Dr. Javier de Belaunde Lopez de Romaña, "a review of the judicial literature over the last 25 years reveals two things. On the one hand, an overly reverential attitude towards the constitution, the terms of which depend on prevailing judicial values. On the other hand, a paradoxical neglect of the rule of *de facto* [arbitrary] governments."[8] The Supreme Court added to the problem when, in 1965, it declared that, "the decree-laws of *de facto governments* remain in force as long as they are not ratified, rescinded, modified or substituted by new legislation."[9]

Nevertheless, some constitutional issues are unambiguous. The president is the commander in chief of the armed forces and the supreme director of the nation's defense policy. The president's ministers, who serve at his pleasure, are responsible for carrying out the executive's security policy. The president is accountable to the people, not the military.

But the Belaúnde government (1980–1985) compromised the principle of absolute presidential control of the armed forces when it ratified two decree-laws issued during the administration of General Morales Bermúdez. First, the national defense law (no. 22,653) placed authority for national security in the hands of a National Defense Council. Its permanent members include: the president of the Republic, who is also the Council's chairman; the ministers of defense of the army, navy, and air force, who are either active-duty or retired officers; the foreign minister and the ministers of interior, economy, and finance, who are in principle civilians; the chairman of the Joint Chiefs of Staff; and the head of the National Defense Secretariat, who has a voice but no vote on the Council. The commanders in chief of the three service branches, the director of the National Planning Institute, and the director of the National Intelligence Service may also be called to participate in the National Defense Council's deliberations. The Council's function is to participate in the framing of society-wide goals as well as in the formulation of national security policies.

Second, a mobilization law (decree-law no. 23,118) assigned a number of additional functions to the National Defense Council. It gave the Council authority to plan and execute national mobilization policy, and defined mobilization in such a way that it covered not only persons but also goods and services. The Council could ration goods and services, restructure economic production, and expropriate, requisition, and intervene in firms according to necessity.

The Defense Council's functions leave no doubt that it is a deliberant body that undermines constitutionally established authorities. According to the constitution, security policy is the president's responsibility, and if he is to have an advisory council that task belongs to his ministers. The way things stand now, most of the cabinet is excluded from policy making in security matters broadly defined. Instead, the chairman of the Joint Chiefs of Staff, and the commanders in chief of the army, navy, and air force, have acquired substantial policy-making capabilities.

A reorganization of the defense ministries in 1981 added to the military's political influence because it made the ministries dependent on them. Legislative decrees nos. 130, 131, and 132 left the defense ministries with inadequate resources to independently carry out their mandated functions. The commanders in chief of the three service branches, however, possessed the administrative means that the ministries lacked. Thus, although the commanders in chief—and hence their respective institutions—lacked formal policy-making authority, informally they marshalled significant capabilities. They controlled administrative resources crucial to the functioning of the defense ministries, and they participated in the National Defense Council.

In other words, a number of arrangements that give the military significant participation in policy decisions have diminished the president's authority over the armed forces. This presents a clear contradiction between the constitutionally mandated powers of the presidency and the de facto power of the military. This is largely due to the civilian politicians' inability to design alternative constitutional frameworks. Such frameworks need to reconcile the rule of law with the military's need to participate in national policy making. That would allow them to make their contribution to national politics in a subordinate position to constitutionally mandated authorities.

At present, however, the Peruvian armed forces have substantial independent policy-making capabilities that are sanctioned by the law of the land. This supports the hypothesis that the military's autonomy has increased over the last few years. By the same token, the capacity of civilian political authorities to control the armed forces and shape national policy making has declined. The military's burgeoning managerial and technical competence buttresses their influence in policy debates.

A number of events in the 1980–1985 period tend to confirm these conclusions. One of the clearest examples is the Peruvian military's behavior during the Malvinas War, when they forced several of the government's decisions and acted with complete independence on a number of occasions. Although the deliberations on these matters were secret, it is possible to draw inferences from certain actions and public discrepancies. For example, France stopped an arms shipment to Peru claiming that it feared that Peru would relay the arms to Argentina. The armed forces were openly sympathetic to the cause of their Argentine comrades, and that frequently clashed with the government's official posture.

The military's counterinsurgency activity also highlights their increased autonomy with respect to civilian control. Although the president has not granted the military their every request, it is nevertheless clear that the military have tremendous leeway within the "emergency zone"; for example, their authority supersedes that of local officeholders, and they frequently engage in extra-constitutional activities, such as human rights atrocities. When the men responsible for these violations, which may be interpreted as common crimes against life and liberty, go to trial, they do so before military tribunals. These mete out light penalties for excessive zeal in the line of duty, which suggests that military justice is granting soldiers the right to behave in a lawless manner. Recent legislation has ratified the military's legal jurisdiction over these matters in the "emergency zone." And, whenever these issues reach the Supreme Court it too usually decides that military courts, not civilian courts, have jurisdiction when soldiers violate the rights of citizens.

Lastly, the public record on human rights violations demonstrates that both the judicial and the legislative branches of the government lack the resources to successfully carry out their functions. This is especially true if those functions involve taking actions that the military opposes.

Despite these problems there is a positive side to civil–military relations. Since 1980, the armed forces have committed themselves to maintaining the democratic regime and to upholding constitutionally defined rules of the game. The clearest example is the fact that they have de facto abrogated their opposition to APRA— the current ruling party—in spite of the fact that it is once again a progressive political party and has allied with the left.

THE PERUVIAN ARMED FORCES IN THE FUTURE

Understanding the Peruvian military's medium-term prospects requires a brief examination of three factors: civil–military relations, military doctrine, and military spending. Although in reality these three areas clearly overlap, they may be kept distinct for the purpose of analysis.

Civil–Military Relations

In all probability, the Peruvian armed forces will retain their substantial presence in the nation's decision-making processes. At present, Peru's institutional structure gives them substantial negotiating power in governmental circles, and, if things go drastically wrong, they can always stage another coup d'etat. The military seems to be the most competent and cohesive political institution in Peru, since neither civil society nor the political parties are well organized.

Of course, coups d'etat do not solely rest with the military. They also depend on factors such as the maturation and consolidation of democratic processes and the organization of the masses. The fact that the present democratic regime has lasted five years and that the people are more organized offers some room for cautious optimism that the military will, at least formally, stay in the barracks. Although, of course, a coup d'etat is always a real possibility.

But two other factors are the truly decisive ones. The democratic regime must contain the peasant insurgency, now in its fifth year, and it must find an efficacious solution to the nation's economic and social crisis. If democratic governments prove incapable of controlling either one of these factors, Peru may slowly disintegrate as violence and anomie rise to unimagined levels. Under these circumstances, the military would be sorely tempted to intervene.

Military Doctrine

The Peruvian armed forces have developed their own defense doctrine, but have so far accepted standard counterinsurgency strategies. Unfortunately, some of the fundamental concepts of these doctrines do not complement each other, but conflict. It is hoped that the military will concentrate on reformulating their counterinsurgency doctrine. But how the military resolves this problem depends on the ability of their academic institutions to preserve the main thrust of their defense doctrine, while adding to it a counterinsurgency strategy. At present the outcome remains uncertain. It is impossible to foresee if CAEM's developmentalist and progressive faction will prevail.

Circumstance may tip the balance in favor of the hawks, who back more repressive and antipopular measures that resemble the posture of most South American military institutions. In any case, the government's actions will play an important part in determining which faction wins. It will help the progressive faction to the degree that it stops relying on purely military counterinsurgency strategies, which have failed to curb guerrilla activity.

Military Spending

Weapons procurements have garnered a relatively high share of GDP and foreign exchange expenditures over the last 15 years. These outlays, however, have placed a considerable strain on the nation's finances. Thus, the current economic crisis calls into question whether the state can continue dedicating such a large share of the national income to the military.

But it is also evident that to the degree that advanced nations develop new generations of weapons, Latin American armed forces will be compelled to undertake expensive modernization programs. Efficient use of these new weapons systems requires periodic restructuring of the armed forces, which is also expensive. For now, it is impossible to predict whether the Peruvian military will inflexibly push their demands for these types of goods. If they do, they will most likely force the issue of whether or not they should govern directly.

NOTES

1. The army tried for several years to establish a single Defense Ministry, but the navy and the air force opposed such plans. Since military officers traditionally become defense ministers, the other branches of the service were concerned that such a proposal might reduce their power.

2. Strictly speaking, CAEM developed this concept in the 1980s. But its core ideas were already in evidence during the 1960s, especially after the 1968 coup d'etat.

3. CAEM ideology stated, first, that the state should be concerned with the general well-being, defined as the adequate and timely satisfaction of material and spiritual needs. Development constitutes the means to achieve this end. Instead of relying on the usual economic indicators it emphasizes income redistribution, which requires a transformation of Peruvian economic and social structures. Second, CAEM theorists developed the concept of integral security, defined as a situation that guarantees the state its existence, the integrity of its patrimony, its autonomy, and its freedom from external subordination. "National defense" provided the means for attaining these goals.

4. For good overviews of this period, see Abraham F. Lowenthal, *The Peruvian Experiment: Continuity and Change under Military Rule* (Princeton: Princeton University

Press, 1975); and Alfred Stepan, *The State and Society: Peru in Comparative Perspective* (Princeton: Princeton University Press, 1978).

5. *Congressional Record*, vol. 7 (Lima: Official Publication of the Republic of Peru, 1978), 459.

6. Ibid., 479.

7. *Derecho Constitucional Peruano*, vol. 2 (Lima: n.p., 1980), 804.

8. *Derecho,* no. 32 (1974), 4.

9. This resolution reinforced the actual political role of the military.

4 DEMOCRATIZATION AND MILITARY REFORM IN ARGENTINA

Augusto Varas

Because Argentina's fledgling democracy has met with resistance, especially within the armed forces, it stands out as a critical case for understanding the process of democratic consolidation in Latin America. So far, the government's attempts to submit the military to tight civilian control have succeeded, but the military have also begun to resist that control. President Raúl Alfonsin's administration took quick, decisive action to keep the situation in hand: it retired a substantial number of officers who were holdovers from the previous dictatorial regime. Nevertheless, the present administration has prudently avoided radical antimilitary policies; perhaps because, on two past occasions, Radical party governments fell as a result of the military's objections to their policies.[1]

Two additional factors compound the difficulties of Argentina's democratic regime. First, the military institution that the regime seeks to bring under control reached the highest degree of autonomy of any in Latin America. Second, because the armed forces themselves largely carried out the repression against civilians in the so-called dirty war, the government has to deal with a very sensitive human rights issue. After all, the military institutionalized one of the most extensive criminal undertakings in the region.[2]

While it may be premature to draw firm conclusions from the Argentine case, it does highlight the main contradictions inherent in the process of subjecting the military to civilian control. On the one hand, there is a democratic regime that mediates between the armed forces and an Argentine society that has mobilized in defense of human rights. Moreover, it is a society that was profoundly traumatized by the cruelty and enormity of the crimes committed against it.[3] On the other hand, we find the military fighting to maintain their corporate integrity. Because they sanctioned human rights violations they now face a situation where the central component of their corporative identity—their autonomy as a political actor—is being challenged. The government undermines the armed forces qua political actor to the degree that it punishes officers for their institutional decision to wage the dirty war. Such actions deny the legitimacy of autonomous political stances on the part of the military. They also weaken the military's capacity to establish political coalitions with civilian forces, or to replace civilian governments when these seemingly break down.

In the final analysis, then, two things are at stake in Argentina: the question of getting the military back to the barracks; and the issue of finding ways in which the armed forces may participate constructively in Argentine political life.

ALFONSIN'S MILITARY POLICIES

Alfonsin outlined the thrust of his military reform policies during his presidential campaign. He promised to cut military spending, punish human rights violations, abolish the doctrine of national security, and demilitarize internal security forces. He also promised to transfer control of federal and provincial forces, border and coast guards, and the aeronautical police to the Interior Ministry. Moreover, his campaign platform promised a reform of military intelligence agencies and a transfer of the industries under military control to the Defense Ministry.

These policies reflected Alfonsin's vision of the military's proper role in Argentine society. He confronted the military with these issues during a luncheon at the Granaderos regiment, where he told them that they should not take refuge in an apolitical corporativism, but instead should make a commitment to the nation within a democratic framework.[4] In other words, the armed forces should adopt a non-deliberant role in politics, and should subordinate themselves to civilian authorities sanctioned by the nation's constitution.

The stability of Argentine democracy depended on subordinating the military to the democratic rules of the game. Alfonsin argued that the nation's international isolation fundamentally rested on the bad reputation it had acquired as a result of military dictatorship.[5] A constitutionally subordinate military would thus give Argentina's international prestige a sorely needed boost, and Argentina needed all the respect it could get in order to carry out delicate international negotiations.[6] This definition of the military's role in society was a core element of Alfonsin's blueprint for reordering civil–military relations in Argentina. But he has also criticized civilians for their management of Argentine politics. For example, at a dinner with three hundred officers he said that "civil society [had] not conducted itself as well as it should."[7]

Of course, the Malvinas War had unequivocally exposed the tragic consequences of an autonomous military. Alfonsin underscored this fact when he declared, "the armed forces had already demonstrated that they were incapable of running either the government or the economy, now they have shown that they cannot even fight a war."[8] The military themselves officially recognized their incapacity to wage conventional warfare in a document released to the press by the chairman of the Joint Chiefs of Staff, Edgardo Calvi, in October 1984.[9]

During the Radical party's presidential primaries, Alfonsin also made it clear that his administration would repeal the amnesty law decreed by the military government on September 23, 1983.[10] That law had absolved the security forces from all responsibility for their actions between May 25, 1973 and June 17, 1982. The so-called national pacification law made it impossible to punish anyone, "regardless of the nature of the transgression."[11]

THE RADICAL ADMINISTRATION'S MILITARY REFORM

During the transition to political democracy, all Argentine political groups were aware of the need to reform the armed forces' functions and structures. As a result, shortly after the democratic regime's inauguration, the Peronist bloc in the Chamber of Deputies introduced a bill called the National Defense Law. This bill was a reworking of law no. 16,970, which had been passed during General Ongania's administration.[12]

Toward the beginning of November, Juan Carlos Pugliese, Afonsin's principal advisor for military affairs, made a series of recommendations regarding the restructuring of the armed forces. During his presidential campaign, Alfonsin had mentioned the necessity of abolishing separate chief-of-staff structures for each branch of the military. Instead, Alfonsin advocated creating a joint chief-of-staff structure that would be the military's highest organizational expression.[13]

Although the outline of the government's military reform proposals originated among Radical party stalwarts, the military actually drew up the bill. This generated a basic agreement between the government and the military regarding both the spirit and the central tenets that would guide the restructuring of the armed forces. The reform bill emphasized joint planning of, and cooperation during, operations among the three branches of the service. Moreover, the military would have to draw up their orders based on directives from the Defense Ministry and the presidency.[14]

The Radical party's National Defense Law envisioned close cooperation between the Joint Chiefs of Staff and the Defense Ministry in the formulation of military strategy. The bill included provisions, first expressed during the presidential campaign, to create a National Defense Council (*Consejo de Defensa Nacional*—CODENA). CODENA would consist of the president, cabinet, and the general secretary of the presidency.[15] These new norms would undoubtedly affect national planning defense-related civil service, national mobilization, conscription, and military personnel statutes.

But the National Defense Law delegated the actual planning of operations to new organizational structures–the joint commands–under the direction of a chief of theater operations who would work closely with the members of all three branches of the service. During a conflict, the president of the republic would take direct control of the joint commands. In peace time, they would be under the control of the Joint Chiefs of Staff. A war cabinet–the regular cabinet plus the chairman of the Joint Chiefs of Staff–would advise the president in a conflict situation. The bill also provided the president with a second advisory board–the military cabinet–consisting of the defense minister, the chairman of the Joint Chiefs of Staff, and the heads of the general staffs of the army, the air force, and the navy.

Alfonsin's military reform proposals turned on the need to reprofessionalize the armed forces.[16] Thus, modernizing the doctrine of national security became one of his principal goals.[17] The government applied the same criteria to Argentina's police forces. For example, in March 1984 the interior minister declared that "police training [must] teach that a democratic republic, framed by the Constitution, is superior to and more desirable than any other system." In his eyes, this was the only way to recuperate the self-esteem that should come with the job.[18]

From this perspective it becomes easier to understand the government's initial emphasis on modifying both the structure and content of educational programs. One of the initial ideas consisted of making the entire officer corps attend a Unified Military College.[19] A conversation between the defense minister, Raúl Borras, and the defense committee of the Chamber of Deputies in August 1984 underscored the government's intention to transform military education. The minister emphasized two things: first, he indicated that the government would immediately implement plans to restructure the military's curriculum; second, he wanted to make officers seeking promotions take required university courses in the humanities, and to replace some professors with others whose outlook was more compatible with the new civilian government's goals.[20]

Furthermore, the government's military reform policies strove to transfer industries previously controlled by the armed forces to the Defense Ministry, thus placing them under the direction of civilians.[21] The government issued an executive decree at the beginning of 1984 to implement these shifts.[22]

Alfonsin continued to demonstrate his resolve to bring the military under civilian control by reducing a number of their prerogatives. The new statutes, effective December 1983, concentrated war-making powers in the presidency and the Defense Ministry.[23] Alfonsin also delegated new authority to the Defense Ministry. These new powers allowed the minister to preside over the promotion and retirement of high-ranking officers. But the military would continue to exercise control over disciplinary matters, courts martial, and obligatory retirements.[24] Civilian leaders also sought to curtail the armed forces' international connections, as when Alfonsin denied a United States request for Argentine participation in UNITAS operations.[25]

CIVILIAN CONTROL OVER THE DEFENSE ESTABLISHMENT

There is little doubt that the government's forced retirement and promotions policy constituted its boldest act with regard to bringing the military under civilian control. With respect to promotions, Alfonsin first turned his attention to the Joint Chiefs of Staff (JCS). He appointed Julio Fernandez Torres chairman of the JCS. He then nominated Jorge Arguindeguy, Rear Admiral Ramon Arosa, and Brigadier General Teodoro Waldner to be the army, navy, and air force representatives to the JCS.[26]

Since most of these men did not have seniority among high-ranking officers, their appointment signaled the forced retirement of many others. For example, General Arguindeguy was 27th in line. That meant that the 26 men ahead of him had to go into retirement. Arosa's and Waldner's nominations required the retirement of 16 admirals and 3 brigadier generals respectively. By the same token, Alfonsin also reduced the overall number of army generals to 18 and eliminated the IV Army Corps. By the end of December 1983, he had retired a total of 44 generals. Moreover, Alfonsin replaced the head of the National Atomic Energy Commission, Admiral Carlos Castro Madero (ret.), with an engineer, Alberto Constantino, although Castro Madero became a private consultant for the Commission.[27] Finally, on April 22, 1984, the government carried out an extensive housecleaning operation in the air force when it forced the retirement of 22 brigadier generals.[28]

The armed forces soon reacted against the government's massive forced retirement policy and began to pressure the authorities to change it.[29] The government, in turn, sent a bill to Congress in order to promote 213 officers, mostly colonels and generals.[30] The situation took a turn for the worse when close to 2,000 noncommissioned officers left the army in the beginning of 1984 because of inadequate salaries. Their monthly pay fluctuated from a low of US$100 to a high of US$350 for men with 30 years of service.[31]

In addition to consolidating the military's command structure and improving their curriculum, Argentina's democratic regime also addressed the issue of military budget cuts. After the defeat in the Malvinas War, General Bignone's administration increased military spending to its highest levels in the past few decades: for example, his administration witnessed the inauguration of Argentina's second nuclear plant, with an output of six hundred megawatts; and, in April 1983, the director of the Nuclear Energy Commission announced plans to construct a nuclear submarine.

Meanwhile, the navy's budget for refitting the fleet reached five billion dollars, two billion of which were already in the pipeline in the first months of 1983. The navy also increased its arms deals with France with the purchase of 10 Super Etendard and 20 Exocet missiles.[32] Moreover, in the first quarter of 1983 the navy bought 12 Xavante that cost a total of four million dollars. In addition to these acquisitions, it had five coast guard ships on order with the Spanish ship-builders FERROL, and Argentina's state-owned shipyards were constructing six corvettes Meko—140, four frigates Meko—360, and several submarines of the TR—1700 class.

The air force also embarked on an ambitious refitting program. To begin with, it ordered its manufacturing plants–the Military Aeronautic Industries–to build the training jet IA—63 Puma, and commissioned feasibility studies for the Lavi, an aircraft recently developed by Israel. The air force also replaced the 109 airplanes lost in the war with 200 more modern aircraft.

But it was the army that consumed the largest share of the military budget– 54 percent–much of which went to pay the salaries of the 120,000 people it employed, including civilian personnel. After the Malvinas War, the army ordered the manufacture of the new Argentine Assault Rifle Model 81 (FAA-81). And after the inauguration of the new democratic regime, it organized an airborne assault unit composed of 24 Super Puma helicopters. This force was attached to the Army Air Corps.[33]

When the government-elect took over the reins of power, military spending ate up 8 percent of GDP. Alfonsin planned to cut it down to 2 percent of GDP. To achieve this goal, the Alfonsin administration wanted to reduce conscription and pare down operations and materiel. They intended to discontinue construction of the Argentine Medium Tank and the IA–63 airplane, and decided to stop all equipment orders that were not already in the works. They also wanted to restructure the financing of existing military purchases (longer payment terms) as well as those of military research and development. Current financing consumed US$130 million per year.[34]

In April 1984, the Defense Ministry announced its intention to cut military spending by 39 percent compared to the 1983 budget. These cuts slashed military spending to a little over 3 percent of GDP, compared to 5.8 percent for 1983.[35] According to press releases, the government's military budget looked something like the following: salaries accounted for about 3 percent of GDP, and 0.94 percent went for maintenance.[36] These figures, however, did not take into account about 0.62 percent of GDP for pensions. In any case, these numbers contrasted sharply with what the military demanded, 5.48 percent of GDP.

The government's military reform measures also included reassigning military units to their natural theaters of operations. Thus, in August 1984, Defense Minister Borras announced that they would be stationed close to Argentina's borders, rather than at the major cities. In October, the government disbanded Buenos Aires' First Army Corps, dismantled 14 smaller units, and transferred command of the Argentine navy prefecture from the navy to the Defense Ministry. These changes resulted in a 75 percent reduction in the number of conscripts compared to 1965, leaving the army about 40,000 strong. Finally, the government cut obligatory military service from 14 to 13 months.[37]

The armed forces also controlled Argentina's military industries, and expressed their industrial autonomy by selling arms to Central American governments. The General Directorate of Military Manufacturers (GDMF) made the last sale on May 27, 1983 (resolution 0639-D). The National Savings and Loan Bank extended a US$113.6 million credit line to finance GDMF promotional arms exports. Buyers could begin payments in 1985 at 7.5 percent annual interest rates. Honduras took out a US$17 million loan, El Salvador borrowed US$19 million,

Guatemala got US$28.5 million, Haiti accepted US$1.5 million, and Ecuador received US$47.5 million.[38]

The ruling Radical party's policy has been to continue promoting the export of Argentine arms manufactures, but under the direction of civilian political authorities. That is why in mid–1984 the government studied the possibility of establishing a unified distribution system. The idea was to have this organization attend to the import needs and export capacity of the industries under the wing of the Defense Ministry.

The Defense Ministry inherited a headache. The GDMF's 24 firms alone had accumulated a staggering US$1.5 billion foreign debt. The debt burden was actually higher because the Defense Ministry also took control of another 23 companies tied to the GDMF enterprises.[39] The General Directorate of Military Manufactures managed sulfur factories, steel mills, ironworks, and petrochemical plants. But the incoming government had no reliable balance sheets for their operations. Not even the Minister of Economy, Miguel Aleman, knew how they functioned.

It has been estimated that the GDMF employed some forty thousand persons, making it an important state-owned conglomerate. This placed it in conflict with the private sector. For example, in the steel industry the GDMF's mills enjoyed a number of privileges that gave them a competitive edge. The same held true for the aluminum industry, where plants managed by the air force received subsidies not available to private sector firms. Meanwhile, the navy controlled the nuclear energy program and the shipyards that built corvettes, frigates, and submarines.

The GDMF's nuclear research and development enterprise exemplified this conglomerate's autonomy. This R&D firm, the INVAP, employed eight hundred persons in the Rio Negro province, and its balance sheet, plans, and programs remained unknown. The INVAP was the product of an agreement between the Rio Negro province and the National Atomic Energy Commission.

Sharp competition characterized the relations among firms under the direction of different branches of the military. Sometimes this competition led them to take extreme measures, such as sabotage, against their competitors. These industries did not keep track of costs, they sold 80 percent of their products to the private sector, and roughly 70 to 80 percent of their production was in nonmilitary merchandise. Their products were generally of low quality, and upon occasion did not work at all, such as the communications equipment used in the Malvinas War. In the case of the Motorola communications devices, investigators later uncovered fradulent billings and corruption in sales procedures. In short, Argentine military industries exhibited a high degree of unmanageability and had a negligible spillover effect in technologies with civilian application.[40]

The new democratic regime quickly set about to rectify this condition. Raul Tomas, undersecretary of defense production, declared that all military industries would undergo an audit conducted by an independent auditor. He also sacked all officers in top management positions. These policies sprang from the government's determination to remove military men from public administration, "even if the corresponding activities were under military jurisdiction." Tomas also revealed the government's intention to include military industries in general economic planning. He hoped that this would harmonize private and public sector economic interests, which had come into conflict over the expansion of state-owned enterprises.[41]

In October 1984, the government decided to go ahead with the production of the Argentine Medium Tank and associated support vehicles, artillery, small arms, the training jet aircraft IA–63 Pampa, and the local construction, with German technology, of submarines and missile-carrying corvettes. The government hoped to export as many of these as it could. The German press later reported that Argentina had sold some of its submarines abroad, about one hundred tanks—which have gained international recognition—to Iran.[42] As a result of the government's export promotion, industrialists in the province of Cordoba looked forward to a Franco-Argentine joint venture, with SOFMA as a showcase firm, dedicated to the production of replacement parts for ground equipment.[43]

HUMAN RIGHTS: AN ARENA OF CIVIL–MILITARY CONFRONTATION

In the final analysis, the military accepted the democratic regime's policies, which were designed to establish civilian control over them, revamp their command structure, and reduce their share of the national budget. The armed forces' high command, especially those officers recently appointed by the new government, realized that these reforms were aimed at reprofessionalizing their institution. In other words, they would heal the damage done by years of intense politicization.[44]

However, an intense confrontation between the military and the new democratic regime developed over the human rights issue. It is this conflict that truly redefined the relationship between these two actors. The main conflict was over the investigation, prosecution, and punishment of military personnel and civilian accomplices who were responsible for massive human rights violations during the so-called dirty war.

In December of 1983, the ruling Radical party took two measures to deal with the human rights question. On December 16, as promised in the party's electoral platform, the Chamber of Deputies repealed the outgoing military government's amnesty law by a virtually unanimous vote. The Senate followed suit on December 23. Meanwhile, the executive introduced a bill to reform the military justice code, and announced that it would abolish the armed forces' internal security function. The Alfonsin administration wanted to reform the military justice code in order to make it possible for the armed forces to handle the trials themselves. Of course, this plan provoked sharp criticism from human rights organizations, who rejected the measure.

The congressional debate over these reforms divided Argentine political forces. Juan M. Casella, chairperson of the Chamber of Deputies' Defense Committee, defended the government's position. He pointed out that the reforms reduced the military tribunals' legal authority and made it possible to transfer sentencing to other judicial bodies. But the Peronist bloc favored another alternative: they wanted judges from the civilian justice system to carry out the trials. They also demanded the removal of all military judges who were comrades in arms of those under investigation.[45] But the Radicals were the majority party in the Chamber of Deputies, and thus the government's bill passed in January 1984. The Supreme Council of the Armed Forces would try military and security personnel under investigation for human rights abuses under peacetime summary court martial proceedings.[46]

The newly elected government nevertheless firmly believed that autonomous military intelligence organizations represented the most serious threat to democratic stability. This prompted Interior Minister Antonio Troccoli to announce the government's intention to limit their functions.[47] Subsequently, in March 1984, the administration transferred 90 retired high-ranking and junior officers of the armed forces to the State Information Agency (Secretaría de Informaciones del Estado, SIDE).

On December 13, President Alfonsin issued a decree filing suit against the first three juntas that had ruled from 1976 to 1983. The charges read: homicide, illegal privation of liberty, and torture. The government also established a national commission, headed by the distinguished literary figure Ernesto Sábato, to investigate the fate of the disappeared. This measure, however, killed presidential electoral platform proposals for a bicameral congressional investigating committee.

The government's decision to have the Supreme Council of the Armed Forces try human rights violators not only drew criticism from Argentine civil society, but from the military themselves. The military defined their relationship to the democratic government from a strictly corporative standpoint, which is why they resented the government's position on this issue. As a result, the government's attempt to submit the armed forces to the rule of law increasingly depended on how it handled the thorny problem of human rights violations. In other words, the military accepted institutional reform as long as it did not undermine nonnegotiable corporative principles, such as blind obedience and strict observance of hierarchy in its decision-making processes.

Of course, the new government officials harbored no illusions about the nature of the task they had undertaken.[48] They fully recognized the difficulties inherent in dismantling a hypertrophic organization such as the armed forces.[49] For example, estimates of secret detention centers run by military security agencies varied from 280 to 271 to 340, as reported by the press, Centro de Estudios Legales y Sociales (CELS), and Comision Nacional de Desaparecidos (CONADEP), respectively. By one reckoning, the army ran 75 of the detention and torture centers, the navy ran 18, the security forces operated 135, and the air force had only three. And this is not counting facilities kept by the federal and provincial police forces, the gendarmes, rural prefectures, the aeronautic police, or the SIDE. Furthermore, CELS believed that it had sufficient evidence to convict 896 officers involved in human rights violations. Of these, 225 directly participated in criminal activities, while the other 671 were liable for related actions.[50]

The magnitude of the crimes placed the government in difficult straits, and inevitably led to a confrontation with the military. The first rumblings of discontent within the armed forces expressed a double meaning. On the one hand, the military accepted reforms primarily geared to modernizing the institution, on the other hand, they rejected reforms that attacked their politico-military role, especially with regard to repression and subsequent massive human rights violations. The statements of General Mario Aguado, commander of the Fifth Army Corps, typify this situation. In January 1984 he signed a declaration stating that he subordinated himself to constitutional authorities, but that he did not think that any excesses had been committed during the dirty war. The government limited itself to reprimanding the general. This slap on the wrist prompted sharp criticisms from the Peronist party and the CELS, who had expected the government to force him into retirement.

The arrests of Rear Admiral R. Chamorro (ret.) (former director of the navy's infamous mechanics school) and General Ramon Camps (former chief of Buenos Aires province police), along with the forced retirement of Brigadier General Alberto Simari, fanned the flames of the military's discontent. Although these actions represented responses to two different types of problems—criminal and disciplinary respectively—they nevertheless pitted the high command against the chairman of the Joint Chiefs of Staff, General Fernández Torres. Toward the end of March 1984, the government discovered a conspiracy among a group of junior officers; in April, the commanding officer of the First Marine Artillery Infantry Brigade, Captain Pérez Froio, was relieved from his duties.

The military's response to these government actions began to take shape in April 1984. At that time, General Jorge Arguindegui, the head of the army general staff, stated that a number of officers refused to testify, and were taking refuge behind the military secrets acts. Their stance seriously hampered further investigations.[51] A more overt effort followed shortly after these events. In April, 67 recently retired high-ranking officers claimed that the trials merely represented a campaign to discredit the armed forces. Meanwhile, General Videla called for a ''restoration of the honor due to them for having vanquished subversion, and denounced efforts to twist the true meaning of the armed forces' military actions.''[52] Retired senior officers demanded General Arguindegui's court martial in mid–1984 because he had forbidden them to participate in Army Day celebrations. Arguindegui himself, the government's man, walked a tightrope. While he joined the officers in denouncing human rights organizations for their attempt to besmirch the military, he also argued that the government's actions were of an entirely different nature.

A Radical party bill in the Chamber of Deputies to create a permanent Commission for Military Affairs heightened the confrontation between the armed forces and the government. The armed forces interpreted this as an attack on their vertical command structure, because the commission would be empowered to guarantee the individual rights of all military personnel.[53]

The relations between General Arguindegui, the head of the army's general staff, and the rest of the officer corps had reached their nadir by July. To begin with, Arguindegui asked Defense Minister Raúl Borras to retire another seven generals. Moreover, his conflict with the Chairman of the Joint Chiefs of Staff, General Julio Fernández Torres, a more staunch supporter of the government's human rights policy, reached a head. Arguindegui lost and resigned from his post. But despite his departure, CELS's Emilio Mignione declared that nothing had changed.

The government, then, faced serious problems in continuing with the prosecution of the nine junta leaders under indictment. In mid–1984, civil courts were investigating 400 cases involving military personnel, and human rights organizations had targeted 8,800 disappearances. Meanwhile, human rights organizations became the target of violent acts; they suffered roughly 300 bombings in Buenos Aires alone. In this climate, Dante Giadone, a member of the president's staff, said: "People have to remember that this is a transitional period. The hearts of many officers are still with the dictatorship."[54]

DEMOCRATIZATION AND CIVILIAN CONTROL OF THE MILITARY

The confrontation between the military and the government led the latter to moderate its policies, while the military's attitude took a radical turn. In any case, as of mid–1984, the two contenders began to reformulate their tactics. President Alfonsin announced in July 1984 his intention to place military men in advisory capacities "in the *most sensitive and powerful spheres of government*" (emphasis ours). He also exhorted the navy high command to "behave as subordinates, but without submissiveness."[55] Vice President Victor Martínez later echoed these sentiments.[56]

The president's appeal for collaboration signaled a substantial shift in his military policy, born of his need both to placate an aroused institution and to mend his strained relationship with it. But the presidency neglected to see that bringing the three military juntas to trial was enough to throw the armed forces and the government into conflict. Calls for collaboration could not soothe a riled military. The government's decision to bring the military under civilian control, and its questioning of their political decision to repress the population in such a brutal manner, were ample grounds to pit the armed forces against the democratic regime.

Under these circumstances, one could argue that the government's excessively moderate stance on human rights gave the military the respite they needed to regroup, recover from the government's offensive, and launch a counteroffensive capable of taking the initiative away from the administration. Meanwhile, declining support for the government from disenchanted human rights organizations weakened Alfonsin's ability to contemplate a more vigorous policy. In other words, the government's attempt to place the military under civilian control had foundered on the sensitive human rights question.

These events, then, forced the government to abandon its original blueprint for articulating its relationship with the armed forces. Instead, new ground rules for civil–military cooperation were hammered out in a meeting held between the high command, President Alfonsin, and the ministers of interior, defense, and economy. At first they analyzed proposals submitted by the Joint Chiefs of Staff. But the heart of the often heated discussions turned on the armed forces' displeasure over the accusations that had been hurled against them, and over a wave of arrests—ordered by civil courts—of officers who had allegedly committed human rights atrocities.[57]

The defense minister's position on the military engineers also revealed the government's defensive posture. The engineers had systematically resisted the administration's attempts to control military industries (the GDMF). But now, Defense Minister Borras attempted to mollify them by denying that the government held a negative view of them. He further declared that "the army of the future, to which we aspire, is a modern one, in which the military engineer will be faced with even greater tasks than those of the past."[58]

Rumors that the government had reached an impasse over the human rights issue began to circulate in mid–1984 and in 1985. The public speculated that the administration was contemplating proposing an amnesty law for junior officers involved in the atrocities.[59] But the executive also took more aggressive action, by appointing more officers to the Supreme Council in order to lighten the case load and by instructing officers not to stand on the military secrets act in order to compel their testimony at human rights trials.[60]

Despite the government's efforts, it could not keep its human rights policy under tight control. The Sabato Commission's findings wrecked the administration's conciliatory overtures toward the military. The commission had brought to light a repugnant reality, one that the trial of only nine officers could not do justice to. The National Commission of Disappeared Persons estimated that there were 8,780 victims, 175 detention centers, and 1,300 military personnel directly and indirectly involved in the atrocities. The Commission's televised findings stunned the Argentine public. The government conceded that many of those responsible for the horror might go unpunished for lack of evidence.[61] The Supreme Council declared shortly thereafter that it would not sentence the nine men who had headed the first three juntas of Argentina's recently departed military regime because the evidence did not warrant it. The Supreme Council argued that the juntas' orders were commensurate to the times, and they could only be faulted for their lack of ability to control excesses.

Following these events, two Supreme Council judges resigned in mid-November, and the rest followed suit shortly thereafter. Their resignations sparked accusations that the members of the armed forces had entered into a "blood pact" that made it impossible for the military to try their own. In the midst of this confrontation between the government and the military, the Astiz case, in which he was accused of assassinating a Swedish citizen, only served to heighten the tension. His arrest, ordered by the civil justice system, boosted fears within the service that the government's moderate policy was disintegrating.

The resignation en masse of the Supreme Council of the Armed Forces represented a watershed in the confrontation between the government and the military. It amounted to their first intrinsically institutional reaction to their critics in the human rights organizations, and to governmental pressure to speed up the trials of the first three juntas. Their resignations undoubtedly had the moral support of the high-ranking officers forced into early retirement, for they were responsible for the counteroffensive against the government in the first place. In effect, the resignations amounted to a quasi-insubordination, which suggests that the armed forces had rebounded and recovered the initiative. They had acquired the capability to directly confront a government that, in the final analysis, merely mediated between the armed forces and Argentine society.

The crisis came to a head in mid–1985. The government proceeded to order the arrest of the leaders of the military juntas. President Alfonsin also forced the retirement of a significant proportion of the high command, including that of the chairman of the Joint Chiefs of Staff. Moreover, Alfonsin forced the departure of four high-ranking naval officers and two air force brigadiers. All together, by March 1985, the government had removed 50 of the 53 generals on active duty when Alfonsin assumed office.[62] The forced retirements represented the government's reply to the armed forces' institutional response to its human rights policies. But the new high command found themselves equally pressured by their comrades in arms not to give in to the politicians.[63] That, in turn, led to more forced retirements.[64] In short, the government used forced resignations as a tool to gain political control over the military. It was a means to squash antidemocratic conspiracies and to derail political meddling by the generals.

Nevertheless, this policy of "pruning the Hydra" (the thousand heads of Argentine *gorilismo*) has its limitations. It is limited to the degree that punishment for the brutalities committed during the dirty war are confined to the leaders of the three military juntas. The government's lack of resolve in pushing for the prosecution of the many persons implicated in the atrocities has had another consequence: it has provided the groundwork for an unusual civil–military coalition that opposes the very idea of human rights investigations.

Thus, even though Alfonsin took a firm stance in resolving the confrontation with the military, it was not enough. He left the door open for his civilian opponents to mount political attacks against him. Former President Frondizi warned that from now on, opposition forces would use the conflict between the government and the military for their own ends. That would, in the final analysis, represent a destabilizing factor for Argentine democracy.[65]

MILITARY AUTONOMY AND ARGENTINE DEMOCRACY

Alain Rouquié has observed that, "until the 1930s, democratic governments entrusted the military with technical and administrative functions."[66] In Argentina, however, this situation began to change during the 1940s, when the armed forces began to get directly involved in economic production. From the GDMF they expanded into the hydrocarbon sector (Yacimientos Petrolíferos Federales), and learned management skills at the Argentine Institute for Executive Training. In 1941 they created SOMISA and ANTOR, a petrochemical industry, not to mention the many economic activities they directed in the 1970s.[67]

The military's autonomy resulted from a twofold process within Argentine society. On the one hand, "the nation witnessed a complete divorce between the system of formal institutions and the power structure. Behind the formal–legal structures lie the realities of power that inform every decision." In other words, although the constitution forbids it, the military participate in politics by exercising their veto power over political, economic, and social processes.[68] On the other hand, beginning in the 1940s, the military managed to build an independent institutional identity, which allowed them to pursue their own corporative interests. From this perspective, the armed forces used the development of military industries as their principal means for penetrating the Argentine economy and state. If to this we add the military's proven disposition to directly intervene in politics, we may conclude that the armed forces have played a stable role in Argentine politics.

Rouquié nicely sums up this state of affairs: "The military is the only institution that possesses undeniable cohesion and an authority that is rarely challenged, which allows them to temporarily replace a hopelessly divided political class. During times of severe crisis that threaten total social collapse, they try to provide a kind of substitute bureaucratic hegemony, that is, they attempt to organize societal consent around a national project."[69] This suggests that the military's political interventions are an autonomous application of their veto power in situations where hegemony has broken down in society.[70]

Nevertheless, it seems that the military's most recent political intervention exhibited some rather distinctive characteristics which were somehow different from their past experiences. For example, Argentina's latest transition to democracy took place after the armed forces had collapsed; the military had fallen under the weight of their own incompetence even before they threw themselves into the Malvinas adventure, rather than as a result of popular mobilization as in other Latin American countries.[71]

Because the military did not fall as a result of popular mobilization,[72] even if the democratic regime applies a policy of firm civilian control, institutional modernization, and professionalization, and punishes human rights violators, the armed forces were nevertheless assured of their institutional continuity as they "exit" from political office. Alfonsin himself provided that assurance to the degree that he stressed his interest in professionalizing the institution. That tack intitially allowed him to find a place for the military within a democratic framework, and won him some support on their part. It also let him reduce the military's political space and expand the role of trusted civilians within the institution.

Although these policies enjoyed a certain measure of success, they began to founder early on with respect to their central purposes. In effect, as Jorge Sábato noted, civilian control over the armed forces was a function of the government's efficacy, of its capacity to regulate the political system as a whole. This is precisely where Alfonsin faced his greatest obstacles. His military reform policies began to crumble once he grasped the full extent of the nation's economic crisis in March 1984 and found himself incapable of continuing with plans to democratize the trade unions. As if that were not enough, the ruling Radical party began to experience serious internal conflicts over these issues.

These events led the government to subordinate its military reform policy—among others—to the management of the nation's staggering economic problems. It could not afford to antagonize the armed forces and risk the loss of their support, no matter how grudging it might be. The administration tried to keep a low profile on its military policy and only addressed urgent problems, such as the high command's insubordination and other disciplinary issues. As a result, Alfonsin had to pull back on a number of projects that gave teeth to his military reform policy. These included the Unified War College, the National Defense Council, changes in the military's curriculum, the creation of a new Defense School, and a complete restructuring of SIDE and of the military intelligence agencies.

Consequently, with the exception of the human rights issue, the economic crisis has put the government on the defensive. The administration's difficulty in building consensus around a national project has begun to increase the military's veto power. This situation might have ended in a draw between the contending actors but for the conflict engendered by the human rights issue. The trial and punishment of those responsible for the atrocities brings up a key question of the military's "exit" from politics—their institutional continuity. It also places limits on their possibilities for a new "entry."

The human rights violations compromise all branches of the service and taint all of its members to the degree that the atrocities were the product of careful planning by the military institutions. But more important, the investigations and prosecutions endanger the military's survival as a power contender capable of executing the type of "technical" functions that it assumed from 1976 to 1982. To the degree that they face challenges to their legitimacy as autonomous political actors, that is, their capacity to enter into alliances with other power contenders outside of the democratic rules of the game, the military confront the specter of their demise as a stable political actor. Of course, if that happened it would overturn 40 years of Argentine history, that of more than one entire generation of officers.

The obstacles that plague the democratic regime's policy-making capacity have pushed the government's struggle with the military into an arena where it stands at a disadvantage. For example, the military forced the executive branch to implement its housecleaning operation in a halfhearted manner, that is, by prosecuting and punishing only the leaders of the juntas. Actions like these have failed to build broad social support for the government, and for that same reason have alienated the armed forces themselves.

This intermediate solution has allowed the armed forces to recover from the government's initial onslaught. From there, the military have taken the initiative in the defense of their standing as a political actor in Argentine society. That is why they have tenaciously stood up for those on trial. Military men feel that their institutional cohesion—which is what gives them their autonomy and ability to participate in the nations' political struggles—is at stake.

It is difficult to draw conclusions about the outcome of this struggle. But it seems that civilian forces interested in propping up a politically autonomous military have begun to appear on the scene. They seem willing to articulate disparate societal interests around new projects. Unfortunately, these actions not only endanger the outcome of military reforms in Argentina, but they also jeopardize transitions to democracy throughout the continent.

NOTES

1. Robert Cox, "Argentina's Democratic Miracle," *The New Republic,* 19 March 1984.

2. In this sense, the armed forces are highly segregated from the rest of Argentine society, possess relatively unique political interests, and have a well-defined associational identity. This results from a combination of the military's high professional development and low civilian control.

3. See Eduardo Luis Duhaldo, *El Estado Terrorista Argentino* (Buenos Aires: Ediciones Caballito, 1983); Miguel Bonasso, *Recuerdos de la Muerte* (Buenos Aires: Bruguera, 1984); CELS, *Uruguay/Argentina: Coordinación Represiva* (Buenos Aires: Colección Memoria y Juicio, n.d.); Asemblea Permanente de los Derechos Humanos, *La Familia Victima de la Represión* (Neuquen, 1982); CELS, *Los Niños Desaparecidos* (Buenos Aires: n.p., 1982); CELS, *Conscriptos Detenidos-Desaparecidos; El Secuestro como Método de Detención* (Buenos Aires: n.p., 1982); CONADEP, *Nunca Más. Informe de la Comisión Nacional sobre Desaparición de Personas* (Buenos Aires: EUDEBA, 1984).

4. *El Mercurio* (Santiago de Chile), 2 October 1983.

5. Ibid.

6. *Clarín*, 17 March 1984. The same ideas crop up during the Pledge of Allegiance

to the Flag in Rosario (*Clarín Internacional*, 18 June 1984). The speech given on this occasion undoubtedly contains veiled references to the Malvinas War.

7. *El Mercurio*, 9 July 1984.

8. *El Mercurio*, 3 December 1983.

9. *El Mercurio*, 22 October 1984.

10. *El Mercurio*, 24 September 1983.

11. *El Mercurio*, 5 June 1983.

12. *Clarín*, 17 April 1984. For an overview of the general content of the Argentine military reform policies, see Sergio Bitar, ''Poder Militar y Democracia en Argentina,'' *La Opinión*, 13 January 1984.

13. *El Mercurio*, 7 November 1983.

14. *El Observador*, 16 May 1984.

15. *Clarín Internacional*, 2 August 1984.

16. Luis Garasino, ''La Reforma Militar,'' *Clarín*, 11 March 1984.

17. *Clarín Internacional*, 18 December 1983.

18. A speech given by the interior minister during the opening ceremony for the academic year at the Police Academy, 6 March 1984.

19. *Defensa*, no. 74 (June 1984).

20. *Clarín*, 2 August 1984.

21. *Clarín*, 29 June 1984.

22. *El Mercurio*, 10 October 1984.

23. *El Mercurio*, 9 December 1983.

24. *El Bimestre Político y Económico*, 7 February 1984.

25. *El Mercurio*, 16 December 1983.

26. *El Mercurio*, 15 December 1983.

27. *Clarín*, 20 January 1984.

28. *El Mercurio*, 27 April 1984.

29. *Clarín*, 11 April 1984.

30. *Clarín*, 26 June 1984.

31. *El Mercurio*, 22 April 1984.

32. *El Mercurio*, 16 April 1983.

33. *El Mercurio*, 23 March 1984.

34. *El Mercurio*, 21 November 1983.

35. *Clarín*, 11 April 1984.

36. *Clarín Internacional*, 16–22 April 1984.

37. *El Mercurio*, 22 October 1984.

38. *El Día* (Mexico), 20 February 1984.

39. *Tiempo Argentino*, 16 June 1984.

40. I obtained these data from personal interviews with staff members of the Defense Ministry and academic specialists.

41. *Diarios y Noticias*, 19 January 1984.

42. *El Mercurio*, 20 October 1984 and 29 October 1984; *La Tercera* (Santiago de Chile), 20 December 1984; *Defensa*, no. 68 (December 1983); *Defensa*, no. 70 (February 1984).

43. *El Mercurio*, 23 December 1984.

44. These reactions tend to confirm Guillermo O'Donnell's thesis of the Argentine military's cycle of professionalization–politicization–professionalization. See Guillermo

O'Donnell, "Modernización y Golpes Militares: Teoría, Comparación y el Caso Argentino," *Desarrollo Económico*, no. 47 (October–December 1972).

45. *Clarín Internacional*, 2–8 January 1984.

46. *El Mercurio*, 6 January 1984.

47. *El Mercurio*, 26 November 1983.

48. *Noticias Argentinas*, 2 March 1983.

49. *Noticias Argentinas*, 14 March 1984.

50. *Clarín*, 3 August 1984.

51. *Clarín Internacional*, 9–15 April 1984.

52. *Associated Press*, 13 April 1984.

53. *El Bimestre Político y Económico*, 25 April 1984.

54. *The Washington Post*, 31 July 1984.

55. Ibid.

56. *Clarín*, 31 July 1984.

57. *Clarín*, 1 July 1984.

58. *Clarín*, 2 July 1984.

59. *Clarín*, 29 July 1984.

60. *The Washington Post*, op. cit.

61. *El Mercurio*, 21 September 1984.

62. *El Mercurio*, 24 September 1984.

63. *El Mercurio*, 8 March 1985.

64. *The Washington Post*, 9 March 1985.

65. *El Universal* (Caracas), 25 March 1985.

66. Alain Rouquié, *Poder Militar y Sociedad Política en la Argentina* (Buenos Aires: EMECE, 1984), 69.

67. *El Tiempo Argentino*, 14 March 1985.

68. Alain Rouquié, *Poder Militar*, chapter 8.

69. Ibid., 380.

70. *Ibid.*, *419. See also Guillermo O'Donnell, "Las Fuerzas Armadas y el Estado Autoritario del Cono Sur de América Latina," in Estado y Política en América Latina,* ed. Norbert Lechner (México: Siglo XXI, 1981).

71. See Alain Rouquié, "El Poder Militar en la Argentina de Hoy: Cambio y Continuidad," in *El Poder Militar en la Argentina (1976–1981)*, ed. Peter Waldman and Ernesto Garzon (Frankfurt: Verlag Klaus Dieter Verfuert, 1982).

72. See Andrés Fontana, "Fuerzas Armadas, Partidos Políticos y Transición a la Democracia en Argentina," in *Transición a la Democracia: América Latina y Chile*, ed. Augusto Varas et al. (Santiago: Ainavillo and Asociación Chilena de Investigaciones para la Paz, 1984).

5 THE ARMED FORCES AND BRAZIL'S TRANSITION TO DEMOCRACY: THE FIGUEIREDO ADMINISTRATION

Eliézer Rizzo de Oliveira

One of the Brazilian military regime's main characteristics was that it instituted a succession process and won a certain formal legitimacy by retaining the Congress, although its powers were sharply circumscribed. The military, of course, controlled the real center of power: the executive branch, which was dominated by four-star generals. The high command of the armed forces chose presidents in secret, while at the same time maintaining the formal selection machinery of an electoral college in Congress. Brazil's last three military presidents—Generals Medici, Geisel, and Figueiredo—all completed their fixed terms in office.

Geisel skillfully manipulated promotions and retirements in order to assure the election of his protégé, Figueiredo. But his drive to secure a fourth star for Figueiredo generated profound resentment among the high command. It seems that the army found it more difficult to accept his rapid rise than the removal of General Silvio Frota from the Army Ministry in 1978. (On that occasion, Geisel had blocked an attempted coup d'etat and strengthened his political liberalization program.) Public opinion—by virtue of a relaxation of censorship laws—was scandalized at the manner in which Geisel was obviously elevating his protégé, even though he had obtained permission from the army high command for his actions.

THE OPPOSITION'S MILITARY CANDIDACY

General Figueiredo, the official candidate, was not the only military man vying for the presidency. A legal opposition party, the Brazilian Democratic Movement (*Movimento Democrático Brasileiro*—MDB), decided to compete against Figueiredo in the electoral college and announced the candidacy of Army General Euler Bentes Monteiro. His frankly opposition platform contained issues that the National Assembly passed into law later in the Figueiredo administration—most notably, the amnesty law championed by Tancredo Neves. General Bentes Monteiro's National Redemocratization Front was a necessarily heterogeneous alliance that included right wing military men (with nationalist overtones reminiscent of Costa e Silva's government) coordinated by General Abreu (who had resigned from his post as head of the *Casa Militar* due to his differences with Geisel over the succession), and the MDB's "auténtico" faction, which harbored parliamentarians linked to proscribed political parties.

Although Figueiredo defeated Bentes Monteiro in the electoral college, the opposition had demonstrated that the military government could be defeated in the very arena that gave it formal legitimacy. The election proved that an opposition victory required solid mass support, high levels of social mobilization, and the ability to mediate conflicts within the military over the democratization issue. Moreover, the MDB would have to reconcile itself to the changes that had occurred in Brazilian politics and society and seriously prepare to govern. In other words, the MDB could no longer afford the luxury of presenting anti-candidacies, such as Deputy Ulisses Guimarães's in 1973–1974 (although at the time it served the positive purpose of winning more seats in Congress for the opposition). Consequently, the National Redemocratization Front's experience taught the opposition—especially the sector that the later became the *Partido de Movimento Democrático Brasileiro* or PMDB which maintained ties with the military—useful tactics, which after the defeat of the "Direct Elections Now" campaign of 1984 led to the creation of the Democratic Alliance and the victory of Tancredo Neves's candidacy on January 15, 1985.[1]

The Intelligence Community

The process that culminated in General Figueiredo's presidential appointment strengthened the power of the "intelligence community." This community is best understood as a system of intelligence services that has "locals" in each ministry and is centralized by the National Information Service (SNI), which also has cabinet-level ranking.[2] Although the SNI has no formal place in the military hierarchy (compared to the National Security Council), it is under the direction of superior officers. One may also think of it as a direct expression of the military's political power, since it is practically immune from military regulations by virtue of special, and sometimes secret, legislation. Given the nature of its functions, the SNI is protected by a web of complicity and silence, by professional and political stealth, and by its "legislated" extralegality. The SNI exists as cause and effect of the military regime, and has transformed itself into a highly autonomous agency in its political, military, and financial aspects.[3]

Even in the present democratic regime, it is virtually impossible to determine the SNI's influence in the government and the military with any kind of certainty. Moreover, within the armed forces it virtually constitutes a parallel command structure. Brazilians believe that it is responsible for blocking the promotions of officers who stray from accepted doctrine or who are otherwise not trustworthy. In this manner, the SNI strongly influences the selection of men destined to control important positions in each branch of the service, as well as in the civilian government.[4]

The Repressive Apparatus

The military's struggle against rural and urban guerrilla movements, especially between 1969–1970, profoundly influenced the development of the intelligence community. The armed forces created special commando units in order to exterminate the insurgents. These units enjoyed such a wide freedom of action that the SNI acquired the status of a parallel command structure.[5] As a result, the Brazilian military precipitated a bloodbath that involved torture, disappearances, and murders of political prisoners.

The repressive forces acted with great operational and political autonomy and had at their disposal enormous human and material resources, from both secret government appropriations and private sector contributions. The private sector first began to support and participate in the repression during Operation Bandeirante in Sao Paulo. This experience served as a model for subsequent business involvement in counterinsurgency activities. Operation Bandeirante placed all federal and state police and security forces under military command. Businessmen supplied funds, vehicles, detention and torture centers, and political support, among other things. Sometimes the security forces blackmailed businessmen in order to secure their cooperation.

This repressive system became the creature of military and political interests. It depended on the maintenance of the authoritarian regime for its survival in the sinister interaction between repression, bids for increased power, and access to resources. This condition spawned state terrorism. From a military point of view the repression succeeded in destroying the various guerrilla movements. Politically, however, it reverberated both internationally and within Brazil.

Despite the controls that Geisel placed on the repressive apparatus, its clandestine remnants constituted part of Figueiredo's inheritance when he became president. They repeatedly attempted to reverse political liberalization. Finally, the existence of military regimes in the Southern Cone allowed the SNI to forge close links with similar organizations in neighboring countries and to conduct joint operations.

Important ideological changes accompanied Geisel and Figueiredo's attempts to control the repressive machine. Before they rose to power the National Security Doctrine (NSD) provided the regime's only ideological referent. During Geisel's administration, the Superior War College—which had given birth to the NSD—labored to create a National Security Legal Code, which Geisel intended to use as a legal justification and guideline for repressive activities in the name of national objectives and to defend the state. However, while Geisel's rhetoric mainly adapted the NSD to a new conceptualization of the relationship between security and development (a minimum of security for maximum development), Figueiredo hardly ever adorned his speeches with such ideas. Moreover, during his government the Superior War College never played the leading role it had in previous administrations.

THE FIGUEIREDO GOVERNMENT

President Figueiredo pursued two major political goals. Both of them required the military's support for their realization. His first and broadest goal was to prepare the nation for the installation of a civilian government in 1990. The evidence simply does not support the argument that he intended to remain true to Geisel's timetable. Geisel had wanted a civilian government in office by 1985—the end of Figueiredo's term. The success of his plan depended heavily on Justice Minister Petrônio Portela (the military's preferred presidential candidate), and General Golbery in the *Casa Civil*. Portela died, however, and General Golbery (who was widely considered to be the principal agent behind the liberalization policy) left the government. The SNI had exerted considerable pressure to secure his resignation because of their dissatisfaction with the way in which he handled the Riocentro affair.[6]

Petrônio Portela's death resulted in the appointment of Aureliano Chaves (another favorite of Geisel's) to the vice presidency. This strongly suggests that former president Geisel intended to remain true to his original timetable, and that he wanted to assure the election of a civilian successor to Figueiredo. Figueiredo, however, had initially sought to name General Otário Medeiros, head of the SNI, as his successor. His candidacy quickly foundered due to a series of financial scandals which involved the SNI—and even one of the president's sons—and because of the Riocentro affair. Figueiredo then proposed the candidacy of Interior Minister Colonel (ret.) Mario Andreazza.[7] Meanwhile, the president's closest advisers (who represented the high command's point of view) made sure that Aureliano Chaves's candidacy never gathered momentum. The military believed that he favored investigating military personnel for corruption in office, as well as for their part in repressive excesses.

Figueiredo's second major objective required a two-pronged attack. First, he had to win support for his liberalization plan from the air force and navy ministers, who had acquired far more power than their predecessors. Second, he needed to introduce incentives that would stimulate the armed forces to evaluate their professionalism. Raising salaries was one way to reconcile the military to the higher levels of professional and political uncertainty that would inevitably accompany political liberalization and democratiziation. The manner in which the Figueiredo administration implemented these salary hikes in 1984, however, angered the civil service.

Figueiredo's actions, then, aimed to induce the military to dedicate more time to their professional functions. He wanted them to give up the direct exercise of political power without relinquishing their ability to intervene under special circumstances, such as—paradoxically—the defense of the constitution. This meant that the next president would have to enjoy the full confidence of the ruling generals.

Figueiredo also reduced the political influence of the Superior War College, a process initiated by Geisel. The War College had previously been a so-called laboratory for political ideas. Figueiredo, however, placed the creation and articulation of his government's political principles in the hands of various state agencies, such as the Ministers of the *Casa Civil*, the *Casa Militar*, the SNI, the *Planalto* group and the president himself. Following the original Geisel plan, Figueiredo introduced an amnesty bill for political prisioners in order to stimulate political liberalization.[8] Congress passed the bill into law despite stiff opposition from some sectors of the military and paramilitary groups. The new legislation benefitted both victims and perpetrators, the tortured and their torturers.

By introducing these policies, then, Figueiredo managed to secure the armed forces' support for political liberalization. Ironically, some of the reforms that he introduced, such as the direct election of state governors, helped opposition forces to capture the executive much earlier than the ruling elite had thought prudent. Thus, in spite of measures taken by the military government to assure the victory of its supporters (no split tickets, disarticulation of the opposition, and a ban on electoral coalitions) the PMDB won nine governorships in the 1982 elections and the left-leaning Democratic Labor Party garnered one.[9] Moreover, the opposition won these elections in central and southeastern states—the most highly developed and populous regions of Brazil. These victories, won during a period of economic crisis, gave the opposition both governmental experience and the drive to mount a serious challenge for the presidency.

These factors notwithstanding, the military managed to carefully control the pace of political liberalization. Moreover, if Figueiredo had once entertained notions of either extending his own rule or of letting the armed forces deal with the economic crisis, he soon realized that he lacked support within the military for such plans. At least two events drove the armed forces to retreat from government. One of them was the vigorous year-long national campaign for direct elections in 1984, and the obvious signal voters sent by electing opposition governors in ten of Brazil's most important states. These occurrences demonstrated the extent to which civilians were tired of military rule and desired a speedy return to a democratic form of government. Judging from conversations with officers, and despite hard-line statements from certain military ministers, most officers seemed to favor constitutional government. This desire alone did not guarantee that liberalization would proceed to democratization, nor could it stave off a coup d'etat. A number of factors could hinder widespread support against a coup d'etat within the armed forces, such as the loyalty of military men to their institution, the hierarchy of command, discipline, and the unfavorable career consequences of a refusal to participate.

This brings us to the second event that helped to secure the military's support for democratization: former president Geisel's efforts to influence promotions and retirements in the high command. These allowed the electoral college to become an arena for real political competition once the opposition formed an electoral coalition between the PMBD and dissidents from the conservative Democratic Social Party (Partido Democrático Social—PDS). This alliance, which drew on the experience of the National Redemocratization Front, proved crucial for the electoral defeat of the military regime.

These two factors, then, did not allow Figueiredo to extend the period of military rule. He simply lacked sufficient support within the military to do so. Figueiredo was also forced to accept the retirement from the military's governing group of General Newton Cruz, who was the architect of the emergency decrees that the government had used to pressure Congress in order to defeat the movement for direct elections in 1984. Furthermore, the high command disallowed Minister Walter Pires, who had attempted to create favorable conditions for a coup d'etat.

This conjuncture induced politicians who had once had close ties to the military regime to approach the military groups that supported democratization. These politicians decided to support the PMDB because Figueiredo refused to back Aureliano Chaves and had allowed Paulo Maluf to capture the PDS presidential nomination. In this respect, we must not lose sight of General Geisel's enormous influence over the generals he had promoted. They shared with him a desire to curb the power of the intelligence community and the conviction that a wide gulf between the military and civil society was not to the political advantage of the armed forces. As a result, unlike Geisel, Figueiredo could not control the high command—indeed, the latter managed to impose the armed forces' will over the desires of Figueiredo's minister. As a result, the high command played an important role in maintaining the schedule for redemocratization.

Two additional factors must be taken into account to explain the military's role in Brazil's transition to democracy. One was the positive influence of the ministers of a revitalized air force and navy. Navy Minister Maximiliano da Fonseca insisted on refitting his branch of the service. He also worked hard to distance the navy from the remnants of the repressive apparatus, and even introduced plans to thwart a possible coup d'etat. Fonseca recognized that the army could carry out a coup on its own, but he also believed that the navy and the air force had the power to place serious obstacles in its way. Navy Minister Fonseca's anti-coup strategy included blockading Brazil's principal ports, awaiting international reaction, and hoping for support from other branches of the service, including army units. The Navy Minister also cultivated a public image of tolerance and intelligence. Thus, when Figueiredo removed him from office for backing the campaign for direct elections, a representative group of his officers from Rio de Janeiro publicly supported the former minister's stance. Furthermore, although this is very hard to prove given the classified nature of the information, the navy probably revised its relationship to the army and the air force in the aftermath of the Malvinas War. Given the navy's importance in such a war, it probably also acquired more influence in the political processes of the period.

Meanwhile, Air Force Minister Delio Jardim de Matos first decided to "pacify" his branch of the service. This entailed bringing overly expressive officers marginalized by the military regime back into the fold. He then managed to reconcile conflicts between the air force and the army whenever the latter felt that the former had gone too far.[10] Moreover, in his characteristically melancholy style, and perhaps in agreement with the air force high command, he firmly supported Paulo Maluf's presidential candidacy.

In summary, two factors influenced the relatively important role played by the ministers of the navy and air force in the transition to democracy: first, the military regime's difficulties led to conflict between different factions of the military party over the pace of political liberalization, allowing the president to counter army opposition—the most important branch of the service both militarily and politically; second, given their personalities and their commitment to a gradual liberalization of the military regime, these ministers were solid supporters of Figueiredo.

During crucial moments, the positions taken by the ministers of the navy and air force led to differences in the high command of the armed forces over how to deal with the army's preponderant weight. For example, at the start of Figueiredo's term the Navy Minister publicly declared that the next president should be a civilian. This statement is not without political significance, especially since it appeared at a time when the army intended to advance the candidacy of SNI chief General Medeiros. Consequently, during the military regime's final years the position taken by the navy or the air force altered what might otherwise have simply been faits accomplis.

Besides the impact of the navy and the air force, another major factor influenced the transition to democracy: the negative feedback effect of state-sponsored terrorism as a consequence of the Riocentro affair. This affair, the worst of a string of reprehensible acts, focused attention on the existence of an intractable, organized opposition to political change in Brazil. Figueiredo was already attempting to come to terms with the repressive machine directed by the SNI before this incident. The Riocentro explosions accomplished one of the goals of its perpetrators—the resignation of Minister Golbery (ironically, he had been the creator of SNI during the Castelo Branco administration). But it cost the hard-liners their main goal, the perpetuation of the military regime, because their atrocity made it impossible for SNI chief General Medeiros to become president.

Of course, a number of additional elements contributed to the collapse of Medeiros's candidacy, such as the SNI's involvement in crimes which to this day remain unsolved. The SNI still enjoys legal protections against inquiry into its activities, which raises the uncomfortable possibility that active cells of the intelligence community may begin clandestine operations to destabilize the democratic regime, especially if Marxist political parties ever become legal.[11]

THE REAWAKENING OF CIVIL SOCIETY

The processes analyzed above took place at a time when civil society regained its place as an expressive and active force in Brazilian politics. Groups openly advocated direct national elections, democratic liberties, wage increases, human rights, and, in particular, the rights of women and Indians, among other themes. The federal government met rising social conflict with authoritarian measures, such as intervention in the unions, arbitrary manipulation of electoral laws, and direct pressure on Congress through emergency measures. The government did not, however, directly involve the military in assuring social peace (although it did allow state governments to use the military police at their discretion—and it is well known that there is a direct link between the military police and the General Staff of the Army).[12]

Without minimizing the importance of the drive for amnesty and the direct election of governors, the mobilization of social forces for direct presidential elections probably best symbolized the resurgence of civil society as the military regime entered into a crisis phase. Given the massive scale and broad-based character of national mobilization around this issue, the *Diretas-Já* campaign highlighted three factors crucial to the military's exit: first, it demonstrated that a profound gulf separated the armed forces and civil society; second, it created political boundaries for the authoritarian forces; third, civil society rediscovered itself during the course of the most extensive political mobilization in Brazilian history. Never before, since the 1964 coup d'etat, had civil society been able to advance the issues of state power and democracy as short-term realizable goals in such a unified and organized manner. This allowed them to defeat Minister Golbery's divide and rule tactics. Given the difficulties inherent in maintaining such a heterogeneous coalition of political parties and social movements, the *Diretas-Já* campaign represented the triumph of organizational innovation at the service of a national vision that won out over the particularistic interests of these diverse groups.

Three aspects of the transition process deeply affected electoral competition during the presidential campaign and undoubtedly entail consequences for the democratic regime as well: the actions of the PDS's candidates; the PMDB's role; and new problems in the relationship between state and society.

Vice President Aureliano Chaves and Paulo Maluf, former governor of Sao Paulo, represented two distinct factions within the PDS and different approaches to redemocratization in general. Moreover, each in his own way contributed to the disintegration of the PDS and to the maintenance of the rules of the game for the political transition (although the military ruling elite was apparently no longer interested in those rules). From the very beginning of the Figueiredo administration Aureliano Chaves had the support of military men who wanted to return to the barracks and retain general oversight of the political process from a distance.

Vice President Chaves attempted to build a social base that included the middle class, industrial and financial groups, and state technocrats presumably beholden to General Geisel. His position on corruption, his personal and political profile, his national image as a moderate, and his reputed negotiating skills harmonized nicely with the requirements of a "negotiated transition to democracy." The ease with which he assumed his duties as president pro tempore during Figueiredo's illness gave the impression that he was not merely the creature of the military.

However, Chaves's critique of electoral rules in 1984 led to a rift with the ruling group. While he did not actively participate in the campaign for direct presidential elections, he did give it verbal support. He also objected to the rules that governed the selection of the official candidate. Chaves favored primaries within the PDS, but the federal government questioned their results because they benefited Paulo Maluf. Meanwhile, before the issue over direct elections was resolved, the PDS's national leadership (with José Sarney acting as party president) turned against Chaves. Adopting a pragmatic and conservative position, the PDS leadership—with Figueiredo's blessing—decided that Mario Andreazza was their best hope for maintaining the ruling bloc's power. In the process, the PDS defeated the drive for direct presidential elections in Congress. However, Paulo Maluf's acrimonious campaign and ultimate victory for his party's nomination split the PDS. The liberal wing that had supported Aureliano Chaves now backed the candidacy of the PMDB's Tancredo Neves for president and José Sarney of the PDS for vice president.

Figueiredo's and the military ruling group's support for Mario Andreazza and their insistence on indirect elections defeated Aureliano Chaves's bid for the presidency. But they could not impede—rather they aided—Paulo Maluf's rise to power within the PDS. A Maluf victory in the electoral college raised the possibility of regressing to a more fascistic style of authoritarianism. He had the support of officers and their civilian hangers-on who had previously supported a Medeiros or Andreazza candidacy. (As of this writing, Maluf is trying to use the remnants of a badly beaten PDS to mount another presidential campaign. During the last election his political style and alliance choices practically destroyed the PDS, exposing the party's fragility and dependence on the military regime.)

The elements we have chosen to characterize the crisis of the Brazilian authoritarian regime suggest a rather difficult problem for the transition. In the state–society relationship of the period, the state did not have the capacity to impose its will on society, and society did not have the strength to impose a radical redemocratization project. The result was a gradual liberalization controlled by the military that social forces managed to turn into a negotiated transition to democracy by not challenging the fundamental interests of the regime's supporters. Thus, the public and (yet to be disclosed) private bargains that the Aliança Democrática struck with Figueiredo are evidence that it was really, in the apt phrase of journalist Galeno Freitas, a "compromised transition." That settlement will no doubt have serious consequences for the content of

Brazil's new constitution, which must define such delicate issues as agrarian reform, labor legislation, political party laws, and civil rights, among others.

This conjunctural equilibrium between state and society is not only due to a particular configuration of class relations, particularly if we make a distinction between conceptual levels of analysis and political practice. During the 1930s the state acquired a dominant position over society by establishing corporatist mechanisms of social control and cooptation, especially over labor. The nature of the state's supremacy changed radically after 1964 due to a concentration of power in the hands of the military. The armed forces strengthened the state's control over society and politics and developed authoritarian controls over electoral politics, such as they were. Given their lack of freedom to organize in the past, the current political parties probably contain social forces that will seek to use the Constituent Assembly to build new political structures. The current political moment represents a challenge to existing and future political parties to construct a new relationship between state and society, one that is based on the hegemony of society over the state. Accomplishing this task, however, requires more sophisticated theorizing than that which we possess, especially in light of the weakness of Brazil's political parties.

Brazil's political parties are weak in at least two respects. To begin with, they are heterogeneous in their social bases and do not adequately articulate social movements at a national level. Consequently, Brazilian political parties tend to generate a dangerous separation between their political activities and capital–labor relationships. The danger is that during an institutional crisis this separation will most likely destabilize the regime.

Second, political parties are weak in the sense that although for two decades the opposition—for example the PMDB—demonstrated great ability to combat the authoritarian regime, their wits failed them when it came time to negotiate the transition during the days of the National Front. Instead of serving as channels for the redress of the party's grievances, PMDB governors only represented the interests of their states. In fairness however, the PMDB's National Directorate did achieve a modicum of success in unifying the party and negotiating regional interests. Nevertheless, those who argued that the then president-elect Tancredo Neves (now deceased) singlehandedly dominated the party and that he was a master mediator of intraparty conflict—Fernando Henrique Cardoso once compared him to a king—clearly exaggerated.[13]

The PMDB's weakness in negotiating the transition stemmed from its inability to dominate the *Diretas-Já* social movement. The movement was not only too large for the party's organizational capabilities, it also surpassed the PMDB in programmatic content. The same held true for the rest of the political parties. No single party or social movement controlled the *Diretas-Já* campaign. It was simply the more or less coordinated result of the action of all of the parties. Consequently, after great political advances the movement failed to generate a higher level of political organization compared to that which had existed before. The same occurred after the drive for amnesty. In other words, after conquering controversy there was no organizational growth in the political parties or social movements. Arguments that this was due to the PMDB's multiclass character are simply wrong, because the Workers Party (Partido dos Trabalhadores—PT) had a much narrower social base and was no more successful than the other parties. However, the PMDB, especially the factions close to Tancredo Neves, successfully exploited the PDS's difficulties. The reason why the PMDB did not bring the full force of its resources to bear in negotiations with the regime—for example by channeling the *Diretas-Já* movement—was simply that the party was divided on this issue.

The PMDB presidential primary campaigns of Tancredo Neves and Ulisses Guimaraes represented the party's response to two sets of likely electoral rules, indirect elections in the case of the former and direct elections in the case of the latter. They did not conduct a bitter, competitive campaign. To the contrary, their candidacies responded to a deliberate strategy by the party leadership— headed by Ulisses Guimaraes—and backed by PMDB governors. When it was clear that the elections would be indirect, Guimaraes dropped his bid and temporarily ceded party leadership to Tancredo Neves.

After the defeat of the *Diretas-Já* campaign, the Democratic Alliance advanced the slogan "changes now." Although this did not have the same appeal as the call for direct elections, the Democratic Alliance nevertheless skillfully manipulated the symbolism of change and the idea of a national reencounter to its advantage. The Democratic Alliance played upon these themes throughout the second half of 1984. Moreover, they never allowed Brazilians to forget that the choice was between change or a continuation of the status quo with Paulo Maluf.

A final word with regard to civil society. Two things are quite evident in Brazil. On the one hand, civil society has a rich and active existence in the developed southeastern region, that is, in the states of Minas Gerais, Rio de Janeiro, Sao Paulo, Parana, Santa Catarina, and Rio Grande do Sul. On the other hand, northeastern civil society lacks sophisticated political organization. The northeastern oligarchy depends on the federal government for many of its material resources, as well as formal instruments of legitimation; hence, for most of the last quarter century this oligarchy has supported the military regime. The northeast's relative industrialization did not alter traditional patterns of domination, and there is a close relationship between the "drought industry" and the dominant elite. Frustration with this state of affairs periodically spills over into electoral politics. Currently, the Liberal Front party has built a broad base in the region. The Liberal Front not only supports Tancredo Neves, but also exercises considerable influence within his coalition. For example, proposals for agrarian reform and the enfranchisement of illiterates threaten to undermine the regional oligarchy's economic and political power.

Since the Liberal Front carries such weight in the current transitional government, the northeast question will most likely condition the political regime as well as an eventual restructuring of the party system. We should not lose sight of the fact that the historically high levels of exploitation in the northeast have reduced the population to such misery that social relations are close to the breaking point. For these reasons, we may conclude that progressive political parties, given their organizational characteristics, are better equipped to meet the challenges of the day in the south central region than in the northeast. Nevertheless, it is also very likely that conservative parties in both of these regions will soon organize to defend against encroachments of their power and privileges.

THE ARMED FORCES AND DEMOCRACY

The authoritarian regime developed deep roots in Brazilian social structure during the 21 years of its existence. As a result, the consolidation of democracy in Brazil will no doubt have to overcome some of that deeply embedded inheritance. The inheritance influences the outlook and conduct, the expectations and attitudes of Brazilian politicians in parliament, the Church, the state university, the military, and the political parties. The remaining pages will address the most significant of these lingering influences, and, based on preliminary reflections, will suggest some possible solutions.

In the Tancredo Neves administration civil–military relations took on a very cautious character on both sides. The illness that prevented Tancredo Neves from assuming office prompted the PMDB, the Liberal Front Party, and, very discreetly, the Army Ministry to work together. Since then, the military ministries have reaffirmed their faith in the nation's maturity, and have demonstrated their intention not to participate directly in politics and to comply with the Brazilian constitution. The armed forces' behavior is both reassuring and surprising. It is also reversible.

The military, however, does not bear sole responsibility for the success or failure of democratic consolidation. Civil society's lack of knowledge of the armed forces also presents problems, although civilians are making efforts to remedy their ignorance. As both sides cautiously probe and learn more about each other we may be hopeful that they will come to a better and less prejudiced understanding.

We must also recognize that the political parties possess no clear strategy for how to deal with the armed forces. This raises the risk that the parties will repeat past errors, such as attempting to ''conquer the military'' rather than organizing society. If civilian political forces opt for the ''conquest'' strategy they will revive the armed forces' desire to directly participate in politics. For, to the degree that the political parties do not control society and do antagonize the military, they reinforce the armed forces' deeply rooted perception that civilians are inherently incapable of governing.[14]

Consequently, civilian politicians must hone their skills and proceed with extreme caution if they intend to revive the traditional Brazilian practice of ''counting generals and cannons'' instead of mobilizing societal forces. Both civilian politicians and the military have to avoid the temptation to adopt political projects that exclude major political forces. Such actions would surely compromise democratic institution-building. As a result, bringing the military under civilian control will clearly require tremendous ingenuity and resourcefulness on the part of Brazilian civil society.

Since the 1930s, the Brazilian legal code has defined certain activities as crimes against the national security. Fortunately, Brazil's recent reform of the National Security Law has led to a reclassification of crimes admissible under this rubric and to a change in sentences. A fundamental problem remains: the National Security Law is still in effect and it allows military courts to try civilians. Moreover, the National Security Law is based on the Doctrine of National Security, which simplifies social problems in the extreme. Brazil's democratic regime must question this law and its foundations, while seeking to understand the effects that it has on the character of the Brazilian state and society.

Brazil's democratic regime also needs to reorganize the state's intelligence agencies in order to achieve the following objectives: (1) The regime must either demilitarize or replace the National Information Service. It must also depoliticize the SNI, that is, destroy its policy-making capacity. (2) The Foreign Ministry should be in charge of foreign intelligence and the Justice Ministry should oversee agencies concerned with domestic intelligence. (3) For the former objectives to be viable, the authorities will also have to modify the recruitment and training of agents, severing their connection to the extreme right wing, both civilian and military.

The civilian administration will probably be very cautious in its relations with the armed forces; therefore, any reorganization of the intelligence community will require solid backing from both civilian and military political forces. Meanwhile, it is absolutely necessary for the civilian government to weaken the SNI by severing its connections to other ministries and state agencies. The SNI should be placed under the control of Congress and submitted to public scrutiny in order to avoid the consolidation of a shadow command structure that rivals the military. The government must not wait for the SNI to begin destabilizing the regime before taking action, but must preempt the SNI. In undertaking this action, however, the administration must distinguish between democracy's need to separate the SNI from the armed forces and "revenge."

By the same token, Brazilian political forces need to review the functions and composition of the National Security Council (NSC), should they decide not to dismantle it. The NSC, after all, was one of the principal instruments the armed forces used to exercise their tutelary role in politics. According to article 87 of the constitution, the NSC is the "presidency's highest advisory board in the formulation and implementation of national security policies." Article 88 establishes that the president, the vice president, and the cabinet are ex officio members of the NSC. Article 89 defines the NSC's scope very broadly: "It sets national goals, and defends the nations's security from internal and external threats.'' The fact that a majority of the NSC's members are civilian ministers does not obscure its primary function. It is the military institution's—especially the army's—tool for devising government policy.

In addition to these problems and recommendations for action, Brazilian society faces four critical issues in the consolidation of democracy. First, the Brazilian military must develop a new outlook. Brazilian commanders must replace their corporate and personal loyalties with fealty to the constitution and rule by law. They must learn to distinguish between discipline and hierarchy (the organizational bases of all military institutions) and blind obedience and arbitrary decisions. The citizen within the uniform must be encouraged to flourish by guaranteeing him a right to the democratic expression of his interests. This requires a moral rehabilitation of the military. Political disagreements should not lead to truncated careers, and suspicion about loyalties should give way to intellectual ferment. A shift away from the National Security Doctrine and toward a commitment to democratic norms should underpin such changes in the military man's mentality. Instead of preparing to fight against an "internal enemy," the military must somehow be encouraged to think more about traditional military tasks, such as the defense of Brazil against external threats. The armed forces must understand that, contrary to the dictates of the National Security Doctrine, social conflict is not a crime. This understanding must become part of their ideology.

Second, Brazil probably needs to reorganize the relationship between the three branches of the service. The navy and the air force cannot individually or jointly mount a successful coup d'etat unless they have the army's support, but any one of them can destabilize the regime. Any restructuring of the relations among the service branches should depend on highlighting the armed forces' external function and minimizing if not eliminating its role as an internal occupation force. This, of course, requires a military doctrine inspired by democratic principles.

A related change would be the innovation in civil–military relations with respect to the armed forces' monopoly over strategic studies. One way to solve this problem would be to create nonmilitary research centers for strategic affairs (for example, in universities and political parties) and to establish contacts and exchanges between these and their military counterparts. Both sides would benefit from such an arrangement. On the one hand, it might serve to weaken the prevalent authoritarian conception of militarism that sanctions the armed forces' participation in politics. While this view is not limited to the military, it received official support during their government, which strengthened militarism both ideologically and as political practice. On the other hand, restructuring civil–military realtions also requires that the two sides establish a dialogue to define the armed forces' constitutionally mandated functions. Such a dialogue should establish the limits of the military's autonomy. This is a formidable political task, given civil society's ignorance of the military and the great degree of autonomy acquired by the latter throughout Brazilian history.

A third issue of great relevance to the consolidation of democracy turns on the character of relations between the executive and the legislature. If Congress withdraws its support for executive branch initiatives, the president may be forced to turn to the armed forces to guarantee political stability. That would obviously increase the military's influence in the civilian regime. Therefore, Brazil's political forces must never forget that the regime's legitimacy and the hegemony of democratic forces—which recognize and promote the political interests of labor—are the only instruments capable of countering the military's tendency to want to establish a tutelary role over the democratic regime. We must remember that Brazil's transition to democracy was not due to the emergence of a political vacuum. It took place in a political space filled with conflicting pressure groups, including military groups. The armed forces were not defeated during the period of political liberalization. Therefore, their autonomy, far from being diminished, will tend to increase during the transition to democracy, unless civil society and the political parties organize political life to an extent not yet known in Brazil.

All of these factors highlight the need for dialogue and innovative problem-solving among political forces and the military if Brazil is to have a viable democracy. This goal will become an impossibility if both sides refuse to overcome their prejudices. Should that occur, the armed forces will no doubt be more capable than the political parties of setting limits to the transition. If civilian political forces insist on isolating the military politically, the latter will simply shape their own policy with a high degree of autonomy. That is, they will continue to affect policy making but without civilian involvement.[15]

A final condition for successful redemocratization turns on disassociating the military from political repression, except in very special constitutionally and legislatively defined circumstances. All of these proposed changes in civil–military relations should be designed to strengthen the armed forces in their professional and constitutionally defined roles, and to integrate the military institution into society and politics in a manner that is compatible with the consolidation of a democratic polity.

NOTES

1. Two parties formed the Democratic Alliance: the PMDB and the Liberal Front, which later became the Liberal Front Party (PFL). The Liberal Front was a dissident faction of the Democratic Social Party (PDS) linked to Vice President Aureliano Chaves. This faction officially split from the PDS after Deputy Paulo Maluf won the PDS's presidential nomination.

2. See Ana Lagoa, *SNI. Como Nasceu. Como Funciona* (Sao Paulo: Brasiliense, 1983).

3. For details, see Walder de Goes, *O Brasil do General Geisel* (Rio de Janeiro: Nova Fronteira, 1978), 18.

4. For a characterization of the SNI as a power resource, see Fernando Henrique Cardoso in an interview given to the newspaper *O Estado de Sao Paulo*, 7 August 1983.

5. "Parallel" or "shadow command" is a concept that expresses the relationship of the SNI to the military command structure in the planning, coordination, direction, and

implementation of policy. In this relationship, the SNI maintains its autonomy from the military and expresses the needs of the intelligence community.

6. The Riocentro affair refers to an incident that took place on May 1, 1981. On that date, democratic and leftist political movements held a cultural festival in Riocentro, Rio de Janeiro. Two members of the Army Secret Service intended to plant a bomb in order to disrupt the event, but the bomb exploded prematurely in their automobile, which was parked at Riocentro. Minister Golbery wanted to mount a full-scale investigation of the attempted terrorist act. But the SNI head and the commander of the First Army prevailed and proceeded with a cover-up. For more details, see an independent investigation conducted by Colonel (Army Reserve) Dickson M. Grael, *Aventura, Corrupcao e Terrorismo: A Sombra da Impunidade,* 2d ed. (Petropolis: Brasiliense, 1985); Belisa Ribeiro, *Bomba no Riocentro,* in vol. 112 of *Colecao Edicoes do Pasquim* (Rio de Janeiro: CODECRI, 1982).

7. Mario Andreazza was a true creation of the special conditions of Brazilian politics at the time. He was a military reservist exercising political functions; moreover, he and others in his position had also either participated in the 1964 coup d'etat or had served in previous military governments. This gave these men their political identity, which was much more important than just fulfilling the condition of being a reserve officer.

Andreazza used the Interior Ministry to organize a solid political base among northeastern state governors. The new northeastern governors—who gained their seats via direct elections in 1982—were forced to vote for Andreazza in PDS primary elections. They could not support Aureliano Chaves because he had split with the party. Therefore, it is not surprising that today most of those governors have joined the Liberal Front Party so closely associated with Chaves. Some of those governors even joined the PMDB, which had important consequences for regional politics.

8. In accord with the Brazilian constitution of the time, the executive branch was solely responsible for introducing the proposed amnesty law in the Brazilian Congress. This law allowed people who had been proscribed from politics to participate once again, but it did not allow demoted officers to regain their former positions.

9. Nevertheless, practically all of the measures introduced by General Geisel in the April Package (constitutional amendment no. 8 of April 14, 1975) were retained—most notably the "bionic senators." These senators were elected indirectly in order to guarantee the military's dominance in the Senate, and thus to block all attempts at constitutional reform.

10. For details of these events, see *Veja,* 16 January 1985. The Army felt it necessary to issue a disclaimer a few days later. Resistance to the minister's plans is widely attributed to General Leonidas Pires Goncalves, then commander of the Third Army and army minister.

11. The issue of the SNI's immunity has already been dealt with by the Constituent Assembly in 1985.

12. "It is the function of the military police to maintain order in Brazilian states, territories, and the Federal District, moreover, military firemen are considered to be army reserve forces" (Article 13, IX, no. 4 of the constitution). The inspector general's office of the Military Police, which coordinates the activities of all military police forces in Brazil, is part of the Army General Staff.

13. *Folhetim* (Folha de Sao Paulo), 11 March 1985.

14. Michel Debrun, *A Conciliaçao e as outras Estratégias* (Campinas: Unicamp, 1984), 133.

15. For details, see the interview with Fernando Henrique Cardoso in *O Estado de Sao Paulo*, 27 January 1985.

6 Autonomy of the Military in Chile: From Democracy to Authoritarianism

Felipe Agüero

The high levels of autonomy developed by the Chilean military during the authoritarian regime are based on processes which originated within the previous period of democratic rule. The armed forces that staged the coup d'etat in 1973 had reached positions which were grounded on those processes. The dictatorship that took over propelled the autonomy of the military to higher and unprecedented levels.

AUTONOMY

Borrowing freely from discussions held elsewhere, military autonomy means here the ability to independently formulate the goals of the organization.[1] The military may adopt goals that do not go in line with the goals or interests of dominant groups in society. The armed forces may draw off from the hegemony claimed by these groups and from the formal mechanisms through which it is exerted. Autonomy is also related to degrees in the capacity to put into practice the goals defined from within. This capacity stems from institutional cohesion, and from the manner of insertion and power resources obtained within the state apparatus. The levels or degrees of military autonomy vary according to goal definition and capacities. An extreme degree of military autonomy may coincide with the autonomization of the state.[2] However, military autonomization normally takes place as a differentiation process within the state: a gradual process of withdrawal from the scope of decisions of civilian authorities and of expansion of the scope of decisions of the military.

Autonomy is related to the domestic and not the international arena. It is autonomy with regard to domestic social and political groups and the legal-formal means of their power, and not to foreign states or military institutions.

For instance, goals may be defined jointly by the militaries of different countries, or a military may simply adopt goals defined by a foreign counterpart. By the nature of their mission and their location in the state structure, the military are so positioned that they have a view of both the domestic and international realms, and form an institutional complex subjected to transnational political, organizational, and technological connections. But international dependence may very well go together with high levels of autonomy in the domestic arena.

Autonomization of the military initially stems from the process of corporatization, a process which points to the emergence of organizational interests as the military establishment modernizes professionally and technically. Corporatism becomes visible when the military react defensively to what they perceive as interference from without in matters regarded as their exclusive domain. The defensive attitude is in itself political as it implies a debate over what pertains to the exclusive scope of military responsibilities. Since autonomy implies organizational involvement, it is not necessarily related to cases of *caudillismo* in its Caesarist or Bonapartist manifestation. On the other hand, the use of the term corporatization should not imply that the military support corporatist models of societal organization or of interests intermediation.[3]

CRISIS OF MILITARY CONSTITUTIONALISM

The period between the election of socialist Salvador Allende in September 1970 and his inauguration into office in November tested the military's loyalty to the constitution. Though the military passed the test successfully, the argument maintained here is that the process leading to higher levels of military autonomy continued unabated. The views held by army commander General Schneider before and after the elections, until he was assassinated shortly before Allende's inauguration, expressed the strategic stance of a player—the army—that planned his moves independently. With the Schneider Doctrine the military voiced their position and indicated an eventual course of action vis à vis other players in the political field.[4] Whether desired or not, the military ended up as another player, increasingly detached from its subordinate position in the state.

The Schneider Doctrine has been generally understood as the heyday of the democratic orientation of the Chilean military. Undoubtedly, Schneider's views were crucial in facilitating the maintenance of the rule of law at a critical point in Chile's democratic tale. Chile's last constitutional government could be inaugurated partly because of the Schneider Doctrine.[5] Notwithstanding, a careful analysis shows that this doctrine fits well into the trends of autonomy described here.

The Schneider Doctrine has two basic components. The first and best known indicated the position the army was to take during the electoral process to elect the successor to President Frei, a Christian Democrat. Six months before the elections Schneider stated that the army would support the candidate who obtained over 50 percent of the votes or who, having won by a simple majority, was elected in a joint session of Congress. In this regard, Schneider did nothing but repeat unequivocal constitutional prescriptions regarding presidential elections.[6] If the constitution mandated such a position for the armed forces as the one specified by Schneider, why did he have to stipulate it now as the official position of the army?

The answer has to be understood in the context of polarization which fragmented Chilean society at the time. First, the army was fully aware that several civilian groups sought to prevent Allende's eventual election and would resort to unconstitutional means. Conservative sectors disliked the possibility that Congress would choose from two candidates with the largest majority even if former President Alessandri, their candidate, got a slight margin. This was certainly plausible, as the polls showed that elections were going to be very tight. The army had to unequivocally state its position if it did not want to animate strategies which attempted to bypass the constitution.[7] Second, the army realized that Frei's government was giving ambiguous signals and seemed unresolved. Strong leadership from civilian authorities to the army in this regard evidently could not be counted on. Had the government stated its position unmistakably and exerted clear leadership on the issue, the army could have played a much less preponderant role. The army realized it had to let its position be known to the government in order to force the latter to a clear stance and to prevent any misuse of the military.[8] Third, the army chiefs concluded that in the various possible scenarios, "professional independence and military discipline and cohesion" could be maintained only through punctiliously following explicit constitutional prescriptions on the matter. Any other path would have stirred politicization and fragmentation. That is, independently of the sincere democratic feelings that army chiefs might have held and of the mandatory subjection to the constitution, they planned their moves while inspired by the organizational interest in preserving institutional cohesion. Military calculations led them to chose the constitutional path as the one that best served this goal.

The army was forced to an autonomous outline of its strategy in the Schneider Doctrine, and in so doing, military subordination to civilian authorities was revealed as purely nominal. This is why this doctrine is a step further in the crisis of military constitutionalism, despite the fact that, in part, it only represented an explicit statement of a segment of the constitution itself. The "crisis of military constitutionalism" means that military subordination to civilians had long become merely formal; the Schneider Doctrine now added that even the *form* of subordination was under erosion. The "Tacnazo" had been a big leap in this direction, but even then the military demanded concessions from the only hierarchically superior sphere that could assent to them, the civilian administration. The Schneider Doctrine played a role that led the military a step further: the military constituted itself as a player in equal standing with others.[9] The stage thus reached in the process of military autonomization was not the result of a methodic and conscious design by the armed forces. It resulted rather from military reaction to civilian institutions—government and political parties—that neglected their responsibilities in the field of national defense. In the absence of civilian leadership and troubled by the threats of increasing social polarization, the military had no choice except to design a strategy meant to safeguard organizational and doctrinal cohesion.

The second component of the Schneider Doctrine borrowed much from national security conceptions which were widespread among the militaries of South America. It was based on the distinction between nation and state and contended that the armed forces owed loyalty to the former, which is permanent, and not the latter, which is transient. The first component of the doctrine—i.e., that the armed forces should not be sought as a political alternative as long as the rule of law prevails—was complemented by the following: If state authorities abandon legality, then the military is free to act in accordance with its duty to the nation.[10] The nation–state distinction insinuated the conditional character of military dependence from civilian authorities. In this view, the military alone are left to determine the circumstances under which allegiance to the state ought to be transferred to the nation. Military self-determination and the suggested substitution of military interpretation for the democratically expressed sovereignty of the people opened wide possibilities for the merger of the national interest with military will.

ARMED FORCES AND MILITARY GOVERNMENT

Various groups with conflicting interests converged in the overthrow of Allende. Right-wing forces grouped under the National Party pursued the establishment of an authoritarian state. The Christian Democratic Party was ultimately interested in the reestablishment of democracy following what it perceived as an unavoidable military interlude. Bankers, dominant businessmen, and elite technocrats sought a radical turn towards an economy based on free market, international opening, and controlled labor. Organizations representing small business and independent professionals had an interest in "the defense of property" and the restoration of public order. The armed forces reacted against Marxism and "national disintegration," and were interested in the improvement of military capability via armament renovation and enhancement of the profession. The military sought a substantial increase in their material power and the fulfillment of national security tenets. Placed at the core of this broad alliance, the military held the power to set the course of policy.

On the political side, the military opted for the establishment of "authoritarian democracy" as the goal, which substituted for the initial pledge to restore broken-down institutions. Hence, the military prepared to rule for a lengthy period with no deadlines. An important decision made by General Pinochet was to reject any suggestion leading to the organization of a mass movement in support of the government. Pinochet feared that such a movement would make policy making slower and conflictual and would eventually break the buffer zone behind which he wanted to keep the military isolated from social and political pressures.

A complement of this decision was the way he moved to structure military participation and the line of authority in the military and the government.

The chiefs of the army, the navy, the air force, and the *Carabineros* initially shared government responsibilities and were supposed to rotate in the presidency of the junta. Pinochet, the army chief, soon convinced his peers in the other services that he should remain as president of the junta. He later had himself appointed president of the republic and chief of state, while simultaneously keeping the top army post. The junta was then removed from direct government responsibilities and put in charge of legislative functions only. An important source of conflict was thus removed, as air force chiefs had shown greater concern for social policy than economic policy-makers selected by Pinochet were willing to take. Also, Pinochet managed to remove influential army generals who had formed the nucleus that planned the coup and who could threaten his leadership.[11] As president, Pinochet held the power to appoint all mayors, *intendentes*, and *gobernadores* of the administrative regions and provinces, presidents of universities, the Council of State, and the comptroller general; the major intelligence agency is accountable directly to him. His personal control of the whole government structure combined with his control of the army.

On the other hand, Pinochet established a clear separation between government and military structures. Though numerous military officers have been appointed to government positions they have not acted as representatives of the armed forces, but have responded to the government line of authority. The bulk of the military has been kept apart from governmental functions and devoted to professional activities, at least until the crisis begun in 1982–1983 demanded greater use of the army in repressive police functions.

In the context of social demobilization that resulted from repression and the economic model which promoted social atomization, the military remained one of the few organizational powers in society. Withdrawn from direct government responsibilities, the military could maintain high levels of cohesion and upgrade their autonomy. The latter was clearly evidenced in the areas of national defense, foreign policy, and the delineation of the future role of the armed forces in the Constitution of 1980.

NATIONAL DEFENSE, FOREIGN POLICY, AND THE CONSTITUTION

With the military takeover the armed forces established their own views on defense as the national defense policy. A consequence of this was the incorporation of the military notions of domestic security into the defense system. The *Carabineros*, the national police force which had been subordinate to the secretary of the interior since its creation, were transferred to the Ministry of Defense. Shortly after the coup d'etat the government created the National Intelligence Agency (DINA), later renamed National Information Center (CNI), which is presided over by an army general and is directly accountable to Pinochet.

Simultaneously, police and military sections devoted to repression developed significantly and have received the lion's share in military budget allocations.[12] The repressive apparatus developed in response to the new defense notions.

On the other hand, the imposition of military views on defense has resulted in huge increases in military spending, arms imports, and personnel. The government's emphasis on military strength over diplomacy was evidenced in 1974 in the upswing in military spending, which stayed high through the decade: military expenditure in 1980 was 75 percent higher than in 1973.[13] Military expenditure as a percent of Gross National Product (GNP) went from 2.8 in 1972 to 4.8 in 1982. Even when signs of economic crisis were already apparent, the military managed to reach in 1982 the highest spending level in that ten-year period, while cuts were applied elsewhere.[14] The military was thus supporting their own views on the likelihood of armed conflict as well as their ideas about the proper social status of military personnel, since much of the budget was devoted to salaries, social security, and other indirect means of economic support for members of the armed forces.

Also, the difficulties met by the government in finding foreign arms suppliers at a time when tensions with neighboring countries were high led to all kinds of stimuli to local businessmen to produce weapons. New industries were added to those already held by the military, which managed to promote an incipient domestic arms industry under an economic policy that made it rather unorthodox.

The military also broke with the traditional patterns of professionalism which had prevailed in the conduct of foreign policy. Admirals were appointed in the Ministry of Foreign Affairs and a vast array of military officers were placed in embassies while others negotiated directly on behalf of Pinochet, bypassing the ministry's staff. Ideology substituted for pragmatism, and the anti-Marxist and anti-Soviet crusade was made the backbone of foreign policy during the first years. National security notions, which established Soviet manipulation of domestic opposition, also prevailed in this area.

Technocrats conducting economic policy later pressed for a more pragmatic foreign policy which could overcome isolation and concur with the process of capitalist modernization.[15] Even when a civilian was appointed minister, the military's domestic security imperatives kept interfering. Repression always remained more important to the military than the need to overcome persistent international condemnation. Acts of international terrorism promoted from high military quarters have to date hindered attempts to cross the barrier of international political isolation.[16] Also, espionage activities run by the military from Chilean embassies abroad have made ambassadors' missions difficult, especially in neighboring countries. Even though civilians have remained in charge of the Ministry of Foreign Affairs, a new post of vice minister was created which has since been held by an army general, and an army officer has held the third-ranked position in the ministry.

The military has also engaged directly in negotiations with the armed forces of neighboring countries on matters that would have been the domain of the

Ministry of Foreign Affairs under normal circumstances. Delegates of the general staff of the armed forces of Bolivia, Chile, and Peru reached an agreement in 1976 which established mechanisms for military collaboration as a way to address normal state relations. Also, negotiations with Argentina following the latter's rejection of Queen Elizabeth's arbitration on the Beagle Channel dispute were conducted many times by military envoys of Pinochet bypassing the professional team of the ministry. Officers, particularly from the navy, have outspokenly criticized official policy toward Argentina.[17]

Autonomy is evidenced in several other areas, most remarkably in the de facto immunity which military officers have enjoyed even after their responsibility has been unequivocally established in the commission of crimes, torture, and terrorist and other unlawful acts. One must add, however, that this privilege is to a large extent the result of lenient behavior on the part of the judiciary. But perhaps the most forthright expression of autonomy is found in the authoritarian constitution.

The constitution approved in 1980 was not intended to be fully enforced until 1989. It was drafted by a committee appointed by Pinochet, followed his directives, set a timetable for the establishment of an authoritarian system, and addressed the succession problem. Its enactment in 1980 set the government's future free from the pressures unleashed since 1983 by an incipient "semi-opposition," and fixed Pinochet's position in the presidency.[18]

Under constitutional guidelines the legislative power (the junta) had to promulgate a number of laws that would make enforcement of the constitution operational in 1989. Military chiefs have thus engaged in legislation on political parties and the electoral system, that will be inherited as the child of the military. However, full enforcement of the constitution will break with past tradition as well as with current "transitory" practices, such as the legislative function of the junta. The military's role and autonomy are enhanced to such an extent that military control of civilian institutions is constitutionalized.

Under the disguise of an extreme presidential supremacy the constitution establishes firm military control.[19] Presidential supremacy is clear with regard to Congress. In military matters, the president has command over public order, external security, and the armed forces; he appoints and removes military chiefs, and decides promotions. Congress, in turn, has no overseeing capacities regarding the military, with only two meager exceptions: it participates in legislation establishing the size of the forces, and determines whether to proceed in prosecuting admirals or generals should the nation's security or honor be forsaken. The president's powers, however, are severely restrained by the military's. He can appoint chiefs of the services from among five of the highest-ranked officers only, and once appointed they cannot be removed during the four-year period of incumbency. Removal in selected cases is an attribute of the newly created National Security Council, where military chiefs hold an absolute majority. Also, promotions and retirements can be enacted only in accordance with the internal regulations of the services.

The constitution assigns the military the role of overseers of the institutional order. This role is exerted through the National Security Council (which comprises the chiefs of the three services and the *Carabineros* and three civilians). The council sets its own procedural norms and can be convened by two of its members. Sessions require that only four of its members be present. Its mission is to advise the president on security affairs at his request. Most significantly, however, the council can state its views to any authority regarding any action or matter deemed harmful to the nation's institutions or security, and can demand from any institution or public official any information related to the nation's domestic or external security. Response to the council's request is mandatory. The council also designates two of the seven members of the Constitutional Tribunal, which arbitrates constitutional controversies and determines the right of political organizations to legally exist. The council appoints four former military chiefs to the Senate for an eight-year period. The constitution establishes that each of the armed services will have delegates in the regional development committees throughout the country.

THE MILITARY AND AUGUSTO PINOCHET

With the sole temporary exception of the "Chicago technocracy," the government has not counted on any stable team of civilians in government roles, and has called upon individuals with varying political and professional backgrounds. In the absence of any other organized source of support, Pinochet has opted for heavy reliance on the armed forces, and has incorporated a large number of officers into the administration. Almost half of the cabinet members since September 1983 have been military officers and, on the average, they have remained in their posts for a longer period than civilian ministers.[20] Despite the differences between Chile and other authoritarian regimes in South America, the military filled the cabinet in Chile to a much larger extent than in Brazil or Argentina. Also, about one-third of deputy ministers have come from the military. The top positions in the regional administrative units across the territory have been held by generals simultaneously commanding army divisions and by colonels in command of the regiments. Numerous public corporations have been chaired by military officers.[21]

Pinochet has availed himself of a selected group of military advisers for government policy. The general staff of the presidency (*estado mayor presidencial*) and the President's Advisory Committee (formerly the Junta's Advisory Committee), which are staffed exclusively by military officers), handle legislation, draft policy reports, and coordinate government policy. The importance of these bodies, which brief the president periodically, is evidenced by the fact that deputy army chiefs and Pinochet's delegates to the junta have come from them. Also, the CNI, the intelligence agency, performs advisory functions in government policy. In the early years of the regime, CONARA (National Commission for Administrative Reform), staffed by military officers, conducted broad reform programs that ended in the current administrative territorial divisions, following military perspectives. As a result of military role expansion the number of army generals rose from 25 in 1973 to 57 in 1986.[22]

Such an expanded incorporation of active-duty officers in government responsibilities makes it highly unlikely that the "military as institution" has remained totally withdrawn from discussions involving broad government policy.[23] Discrepancies among army generals have on occasion gained notoriety, and a few officers who uttered criticism were assigned short-term government positions. Though there is a slight basis to believe that some space exists for military representation in the government, this is obviously a subject in need of research.

POLITICIZATION, COHESION, AND AUTONOMY

The military may maintain high levels of autonomy if cohesion is high. Active engagement in politics, however, tends to weaken cohesion and to open gaps which may be utilized by civilians in search of military allies. Hence, autonomy severely suffers. Such experience is true of most South American military regimes.

The threats of politicization and framentation in the Chilean military stem not from internal decision-making structures, but from growing exposure to the conflictual situation that has pervaded society since the crisis that began in 1983. That year marked the end of economic policy success, the beginning of a sharp economic decline, the explosion of sectorial pressures, the inauguration of massive antigovernment demonstrations, and the conquering of public space for opposition maneuvering. In the absence of a proper means of channeling demands, the military was brought much closer to divisive politics than Pinochet's policy of seclusion had allowed. Also, the government started daily use of the army in police functions.

Exposure to conflict, and the urgency with which major decisions mandated by the constitution had to be faced, resulted in growing evidence of fissures within the junta. Signs of conflict had already been apparent when General Gustavo Leigh was forced out of the junta, but the episode was then promptly terminated. The new air force chief, General Matthei, later became the voice of internal dissent, stating in 1984 that the armed forces would risk division if the "transition" was not accelerated before 1989. In overt disagreement with his peers in the junta, he showed sympathy for an accord reached by the opposition in 1985. Retired generals also began to voice criticism. The isolation faced by the government forced Pinochet to draw the army along with his own political interests, thus linking the fortunes of the military to the government. He once called upon the minister of defense, a retired admiral, to issue public statements on behalf of his personal political preferences.[24] The later removal of the director general of *Carabineros* from his post and from the junta and the dismissal of a group of police officers for their responsibility in the assassination of three dissidents provided further evidence of internal conflict within the services.

More divisive issues lie ahead for the military and the junta. The most important is the junta's designation of the president for the new eight-year term starting in 1989. Transitory dispositions of the constitution mandate that the junta unanimously designate the president, who shall then be submitted to a plebiscite. Should the junta not reach unanimity, the decision lies with the National Security Council, which shall be formed by the president, the chiefs of the armed services, and three civilians, most of whom will have been appointed by Pinochet. Strong indications exist that unanimity will be hard to reach, thus affecting the junta's activities until its expiration in 1989. Chilean politics has not known such levels of strife between the armed services at least since the early 1930s.[25]

Nonetheless, in current Chilean power politics it is the army that counts, and Pinochet has been able to secure loyalty and cohesion among his subordinates in this service. By imposing the official "transition" course and timetable, he has also subordinated the semi-opposition, and, in passing, the entire opposition. The primacy of the army over the other services has ultimately rendered interservice conflict uneventful and has helped maintain cohesion where it really matters. But regardless of the future course of events, especially the selection of the president for the next term, the full enforcement of the constitution in 1989 will have fixed the military in unprecedented levels of autonomy.

CONCLUDING REMARKS

No imperative reasons exist for the military to relinquish power. Factors which have weakened the military in the authoritarian regimes of other South American countries, or which have produced incentives to support mild democratization, are not present in Chile.[26] On the other hand, for the past decade the military has deepened and solidified ideological positions which assign the armed forces the leading role in resisting an all-embracing and ever-present Soviet penetration in the domestic arena and in Chile's adjoining geopolitical context.[27] Also, during this time the military has gained all kinds of privileges which it treasures very dearly. Finally, the opposition has yet to prove that it can produce a workable and credible civilian alternative. For all these reasons, Chile will be the hardest case in the restoration of levels of military autonomy that are compatible with democracy.

One could, however, postulate the possibility that the military will become aware of shortcomings involved in the constitution. When it becomes fully enforced in 1989, parity will be restored between the three armed services, with the new addition of *Carabineros* and the new encompassing functions of political control. Since the top chiefs of the armed services will remain four years in their posts, pressures from within the generals and admirals corps will mount for the selected chiefs to be true representatives of their collective bodies. This will spur deliberation, which will be further stimulated by the constitutional role of overseeing the political process. As delegates of their bodies (since the president would have to bargain with each service on the appointment of the top commander from among the top five generals) the chiefs' authority over their subordinates will inevitably relapse, much more so because the new chiefs will lack the charisma endowed to junta members as regime founders. Politicization and fragmentation would then appear as serious threats to the military.

For the military to favor reductions in their political power and changes in their status in the constitution, the military would have to enter the reasoning postulated above into their own strategic calculations, based on the interest in preserving institutional cohesion. If this were to be the case, it would certainly take time for the military to perceive the constitutional mechanism for military participation as a shortcoming. Needless to say, it would also take the formation of a visible civilian power alternative that can take command of government and instill in the military a new professionalism and a freshened sense of mission, It is unfortunate that the chances of diminishing military autonomy lie with such an improbable alternative.

NOTES

1. Theda Skocpol, "Bringing the State Back In: Strategies of Analysis in Current Research," in *Bringing the State Back In*, ed. Peter Evans, Dietrich Rueschemeyer, and Theda Skocpol (Cambridge: Cambridge University Press, 1985); and Eric Nordlinger, *On the Autonomy of the Democratic State* (Cambridge: Harvard University Press, 1981).

2. Ellen Kay Trimberger, *Revolution from Above: Military Bureaucrats and Development in Japan, Turkey, Egypt, and Peru* (New Brunswick, N.J.: Transaction Books, 1978); and Alfred Stepan, *The State and Society: Peru in Comparative Perspective* (Princeton: Princeton University Press, 1978).

3. For this meaning in another context, see P. Schmitter and G. Lehmbruch, *Trends toward Corporatist Intermediation* (London: Sage, 1979). Our use of the term is more in line with Amos Perlmutter, *The Military and Politics in Modern Times* (New Haven: Yale University Press, 1977).

4. General Rene Schneider was chief of the army during the latter part of Frei's administration. He issued a number of public statements before the presidential elections of 1970 delineating the position of the army. Schneider's views became the official stance of the army and were later known as the Schneider Doctrine, which became a matter of debate among the political elite.

5. A number of attempts were made to impede Allende's inauguration. The most important was the attempt to kidnap army chief Rene Schneider in order to deter the Congress from electing socialist Salvador Allende, who had a slight majority in the ballots. The kidnapping failed because Schneider was shot in the attempt. His assassination dramatically proved correct his fears about the threats and pressures the army would have to face, and therefore, the need for his doctrine. Despite his death, his views prevailed and helped deter other conspiratorial moves, and Congress was able to freely elect Allende for president.

6. See Carlos Prats Gonzalez, *Memorias: Testimonio de un Soldado* (Santiago: Pehuén, 1985), 148. The Schneider Doctrine repeated, in this regard, the norms prescribed in articles 64 and 65 of the Constitution of 1925 (in force at the time), which referred to the mechanisms for presidential elections.

7. Also, the generals must have been aware of the conspiratorial maneuvers directed by the Central Intelligence Agency (CIA) within the Chilean army. The missions assigned to the CIA—Track I and Track II—were aimed at encouraging a coup d'etat in order to prevent the inauguration of Salvador Allende as president. See United States Congress, Senate, *Covert Action in Chile 1963–1973*, Staff Report of the Select Committee to Study Governmental Operations with respect to Intelligence Activities (Washington, D.C., 1975); and the book by the U.S. Ambassador at the time, Nathaniel Davis, *The Last Two Years of Salvador Allende* (Ithaca, N.Y.: Cornell University Press, 1985), especially 8–11 and 317–18.

8. General Prats has written that on September 8, 1970, four days after socialist Salvador Allende had won a slight majority of the votes over Conservative candidate Alessandri, President Frei summoned the chiefs of the army, the navy, and the air force and told them about his conviction that Allende's inauguration would "irrevocably slip the country into Marxism." In Prats's account, Frei insisted on his concern about the crisis in industry, foreign trade and exchange, and finance that Allende's electoral victory had brought forth. The military chiefs were exposed to identical statements in a series of meetings with members of Frei's cabinet. General Schneider replied in the same way at all these meetings: that the situation called for a political and not a military solution, and it was not the responsibility of the military but of the government party (the Christian Democratic Party) to consider political options. Carlos Prats, op. cit., 167–68.

9. The series of meetings in which government and Christian Democratic leaders had military chiefs explain their position (even if the only acceptable position was the constitutional one) contributed to establishing the military's independent role and to strengthening its autonomy. See Carlos Prats, op. cit., 168–69.

10. See Carlos Prats, *Memorias*, 157.

11. For a thorough analysis of Pinochet's manipulation of promotions and other control measures in the army, see Genaro Arriagada, "The Legal and Institutional Framework of the Armed Forces in Chile," in *Military Rule in Chile*, ed. J. Samuel Valenzuela and Arturo Valenzuela (Baltimore: Johns Hopkins University Press, 1986). Conflicting views of the role of Pinochet in the planning of the coup are offered in: Augusto Pinochet, *El Día Decisivo* (Santiago: Editorial Andrés Bello, 1980); Carlos Prats, op. cit., and "Generales del Golpe Desmientena Pinochet," *APSI* (Santiago), no. 161 (1985). The latter suggests that Pinochet joined the plotters at the very end, while Pinochet portrays himself as the organizer from the start. Prats suggests that while Pinochet was second in command he maintained good connections with both the plotters and generals loyal to the government.

12. Augusto Varas, "Militarización, armamentismo y gasto militar en Chile: 1973–1981," Material de Discusión, no. 36 (Santiago: FLACSO, 1982). For an analysis of military role expansion in repressive functions and other areas, see Hugo Frühling, Carlos Portales, and Augusto Varas, *Estado y Fuerzas Armadas* (Santiago: FLACSO, 1982).

13. Carlos Portales and Augusto Varas, "Gasto militar en Chile: 1950–1980," Documento de Trabajo. Santiago: FLACSO, 1981.

14. Arms Control and Disarmament Agency, *World Military Expenditures and Arms Transfers 1972–1982*, April 1984; Adrian J. English, *Armed Forces of Latin America* (London: Jane's, 1984); and SIPRI *Yearbook 1983* (London: Taylor & Francis).

15. For analysis of foreign policy under military government, see Heraldo Muñoz, *Las relaciones exteriores del gobierno militar chileno*, (Santiago: Ornitorrinco, 1986); Manfred Wilhelmy, "Politics, Bureaucracy, and Foreign Policy in Chile," in *Latin*

American Nations in World Politics, eds. Heraldo Muñoz and Joseph S. Tulchin (Boulder, Colo.: Westview Press, 1984); and Howard Pittman, "Chilean Foreign Policy: The Pragmatic Pursuit of Geopolitical Goals," in *The Dynamics of Latin American Foreign Policies*, eds. Jennie F. Lincoln and Elizabeth G. Ferris (Boulder, Colo.: Westview Press, 1984).

16. DINA agents, with the participation of military officers, assassinated former Allende minister Orlando Letelier in Washington, D.C. in September 1976, as well as killing former army chief General Carlos Prats and his wife in Buenos Aires; former vice president and renowned Christian Democratic leader, exile Bernardo Leighton, escaped alive but was severely injured in an assassination attempt in Rome, Italy.

17. For the agreements with Bolivia and Peru, and statements of officers on the policy toward Argentina, see Felipe Agüero, "Armas y desarme en América del Sur," Documento de Trabajo no. 161 (Santiago: FLACSO, May 1982). The Navy reluctantly supported the final agreements reached with Argentina under the mediation of Pope John Paul II.

18. For the use and meaning of the term *semi-opposition*, see Juan Linz, "Opposition In and Under an Authoritarian Regime: The Case of Spain," in *Regimes and Oppositions*, ed. Robert A. Dahl (New Haven: Yale University Press, 1973).

19. An excellent analysis of the constitution is found in Genaro Arriagada, "El sistema político chileno: una exploración del futuro," *Estudios CIEPLAN*, no. 15 (December 1984). For the military aspects of the constitution see my paper, "The Military in the Constitutions of the Southern Cone Countries and Spain," prepared for the Conference on the Role of Political Parties in the Return to Democracy in the Southern Cone, Washington, D.C., September 1985 (an expanded version in Spanish appeared in *Revista de Ciencia Política* [Santiago] 8, nos. 1–2 [1986]). Also of interest are Carlos Portales, "Militarization and Political Institutions in Chile," in *Global Militarization*, ed. Peter Wallensteen, Johan Galtung, and Carlos Portales (Boulder, Colo.: Westview Press, 1985); and Manuel Antonio Garretón, "Political Processes in an Authoritarian Regime: The Dynamics of Institutionalization and Opposition in Chile 1973–1980," in *Military Rule in Chile*, ed. J. Samuel Valenzuela and Arturo Valenzuela (Baltimore: Johns Hopkins University Press, 1986). The unprecedented role assigned to the armed forces certainly responds to the interests of the civilian groups that helped draft the Constitution. These groups find in the military an everlasting guarantee for the maintenance of the economic system and the exclusion of the Left from power positions. What exactly the military's input was in the sections related to their role and position in the system is still a matter of research.

20. "Ministros y Subsecretarios de don August Pinochet Ugarte desde Septiembre de 1973 hasta Abril de 1983," a document of the Library of Congress (Chile).

21. See Carlos Huneeus, "La política de la *apertura* y sus implicancias para la inauguración de la democracia en Chile," *Revista de Ciencia Política* (Santiago) 8, no. 1 (1985), and his recent study with Jorge Olave, where the authors conclude that Pinochet's authoritarianism is "an army's regime" after a thorough analysis of the share of each armed service in government positions. The study is reported by journalists Gonzalez, Monckeberg, and Verdugo, in *Análisis* (Santiago), no. 185 (August 1987).

22. For the reform programs, see Jorge Chateau, "Geopolítica y regionalización: algunas relaciones," Documento de Trabajo nos. 75–78 (Santiago: FLACSO, August 1978); and Pilar Vergara, "Las transformaciones del Estado chileno bajo el régimen militar," in Manuel A. Garretón et al., *Chile 1973–1983* (Santiago: FLACSO, 1983).

For the figures on generals, see Genaro Arriagada, op. cit., and the study by Huneeus and Olave described in note 21 above.

23. For the distinction between "military as institution" and "military as government," see Alfred Stepan, "Paths toward Redemocratization: Theoretical and Comparative Considerations," in *Transitions from Authoritarian Rule: Comparative Perspective*, eds. Guillermo O'Donnell, Philippe C. Schmitter, and Laurence Whitehead (Baltimore: Johns Hopkins University Press, 1986).

24. For Matthei's statements see Foreign Broadcast Information Service (FBIS), *Latin America Daily Report*, vol. 6, March 9 and 13, September 26, and October 15, 1984; and *Southern Cone Report*, October 11, 1985. For Pinochet's and his defense minister's statements, see FBIS, March 13–14 and April 2, 1984.

25. For a more detailed account of the political process vis à vis the military during the present decade and the alternatives facing the military before and after the full enforcement of the constitution, see the original Spanish version of this paper. See also Manuel Antonio Garretón, *Dictaduras y Democratización* (Santiago: FLACSO, 1984); Carlos Huneeus, "La política de la *apertura*," and Arturo Valenzuela, "Prospects for the Pinochet Regime in Chile," *Current History*, no. 149 (February 1985).

26. Despite the weakening of the Argentine military after a defeat in war, which helped trigger the transition, the military later managed to recover considerable assertiveness. *Faute d'ennemi*, the Chilean military face no such debilitating prospects. Neither do they face feuds with the local bourgeoisie or strong conservative democratic parties as did the Uruguayan military, who suffered bitter defeat in a plebiscite. On the other hand, the Brazilian military developed an interest in promoting liberalization and civilianization, which were perceived as a more suitable framework for the pursuit of military interests. See Alfred Stepan, *Rethinking Military Politics: Brazil and the Southern Cone* (N.J.: Princeton University Press, 1988). Chilean military find no such incentives. Also, the "Argentine factor" showed the military in Brazil the need to recover preponderance in the South Atlantic and to return to higher levels of modernization in the barracks. See Alexandre de Souza Costa Barros, "Back to the Barracks: An Option for the Brazilian Military?" *Third World Quarterly* 7, no. 1 (January 1985). The "Argentine factor" plays in the opposite direction in Chile because of fears of Argentine rearmament and the gloomy prison imagery which nightmarishly fills the minds of human rights violators.

27. *Defense and Foreign Affairs*, July 1985.

7 THE MILITARY IN THE ROLE OF "SUBSTITUTE POLITICAL PARTY" AND REDEMOCRATIZATION IN URUGUAY

Juan Rial

On June 27, 1973 an armored cavalry regiment surrounded the Uruguayan legislature. This action put the finishing touches on a protracted coup d'etat, the visible phase of which began on February 9, 1973. On that date, the high command of the army (which had been reshuffled that same day) and the air force broke with the civilian government. They forced President Bordaberry to institutionalize a form of cogovernment between the armed forces and the executive branch.[1]

The general population reacted in two ways. Many were stunned. Uruguay's apolitical armed forces had suddenly become no better than those of the rest of Latin America—some suspected this of the country in general. The armed forces were now directly involved in the business of rule. The more politically aware citizens realized that the military's action represented the logical culmination of a process that had begun a few years earlier. On September 9, 1971, by presidential decree, the armed forces had assumed the main responsibility for counterinsurgency operations against leftist guerrillas. Of course, they cooperated with the police, who heretofore had shouldered the fight by themselves. In December the military and police detachments involved in counterinsurgency were officially called the Joint Forces.

The military, however, revealed their political ends six days after the government placed them in charge of counterinsurgency. In the first round of deliberations—conducted in secret and made public in 1976—the commanders in chief and the Joint General Staff (*Estado Mayor Conjunto*—EMASCO) indicated that their immediate priority lay in controlling the insurgency and in a guarantee of scheduled elections in 1971.[2] But once they had accomplished that, they made it clear that in the presidential period beginning in March 1972 they intended to crush the subversives' political-military base. Once the subversives were out of the way the armed forces proposed to: "(1) assure security for national development; (2) develop the military's capability to contribute to national development; (3) support national development plans; and (4) directly take charge of some national development programs."[3]

In short, this secret memorandum laid bare the armed forces' desire to take an active role in Uruguay's political process. It also revealed that the military's autonomy and the definitions of its mission were quite advanced at this stage.

THE URUGUAYAN ARMED FORCES AND THE CRISES OF THE 1950s AND 1960s: BUILDING PROFESSIONALISM AND AUTONOMY

This perception of the military, however, did not correspond to reality. Since World War II, the Uruguayan armed forces' contact with their U.S. counterparts had led to a gradual but sustained process of modernization. For example, shortly after the end of the war, Uruguay acquired M3A1 tanks that had been used in the Africa campaign to replace horses in a number of cavalry units. Truck-drawn 105mm howitzers supplanted the old horse-drawn German Krupp or French Schneider artillery, and World War II vintage American light arms for soldiers gradually became standard issue. The Uruguayan navy also received U.S. equipment, such as a number of World War II surplus destroyers.

But the Uruguayan military modernized more than their equipment. They also adopted U.S. technical and combat manuals, and either copied or adapted U.S. military organization.[4] For example, in 1953 Uruguay passed legislation establishing an air force that was independent of the army. Many officers, moreover, received training at Fort Gulick, the U.S. Army's Americas School, and Fort Bragg.[5]

Uruguay also signed a hotly debated military cooperation treaty with the United States in 1952, but refrained from sending an infantry battalion to Korea.[6] Nevertheless, during the Cold War, Latin American military establishments became part of a continental defense system designed to contain Communism. Thus, it should come as no surprise that anticommunism turned into a central component of Uruguayan military thought.[7]

Although the Uruguayan armed forces were enclosed and isolated, they managed to maintain a relatively high level of professionalism as a result of their contact with U.S. military assistance programs. The largely middle-class officer corps, then, busied itself on two fronts: the officers competed among themselves for promotions, and pressured the legislature for more benefits. Within the context of the welfare state, their opportunity to increase their benefits came in 1958— an electoral year in which the traditional ruling party, the Colorados, lost to the National or Blanco (White) party. For historical reasons, most officers sympathized with the Colorado party, although they did not support its Batllista faction. Thus, the National party faced the problem of how to "whiten" its ranks.

The solution consisted of accentuating "military clientelism." Toward the end of the 1940s and the beginning of the 1950s, Colorado administrations had promoted high-ranking officers by appointment. The Blancos built support by radically shortening the time it took officers to be eligible for their next promotion. For cadets of the class of 1963, law no. 13,145, promulgated on July 4, 1963, topped off two years for promotion from second lieutenant to lieutenant, and from lieutenant to first lieutenant. The same applied for equivalent ranks in the air force. For equivalent ranks in the navy, the law reduced intervals between promotions by three years. Officers of previous classes, from the rank of second lieutenant to lieutenant colonel, had two years cut between promotions. In some cases, this required newly promoted officers to take courses that were supposed to qualify them for their new assignments.

The new law significantly changed the composition of the officer corps. The ranking pyramid became inverted from colonel down. Although the proportion of junior officers remained roughly the same due to increases in enrollments at military academies, the number of captains, majors, and colonels increased rapidly. In other words, career paths that had spanned 40 years were progressively shortened to the point where a second lieutenant could make colonel in 16 years. By contrast, in the 1940s it took at least 22 to 25 years for a newly commissioned officer to become a colonel.

Such a sharp increase in the number of high-ranking officers required creating positions for them to fill. This was done, and thus military academy graduates could reasonably expect to finish their military careers with the rank of lieutenant colonel or better. For example, toward the end of the 1960s and the beginning of the 1970s 73 percent of one class became colonels or generals. These men achieved high degrees of skill in bureaucratic management as a result of the continual training required to be eligible for promotions. Politicians, of course, realized that the creation of such a large body of "reserve" leaders without well-defined functions represented a potential problem. For example, circa 1970 the army alone had about 300 high-ranking officers and there were not enough military postings to go around.[8] Many of these officers, especially colonels, remained on active duty but had nothing to do. As a result, for the purpose of computing seniority, colonels had to complete only one year in a military post in order to be eligible for promotion to general.

The clientelistic methods by which the "political class" sought to coopt officers, and thus assure their integration into the political system, resulted in the deprofessionalization of the officer corps. Furthermore, this process was taking place during a period of crisis in Uruguayan society, in which politics had taken on a more defensive style. Populism had gradually given way to repression. This provided the military with an alternative course of action. Many high-ranking officers in the general staff, or who had taken courses at the Military Institute for Superior Studies, started to work on blueprints for righting the country's economic and political ills. And towards the end of the 1960s they also developed a counterinsurgency strategy.

By the end of the 1960s, then, the Uruguayan military had reached a level of professionalism that enabled them to fight a Korea-style conventional war, and they were learning how to wage internal war. Meanwhile, most Uruguayans thought of the armed forces as a decorative appendage of the state that was mainly capable of mounting colorful parades. The political class, however, always knew that Uruguay's military establishment represented a potential threat to them.

The crisis of the welfare state thrust the military, who never wanted any part of it, into a policing role—they had to keep order as the conflict between state and society sharpened. Many Uruguayans for the first time saw their military in a new light, and were surprised by its roughness.[9] Meanwhile, divisions among officers over the armed forces' proper role in society deepened. They split along ideological lines that shattered the bonds that once united them, such as academic class, family, and service branch. The result was an internal war within the military itself.

THE URUGUAYAN ARMED FORCES AND THE CHALLENGE OF THE 1970s: THE MILITARY PARTY'S "POPULIST–PATERNAL" PROJECT

Between 1968 and 1973, the armed forces gradually appropriated a leading role for themselves in Uruguayan politics. It would be difficult to argue that they did so exclusively in the interest of a particular social group. Although industrialists welcomed the military's intervention because of a perceived threat to capitalism in Uruguay, the armed forces themselves mainly wanted to defend the state; they were, after all, an organ of the state.[10] That state, however, no longer represented civil society. Instead, the state had separated itself from civil society in order to repress it, because without substantial reform it could not continue to implement progressive populist policies.

As a result, the Uruguayan military adapted the doctrine of national security to local conditions.[11] They essentially sought to protect the state because their existence depended on it. Thus, the armed forces tried to justify their political intervention by fusing the concepts of national security and economic development: "Once the military began to act with sufficient force and coherence to restore confidence in the state, it took only seven months to destroy the seditious forces, the armed branch of subversion; for during the preceding years the indolence and squabbling of politicians had gradually weakened the state to the point where it had lost its capacity to serve as an instrument of order, peace and progress."[12] Consequently, the military assumed the responsibility for providing the security that development required. From there, it was but a short step to the codification of a distinction between security and national defense in 1974. Needless to say, the military gave these concepts very broad definitions.[13]

Of course, the Uruguayan military faced the problem of defining the objectives for which they needed to provide security. They had to find an answer to the question of why it was necessary to constantly "patrol" society. The military's response had two sides to it. On the one hand, they simply repressed real or imagined enemies. On the other, the armed forces wanted to transform the Uruguayan polity by "debatlletizing" it. After all, in the previous decades, Batllism had permeated Uruguay's social fabric and built a state designed to serve the needs of civil society. In that scheme, the armed forces had no real role to play in the building of a "model country" (a Uruguayan aspiration born in the early twentieth century) or in the definition of national priorities.[14]

But in the 1970s, the armed forces turned the tables on the civilians, for now it was the military who sought to influence society. That required, in part, the elaboration of a new societal model, a new objective. The famous communiqués numbered four and seven of February 9 led many Uruguayans to the delusion that their armed forces were about to embark on a Peruvian-style populist project.[15] But in reality it was a "populist–paternal military" that attempted to mold society.[16] The army built its strength on, and sought the support of, the lower strata of society. During its expansion drives, it recruited fresh troops from the lower classes because they were the ones least likely to question military structure, hierarchy, and discipline. That expansion involved a significant number of people: for example, when the armed forces began their counterinsurgency campaign in 1970, military personnel assigned to the Defense Ministry numbered 21,269 persons; in 1978, during a time of peace imposed by repression, military personnel had increased to 38,545 persons.[17] Since many of these troops were not assigned to combat units, it seems evident that the military were trying to coopt the lower classes. They used the public administration system for the same purpose. Adopting the usual clientelistic methods, the armed forces filled the civil service with personnel from all sectors of society, but a disproportionate number were of lower-class extraction, mainly urban slum dwellers. In this fashion, then, the armed forces incorporated and extended their protection to a social group that had heretofore been under the wing of the political class.

Not all officers agreed that the military should take such an active role in politics; thus, the armed forces experienced a number of purges before and during the time they were actively involved in the government. In 1973 all but a small group of officers who supported the guerrilla movement agreed that the subversives had to be crushed.[18] But there was less of a consensus on getting directly involved in the business of rule. Some officers were loath to abandon their strictly professional role and feared that the military's direct entanglement in counterinsurgency actions would lead them to take over the government; to avoid this outcome, they proposed creating a special police force to deal with the insurgents. As a compromise solution, some army units received specialized counterinsurgency training and were assigned to combat the guerrillas.[19] It did not take the army long to defeat the foe in the field; from then on, these specialized units essentially only conducted police dragnets.

The armed forces had still not agreed on how far they should get involved in national politics. They had already played a mild moderating role during the crisis of the 1960s. During those years, the presidency had authorized the army to engage in strikebreaking actions and had given it custody of troublesome union leaders. The idea was simply to introduce a Caesarist parenthesis, although military activity increased sharply at the margin, especially in 1968 with the militarization of the civil service.

Then, in 1973, a subgroup, the "military party," gained control of the armed forces and imposed its new project. On one hand, it consisted of officers involved in the counterinsurgency campaign who had exclusive access to classified information that had brought them very close to the levers of power. On the other hand, some other factions in the military had old scores to settle with the political class. Moreover, they were imbued with a strong anti-Batllist ideology that at best exalted conservative values, and at worst openly embraced neo-Nazi views.[20] These groups allied against the officers who wanted to maintain the military's professionalism and eliminated them. After all, the deposed officers would have at most only settled for a moderating role, such as the one proposed by Senator Wilson Ferreira Aldunate in 1973.[21]

Once this dominant group of officers overcame the resistance of the navy on February 1973, they embarked on a gradual purge of their opponents within the armed forces. In 1974, this process was institutionalized with the adoption of a new Organic Military Law that permitted them to force the retirement of officers whose points of view dissented from those of the high command.[22] In short, over time it became clear that throughout the armed forces the dominating *camarillas* had almost imperceptibly begun to meld their political and military roles into one.

Meanwhile, Uruguayan politics were at an impasse. The nation's social and political forces were deadlocked, and thus incapable of adapting their style to a new international conjuncture. Under these circumstances it soon became evident that the military faced a similar problem, but with one difference: they might be able to break the stalemate. Two factors facilitated their task. The armed forces were autonomous from civil society and identified strongly with the state, upon which they depended for their existence. Meanwhile, Uruguay's civil society was weak and subordinated to a paternalist state.

Once the military took charge of the state, however, they hesitated. Should they reduce public sector involvement in society, as advocated by neoconservative economists (who, when all is said and done, were the only ones who proposed a substantive alternative project)? Or should the state continue to play the role of "philanthropic ogre," albeit in such a manner that there could be no doubt that its largesse came from the military (especially the army), not the state.

THE MILITARY AS A "SUBSTITUTE PARTY": THE PUSH
FOR AUTONOMY AND PROFESSIONALISM

Once in the government, one of the Uruguayan military's goals, much like that of similar authoritarian regimes in the rest of the Southern Cone, consisted of administering political affairs from above while suppressing politics. At the same time, the military found it necessary to ally with business sectors who supported the economic policies favored by neoconservative economists. These goals led to a very heterodoxical policy mix.

On one hand, the armed forces agreed to liberalize some economic sectors, especially the financial sector, and to lower tariff barriers and subsidies for industry. On the other hand, the military reinforced the state to the point where, today, the ruling Batllist Colorado Party has been forced to downplay its ideological heritage and adopt a more pragmatic style.

The military's suppression of politics led them to take contradictory positions. They tried to run the government on a technocratic basis. That meant that for the purposes of public administration they sought the help, and hence political support, of the burgeoning financial sector (generally represented by economists with strong international connections), and from "hidden" professionals of the major political parties who were willing to collaborate. But somebody had to make the big political decisions. The military reserved the right of supreme decision-making authority for themselves, and institutionalized a number of mechanisms through which they directed the nation's political affairs. In this manner, the military became a "substitute political party."

The Uruguayan armed forces' principle decision-making body was the Junta of General Officers, to which the highest-ranking officers of all three service branches belonged. When the military first took over the government, this board consisted of 12 army generals, 3 air force brigadiers, and 3 rear admirals. In 1977, the army added two generals and the air force and navy each received an additional representative.

Membership in the Junta of General Officers, that is, the entire high command, was not formally codified. The high command of the armed forces discarded the previous system of promotions to general in which a third of the officers were advanced by competition, another third by seniority, and the final third by appointment. They replaced that system with one in which they, the existing generals, brigadiers, and rear admirals, promoted fellow officers strictly by appointment as vacancies occurred. Naturally, this facilitated the cooptation of the officer corps. The military thus not only became autonomous from civil society, but also independent from the state itself. The president and the executive branch lost all control over the armed forces. The Defense Ministry, headed by civilians throughout the period of military rule, was little more than an administrative and logistical coordinating office.

The Junta of General Officers, then, used promotions to coopt the officer corps (they could also force the retirement of dissidents), and only those officers with good connections could aspire to the highest ranks every January. By the same token, this style of leadership selection also guarded the military from the emergence of a strongman, for the appearance of a charismatic leader was inhibited by automatic retirement rules.[23]

The Junta members also nominated their primus inter pares, the commanders in chief of each branch of the service, as well as the members of the National

Council as of 1976—although this latter function was codified. The National Council appointed the president of the republic, the president and members of the Council of State (a civilian body that replaced the Parliament), the Supreme Court and the Electoral Court. Generals, brigadiers, rear admirals (28 in all) and the members of the Council of State (25 civilians) elected individuals to all other important government positions. Since officers outweighed civilians, the military was assured that it would prevail in the unlikely event that the latter opposed the armed forces' choice. In short, the civilians were essentially "yes men."[24]

Toward the end of 1979, the Junta of General Officers also appointed the members of the newly created Armed Forces' Political Commission (*Comisión Política de las Fuerzas Armadas*, COMAPSO). These include four members of the army, two from the navy, and two from the air force. The commission was charged with finding a formula that would put an end to Uruguay's authoritarian solution. Its failure to find an adequate political solution to the military's exit from government prompted the Junta of General Officers to take the problem up directly in 1984. All things considered, then, the Junta took it upon itself to make the most sensitive and fundamental political decisions.[25]

Meanwhile, the crisis of February 1973 gave birth to three additional military organizations. Two of those were the Junta of the Commanders in Chief, which was charged with coordinating action among the three branches of the service, and the Joint Chiefs of Staff, whose function it was to plan and coordinate interservice branch affairs. In reality, however, the Joint Chiefs of Staff coordinated interministerial functions. Officers attached to the Joint Chiefs served as a liaison among the ministries, public enterprises, and decentralized services. The third institution, the National Security Council (NSC), which eventually received its own statutes in the Organic Military Law of 1974, carried out the routine executive branch functions of the government. Its members—the three commanders in chief, the interior minister (who was always a military man), the defense minister (a civilian puppet), the external relations minister, the chariman of the Joint Chiefs of Staff, and the president of the Republic—met once a week to discuss the business of rule, and always couched their decisions in terms of strengthening national security. Five of the eight members of the NSC were generals who also served in the Junta of General Officers. These five men were the principal decision-makers. However, policy choices that involved fundamental strategic issues were discussed with the entire Junta of General Officers.

The Uruguayan military government, then, revealed several characteristics of the armed forces, the first being that they exhibited a very marked autonomy with respect to civil society. In other words, the divisions between social groups gave the military and their civilian advisers the ability to make decisions that went against certain business pressure groups, although their policies favored new groups that emerged during this period. The military also became autonomous with respect to the state; they ceased to be the armed branch of the state, and regulated their affairs (budget, doctrine, and objectives) by themselves. The armed forces also ran the government, dominating the executive and legislative branches, and exercised a strong supervisory function over the judicial branch through the power of appointment and the legislation of judicial norms.[26]

The armed forces, in effect, behaved like a substitute political party, that is, they displaced the civilian parties.[27] Political parties are supposed to articulate relations between state and society. But at first the military government tried to substitute politics for administration. Events, however, forced the armed forces to contemplate the imposition of an institutional scheme that could in some measure mediate between the interests of certain social groups and the state. In Philippe Schmitter's terms, they tried to build a *democradura*—a conservative, restricted democracy.[28]

The Uruguayan military corporation also managed to solve the contradiction between their professionalizing and deprofessionalizing functions. The armed forces' involvement in government put them in danger of neglecting their martial function. In order to avoid this problem, they instituted a division of responsibility among officers in the high command. Some attended to the business of rule, while others made sure that the strictly professional standards of the military did not suffer. In this fashion, the armed forces managed to maintain their cohesion.

In another move to shore up the military's professional standards, the high command decided to increase the number of combat units and to modernize their equipment. This modernization acquired a highly discriminatory profile. The army benefitted the most by far, although the air force was not entirely neglected. The navy, however, due to its reticent stance in 1973, was passed by.[29]

The Uruguayan armed forces thus experienced a twofold process: on one hand, the corporateness of the military establishment—and hence its cohesiveness—increased noticeably; on the other, the armed forces made serious efforts to maintain professional standards while they were engaged in the deprofessionalizing task of running the country and acting as a substitute party. The military's subsistence depended on strengthening their corporateness because the recruitment system effectively cut them off from society.[30] Most officers came from a lower-middle-class background, many from small towns in Uruguay's heartland. Most of the troops came from the rural lower classes. The accentuation of the military's corporate identity also affected their autonomy—all in all, they became even more isolated from society, and increasingly independent from the state itself.

Beginning in 1973, the military's involvement in politics induced them to mold society, a task which heretofore had been the purview of the political class. But the armed forces clearly wanted to replace civilian politicians, which was why they developed their paternal–populist national project and selectively repressed the most bothersome social groups.[31] Given the military's ambition, one of their biggest problems was how to accomplish social goals without seriously disrupting their institutions, their corporateness. If the armed forces aspired to retain their martial professionalism and be active in politics (even if they intended to eliminate politics by privatizing it), they would have to create the "political-soldier''—a figure that had its antecedents in a number of totalitarian regimes.[32] In short, the armed forces recognized that while they needed to maintain their professionalism, they also had to adapt it to a clear political objective.[33]

To successfully carry out this two-sided action required a certain amount of dissociation. Within the chain of command, those who executed orders had to share in the military corporation's ideology while accepting that they had no decision-making function: they simply had to submit themselves to military hierarchy. Those at the top of the hierarchy, however, did enjoy decision-making capability.

It was the high command which had to develop the dual process of professionalization–deprofessionalization, to use the terminology developed by Augusto Varas, in this volume. They had to build and lead a military force—in the words of General Queirolo, ''a small but highly trained technical and professional force.''[34] For this reason the Uruguayan military modernized their forces between 1979 and 1981.[35] Yet General Queirolo was well aware that this modernization also served political ends.[36] Junior and senior officers, moreover, surely recognized that they fulfilled a double function. Aside from their strictly military duties, the commanders of military units were involved in numerous civilian activities, often in government and administration, and many officers had to fulfill strictly political functions. For example, the superintendents of all of Uruguay's departments (territorial administrative units), except for the department of Montevideo, were colonels. They, in turn, were subordinate to their department's division commander. Officers also filled many ministerial positions and became managers of public enterprises.

The military managed to link their administrative and political roles—their professionalizing and deprofessionalizing functions—through two mechanisms. For one, the army dominated the other two branches of the service, essentially directing the armed forces' national project. Given its seniority, the navy should have been second in line of importance, but its initial opposition to military rule precluded such a distinction. Instead, the navy was more or less on a par with the air force, whose officers had a knack for siding with the winning forces, both in the installation of the military government and in the return to liberal democracy.

But the Uruguayan armed forces also disposed of a number of additional mechanisms that safeguarded their cohesion. They remembered what had happened in Argentina in 1962, a time in which the struggle between different factions in the Argentine military had resulted in open and violent confrontation between the blues and the reds.[37] By contrast, the Uruguayan armed forces maintained their unit by adopting a strict hierarchical structure, with the Junta of General Officers at the top.

Three characteristics stand out in the military's organization for rule. (1) The Uruguayan armed forces conducted their internal affairs and their political decision making within a collegiate organizational structure. Fundamental issues (promotions to general, economic and social policy goals) were always settled among the generals by vote. (2) Only the high command debated policy. Once they reached a decision, it was the duty of the rest of the officer corps to implement it.[38] (3) Subordinate officers "participated" in policy making to the degree that they believed in the ideology propagated by the national security doctrine, as interpreted by the Junta of General Officers. New soldiers were socialized in this setting.[39] Dissident senior officers who managed to occupy important positions did so at the sufferance of the high command and could be dismissed at any time.

These, then, were the means by which the Uruguayan armed forces managed to make their military and political roles compatible—in other words, the Uruguayan military establishment was organized along cadre lines. Debate took place only at the very top, in something akin to the Communist Party's "Central Committee." Senior officers, to continue with the analogy, were the "intermediate cadres," and the rest were the "militants." Finally, those who were not in the military, but who had family ties to it, or who shared its ideology, and helped it to achieve its political ends—that is, all of those who benefitted from the military's paternal–populist policies—could be characterized as the "sympathizers." In the meantime, the military continued to modernize in order to perfect its professional standards.

But the new soldier-politicians and their national project failed because civil society rejected them.[40] In the 1980 plebiscite a majority of Uruguayans voted against a measure that would have given the military a green light to institutionalize a conservative, restricted democracy—a *democradura*. After their defeat at the polls the Uruguayan armed forces toned down their lofty rhetoric. But they did not abandon the core of their project: the protection of the military corporation's new ideology. Thus, as the armed forces negotiated their exit from government, they made it clear that they were a political actor and intended to remain one even after Uruguay's return to political democracy was completed.

THE ARMED FORCES AND REDEMOCRATIZATION: IN SEARCH OF A NEW ROLE

The negotiations over the conditions of the military's exit from government culminated in an agreement between the civilian political parties and the armed forces, that is, the commanders in chief of the army, navy, and air force. This accord basically allowed the military to retain a strong measure of autonomy. The pact included the following provisions:

(1) As was usual before the coup d'etat in 1973, the executive branch, with Senate approval, would appoint all officers above the rank of colonel. But they would do so from a list of names submitted by the armed forces—two suggestions per vacant position. Meanwhile, a new organic law designed to regulate all other promotions was signed into law in November 1984. The substance of that law was probably hammered out between the military and a civilian commission in secret sessions in mid–1984.

(2) Generals would still be promoted exclusively by appointment. If the Senate did not confirm either of the military's two nominees, the Executive branch had the right to insist. In that case, the Senate would have to muster a two-thirds majority to maintain their veto.

(3) The president of the republic would elect the commanders in chief of the army, air force, and navy from a list of three candidates. The candidates would be senior officers within the high command. Their appointment did not require confirmation from the legislature, and the criteria of "first among equals" still prevailed.

(4) The military insisted on maintaining the National Security Council. Although it would now function only as an advisory board to the president, the armed forces felt that it still had value as a symbol of their corporation's dominant ideology.

(5) The new organic law also established a new national emergency condition called the "state of insurrection." In the event of a resurgence in subversive activity, the Legislative Assembly was empowered to immediately suspend all civil liberties, the bedrock of liberal political democracy. During a state of insurrection, military justice would prevail for all offenses. This ruling, however, was only a year-long temporary measure (1985), subject to ratification by the Constituent Assembly cum Legislative Assembly and approval or rejection by plebiscite.[41]

A series of additional measures designed to protect the military as they left government were also adopted.[42] The new Organic Law of the Army (November 1984) revised troop strength limits. It also rationalized the composition of the officer corps so that it once again resembled a pyramid and lengthened the time it took for junior officers to advance in rank. The idea was to limit the number of all officers to 1,440, in addition to fresh graduates from the military academy. Of course, achieving this goal required the retirement of a number of colonels. A number of transitory measures allowed the government to remove 85 colonels from active duty, albeit with the highest pensions possible.[43] Other protective rules included placing the Defense Information Service, which had previously been nominally subordinate to the Defense Ministry, under the wing of the Joint Chiefs of Staff. This short-circuited the possibility of establishing civilian control over that agency.[44]

Officially, the new government wanted to restore traditional civilian modes of control over the armed forces. It aspired to reduce the military to its professional role, according to conceptions disseminated by the developed nations of the West. Such was the case when President Sanguinette, in his inaugural speech, declared that he was now the commander in chief of the armed forces.[45] It seemed highly unlikely, however, that in the final analysis the military would resign itself to such a fate. If they went along with it on the surface it was mainly because, according to Varas's conceptual scheme, they were satisfied with "conditioned corporateness" rather than full autonomy. Civilians may have attempted to exercise firm control over the military, but the armed forces' degree of corporateness had already reached such high levels that the military simply exercised "professionalized autonomy." For example, a few days before President Sanguinetti's inauguration, the commander in chief of the army, General Hugo Medina, declared that if the social conditions which had forced the military to act in 1973 recurred, they would once again take over the government. Despite subsequent retractions his threat lingers.

But this is not the only unsettling declaration by the military that has come on the heels of redemocratization. In March 1985, the armed forces' journal *El Soldado* dedicated an entire issue to the defense and justification of the military's actions in government between 1974 and 1984. Moreover, a colonel signed his name to a bedtime story—with a moral—which was nothing more than a thinly veiled threat against the newly installed democratic regime. The gist of the message was: keep the military happy and attend to its felt needs, or else democracy may not survive.[46]

It seems clear, then, that the Uruguayan military's current phase of conditioned corporateness can be characterized as follows: the armed forces oppose all efforts to significantly alter the composition of the officer corps. The commanders in chief who signed the Naval Club Pact—the agreement that set the fundamental terms of the military's exit from government—have not lost their positions in the Sanguinetti administration. Retirements and promotions are expected to follow routine patterns; in fact, it has been clearly stated that there is nothing to gain by replacing them. The military institution ruled between 1974 and 1984, and thus, all senior officers took part in the "process." With regard to human rights abuses and corruption, the Uruguayan armed forces will only book charges in cases where there is an a priori undeniable proof of guilt.[47]

Besides these factors, the military's fundamental interests include four additional issues. (1) They want no changes in promotions policy, which is an important contributing factor to their autonomy from the state. (2) The armed forces want to defend their professional status. This means that they do not want to give up control over their educational system and socialization processes. (3) The soldiers also oppose reductions in their budget. In 1983, the forces of order consumed 49 percent of the state's budget, or 7.7 percent of GDP.[48] The situation is delicate for two reasons: salaries and pensions constitute a large portion of these funds; moreover, the government will surely have difficulty preventing the obsolescence of military equipment, given the cost of modern weapons, communications, and transportation systems. This, of course, will have a negative effect on the armed forces' professional standing. (4) Last but not least, the military feel a need to define the levels of permissible social conflict, and want the formal power to issue warnings when the limits of their tolerance are being taxed.

It seems clear, then, that the Uruguayan armed forces intend to remain a relevant political actor, although nominally they will be under the control of a civilian government that wants them to assume purely professional functions. Individual officers, moreover, may sympathize with this or that political party in order to secure promotions, but on the whole the military corporation has shown a tendency to affirm its own ideological position and autonomy. And, while most Uruguayans would prefer it if the military occupied themselves strictly with military tasks, it seems unlikely that they will do so given the country's political situation. Consequently, what to do with a military establishment that is an "underground" political actor—one that does not have the right to voice but knows how to make its presence felt—is a pressing political problem in Uruguay today.

In fact, the problem is regional in scope. Like in other countries of the Southern Cone—Brazil and Argentina—the Uruguayan military's exit from direct government appears to be more a tactical than a strategic retreat (to use military jargon). As a result, political leaders will have to resort to very imaginative measures to control an institution that has the power to veto their decisions and constantly conditions the actions of civilian political forces. Some Uruguayan politicians entertain the illusion that it may be possible to disband the armed forces sometimes in the distant future—maybe in 40 years, according to Vice President Tarigo. In private, other politicians hope for an earlier date. But it seems highly unlikely that the armed forces would acquiesce in their own demise; even leftists recognize this.[49] Since the soldiers cannot be wished away, Uruguayans need to open a debate on how to deal with this unwanted, underground political actor.

NOTES

1. For the process by which Uruguayan armed forces became autonomous, see María del Huerto Amarillo, "Bases del Proceso de Autonomización de las Fuerzas Armadas en el Uruguay," (Montevideo: *ILESUR*, 1985, Mimeographed).

2. The commanders of the army, air force, and navy constituted the Junta of Commanders in Chief. This junta, which started as an informal organization, began a process of institutionalization in 1973. The Joint Chiefs of Staff was also an informal institution. At first, officers of the three branches of the service met to plan the counterinsurgency campaign. But gradually, they began to analyze broader political issues. By the same token, the creation of a unified intelligence service also started out as an informal initiative; it later became fully institutionalized as the Defense Information Service.

3. Junta de Comandantes en Jefe, *El Proceso Político* (n.p., 1978).

4. These procedures are elaborated by the general staff and adjusted in the Military Institute for Superior Studies. Given the small number of troops, Uruguay has few division-level units; therefore, Uruguay has adopted smaller units based on South Korean *jean*.

5. Between 1946 and 1982 approximately 920 Uruguayan, 693 Argentine, and 2,130 Chilean officers attended Fort Gulick training school in the Panama Canal Zone. Stella

Calloni and Rafael Cribari, *La Guerra Encubierta contra Contadora* (Panamá: Centro de Capacitación Social, 1983).

6. The idea was to form a continental defense system with experienced troops. Only Colombia really complied. Uruguay limited itself to sending some officers as observers.

7. María del Huerto Amarilla, "Bases del Proceso de Autonomización," and "Participación Política de las Fuerzas Armadas," in *Uruguay y la Democracia*, ed. Charles Gillespie, L. Goodman, Juan Rial, and P. Winn (Montevideo: EBO and Wilson Center, 1984).

8. For conflicting estimates on the number of active-duty colonels, see declarations by Luis Hierro López in *Tiempo de Cambio*, no. 13 (28 August 1984): he claims there were 265. The current commander in chief of the army, who held the same post during the military's exit from politics, said that there were 200 colonels. See *El Día*, 16 November 1984. In computing that figure he referred to the 1950 law and the Special Tribunals, but he did not mention the 1963 legislation.

9. In all of the cases where the government applied "immediate security measures"—administrative arrests—the detainees were held in barracks. The armed forces also undertook strikebreaking activity.

10. Guillermo O'Donnell, "Reflections on the Patterns of Change in the Buraucratic–Authoritarian State," *Latin American Research Review* 12, no. 1 (1978); and *El Estado Burocrático Autoritario, 1966–1973. Triunfos, Derrotas y Crisis* (Buenos Aires: Universidad Belgrano, 1982); Howard Handelman, "Labor, Industrial Conflict, and the Collapse of Uruguayan Democracy," *Journal of Interamerican Studies and World Affairs* 23, no. 4 (1981).

11. Joseph Comblin, *Pouvoir Militaire dans l'Amerique Latine* (Paris: Pierre Derbarges, 1977).

12. Junta de Comandantes en Jefe, *El Proceso Político*, 247.

13. Articles 1 through 7 clearly mark this change in the military's understanding of their function. They are now the guarantors of the nation's external and internal security and have the duty to take over the nation's development planning. Article 4 defines national security in the broadest terms possible: "It is that state in which the nation's patrimony, in all of its forms, and the process of development toward national goals find themselves vulnerable to internal or external meddling or aggression." This law also details the functions of the National Security Council and the School for National Security and Defense. These institutions propagate the doctrine of national security among officers and state administrators.

14. Milton Vanger, *El País Modelo. José Batlle y Ordoñez, 1907–1915* (Montevideo: EBO, 1983).

15. One of the participants in these events, Brigadier Borad, played down the importance of the communiqués, saying that they were put together by Colonel Ramon Trebal barely two hours before they were issued without much thought to their content. These declarations appeaed in *Búsqueda*, 10 January 1985. Colonel Trebal was assassinated in Paris shortly afterwards on December 19, 1974. In a statement that appeared in *El Cía* on September 23, 1984, Zorrilla said that the military was only playing a Peruvian line because it was popular at the time, and they thought such rhetoric would broaden their base of support.

16. My colleague Carina Perelli coined this concept, and I developed it in "Los Límites del Terror Controlado," *CIESU* (Montevideo), no. 97 (1985).

17. The forces of order: total employment.

Year	Defense Ministry	Interior Ministry
1970	21,269	20,854
1971	22,332	21,060
1972	25,338	21,473
1973	27,569	21,661
1974	21,921	24,370
1975	33,531	24,934
1976	36,135	24,932
1977	37,704	25,184
1978	38,545	25,758

Source: *Anuario Estadístico del Uruguay 1970–1978*, fasc. 10. There are no official figures for more recent years.

18. Not very many officers were arrested for membership in armed guerrilla groups, perhaps no more than a dozen. Many more, however, were purged from the military for belonging to Marxist organizations such as the Communist party or the Broad Front.

19. This applies especially to the group led by General Alvarez, the founder of the Joint Chiefs of Staff.

20. The former commander of the First Military Region, General E. Cristi, provides the best example of anti-Batllist feuds. In the 1940s, his father came into conflict with President Batlle. This impeded his promotion to general until 1963, when he was awarded the rank after he had already retired. In 1972, his son, then also a general, had Dr. Jorge Batlle arrested. He charged Batlle senior's son with criminal financial dealings, and did so in a way that overstepped all institutional channels. The action of General Cristi, Jr., added to the sense of crisis that ended in the June 1973 coup d'etat.

General Alvarez and his clique joined these conservative forces in the military. Neo-Nazi publications included *Azul y Blanco* and other small journals, such as *Nación*, which published a number (3) titled "Viva el Fascismo."

21. Using General (r) Ventura Rodríguez as an intermediary, Ferreira asked the commander in chief of the army, General Martínez, to take over power and hold a double round election. Martínez did not accept this proposal. Admiral Zorrilla, who toward the end of 1972 had defended President Boraberry against pressure from the army and the air force, also declined to entertain any of Ferreira's plans. Both Martínez and Zorrilla were Batllista Colorados.

22. Article 912, section 6 (incorporated into law no. 14,157 in 1974) facilitated purges. The heaviest purges occurred in the navy, and also touched a few dissenting army officers. It seems that air force officers escaped unscathed.

23. These rules, for example, kept General Cristi from ascending to the rank of commander general and allowed General Alvarez to hold that rank for only a short period of time. These men were the most visible representatives of the two most significant factions in the army. With few exceptions, moreover, successive appointments (Generals Alvarez, Hountou, Aranco, and Medina) were made according to seniority among members of the Junta of General Officers. For the most part, these criteria also held for the other branches of the service.

24. See constitutional decree no. 2, articles 1 and 4, of June 12, 1976.

25. Sometimes administrative positions overlap according to military, governmental, and political function.

26. Institutional acts numbers 8 and 12 essentially transformed an independent judiciary into another branch of the executive power. At the same time, military justice was conceived of as a disciplinary tool, not as a protector of human rights.

27. Juan Rial, *Partidos Políticos, Democracia y Autoritarismo* (Montevideo: EBO, 1984).

28. Philippe Schmitter, "The Transition from Authoritarian Rule to Democracy in Modernizing Society: Can Germani's Proposition and Pessimism Be Reversed?" (Unpublished manuscript, 1984).

29. The army created an infantry brigade, composed of two new battalions, under the direction of the general command. One of those battalions also had an elite paratroop company. Moreover, a fifth branch of the army, communications, was created in 1980. It consisted of a reorganization of army engineers.

With respect to materiel, the army substituted U.S. light weapons for Argentine manufactures, bought reconditioned U.S. light tanks from Belgium, and reconditioned old World War II vintage Stuart-class tanks. Cavalry units received Brazilian armored vehicles. New artillery pieces came from South Korea, and army engineers and communications specialists received high-tech equipment. Meanwhile, the air force acquired new airplanes and ground combat capabilities. For its part, the navy installed a coastal radar network, bought patrol boats, and created a marine detachment—however, the navy did not acquire new ships. See *The Military Balance 1984–1985* (London: International Institute for Strategic Studies, 1984).

30. Unfortunately, the secretiveness of the armed forces with respect to this type of information makes it impossible to provide more precise data. Nevertheless, on the basis of impressionistic data and in accord with what we know about the military in other countries, there are a sizeable number of identifiable families whose sons traditionally become military officers. Furthermore, recently it seems that the sons of noncommissioned officers are also becoming officers in increasing numbers.

31. On this subject see Juan Rial, "Los Límites del Terror Controlado," op. cit., and Carina Perelli, "La Lógica del Miedo," unpublished manuscript (1985). The officer's journal *El Soldado*, no. 75 (1981), in "Soldier's Son: Future Soccer Star," provides a good example of this brand of populism.

32. The idea of creating a *Soldatenbund* (a fraternity of soldiers) and a *Mannerbund* (a fraternity of "real men") was one of the basic goals of the Third Reich's military security service. These ideals led to the formation of special forces such as the *Waffen SS*. See E. K. Bramstedt, *Dictatorship and Political Police* (New York: Oxford University Press, 1945).

33. For further details, see the commencement address by the Director of the Armed Forces School (*Escuela de Armas y Servicio*), General O. Ballestrino, in December 1979. During his career, General Ballestrino was the commander of a paramilitary police organization charged with breaking up demonstrations and other forms of civil disobedience.

34. For details, see the speech by the commander in chief of the Uruguayan armed forces, General Queirolo, before the Interamerican Defense Council, reprinted in *El Soldado*, no. 64 (1980).

35. Out of total public spending, the following percentages went to the security forces:

	1980	1981	1982
Defense Ministry	12.7%	31.2%	15.4%
Interior Ministry	4.6%	7.0%	7.2%
Total	17.3%	38.2%	22.6%

36. See General Queirolo's speech in *El Soldado*, no. 64.

37. Alain Rouquié, *Pouvoir Militaire et Société Politique en la République Argentine* (Paris: Fondation Nationale des Sciences Politiques, 1978).

38. Of course, I recognize that they may meet with officers who have troop commands, although they do not grant them decision-making authority.

39. Since 1972, the year in which the antiguerrilla campaign really got underway, the military academy has given young officers that type of training. Thus today most officers from the rank of second lieutenant to captain, and many senior officers as well, share this same basic educational background.

40. For example, see statements by Colonel Laitano, who was commander of the recently formed First Engineer Brigade, as reported in the Uruguayan press on April 15, 1980. This was the same year that the military lost its bid to establish a *democradura*. For more details on this, see Rial, *Partidos Políticos, Democracia y Autoritarismo*.

41. Institutional act number 19, article 6, promulgated in August 1984.

42. In terms of the categories provided by Alfred Stepan, Uruguay falls within the category in which the military agree to return to the barracks in order to protect their corporate interests. See Alfred Stepan, "Paths toward Redemocratization: Theoretical and Comparative Considerations," in *Transitions from Authoritarian Rule: Comparative Perspectives*, ed. Guillermo O'Donnell, Philippe Schmitter, and Laurence Whitehead (Baltimore: Johns Hopkins University Press, 1986).

43. The Army Organic Law of November 20, 1984, articles 231 and others.

44. In statements to the press, the Sanguinetti administration's defense minister, Dr. J. V. Chiarino, said that in addition to the Defense Information Service, each branch of the military had their own intelligence organizations. See *El Día*, 14 April 1985. The decree that placed the Defense Information Service under the direction of the Joint Chiefs of Staff appeared in the press on October 24, 1984.

45. See statements to the press on the first and second of March, 1985.

46. Colonel Julio Farone was the author of the story, which appeared in an abridged version in *El Soldado*, no. 100 (1985).

47. As a result of a series of denunciations against them, the high command decided to improve the military's image with the public. To that end, it opened La Libertad prison, where the military had held political prisoners, to public scrutiny. For more details, see Rial, "Los Límites del Terror Controlado."

48. See statements by Luis Hierro López, currently a Deputy in the Uruguayan Parliament, in *El País*, 21 September 1984.

49. See Navy Captain (r) Oscar Label, "Las Fuerzas Armadas como Problemas," *Aquí*, nos. 99 and 100 (9 and 16 April 1985). Captain Label belongs to the "Por el Gobierno del Pueblo" faction (list 99) of the Colorado party.

8 THE MODERNIZATION OF THE MEXICAN ARMED FORCES

José Luis Piñeyro

In the past two decades, the Mexican army and air force have experienced significant modernization, which has affected the character of their institutions and the nature of civil-military relations.[1] This chapter presents an overview of those changes, and traces their implications for Mexico's security doctrine and the degree of civilian control over the armed forces.

PROFESSIONALIZATION, TRAINING, AND WEAPONRY

Mexico's current approach to modernizing its military institutions began in 1971. Since then, it has addressed all three of the main factors that influence the military's professional capabilities: training and organization, equipment and logistics, and politico-ideological development.[2] Under President Echeverria, the founding of the Military University in 1976 represented the high point of professionalization for the armed forces.[3]

Lopez Portillo's government (1976–1982) continued the modernizing trend, and authorized spending for ground, air, and sea transportation systems; light and heavy weapons; housing; training, high-technology equipment, such as computers and radars; an increase in administrative personnel; and the creation of new combat units.[4] The Lopez Portillo administration's crowning glory was the founding of the nation's highest military college, the National Defense College, which confers a master's degree in national security and defense management.[5]

Decreasing the armed forces' reliance on civilian professionals and technicians—in order to make them as self-sufficient as possible—constituted the central objective behind these innovations.[6] Although this goal was originally set in 1966, today it has expanded to include logistics—the production, supply, and commercialization of basic necessities. For example, in 1973 the government established a retail chain (SeDeNa) for the distribution of basic necessities and other consumer goods; by 1982 SeDeNa had 95 branch stores throughout Mexico. The government also organized a farm and ranching system in 1976, which operated 24 units in various military zones by 1982. Both the stores and the farms have apparently become self-sufficient, "based on a calculation of sales and profit."[7]

Of course, the military are also interested in technical and professional self-sufficiency. To that end, they have proposed the following educational goals: "First, the development of a higher education curriculum; the establishment of guidelines for the planning, implementation, and evaluation of the military's educational institutions; competent instructors with the necessary professional drive, love of national service, and social responsibility to bestow knowledge in the scientific, technological, and humanistic fields. Second, to assure that the National Defense Secretariat has adequate material and human resources to carry out these objectives."[8]

By 1985, the military education system had 23 schools which offered training in a wide range of professions and vocations. This increased the military's capacity to take on new political functions should Mexico suddenly experience a crisis of governability, or if civil-military relations deteriorated beyond a certain point. A brief list of some of the officer training schools should give an idea of the variety of professions involved: the National Defense College, the Superior War College, the Military Medical School, Engineering School, Dental School, Air School, the Heroic Military College, the Broadcasting School, and the Nursing School.[9]

The United States has played a central role in restructuring the Mexican military's educational system. Updating the Mexicans' store of technical and strategic knowledge has been a crucial U.S. contribution; for example, the 546 Mexican soldiers who received advanced training between 1950 and 1968, 306 (55 percent) took courses in the United States between 1964 and 1968—the formative years of the military educational system's modernization. It is significant that 89 soldiers trained in the United States only one year before the establishment of academies for the infantry, artillery, sappers, services, and cavalry. They took courses in two broad subject areas: how to establish military schools, and counterinsurgency warfare. This pattern was repeated between 1971 and 1976.[10]

Nevertheless, the number of Mexicans who received military training in the United States was far below that of most other Latin American countries: only 1,054 soldiers received U.S. schooling between 1950 and 1984. Two factors accounted for this difference. The first is historical and political in nature. Ruling groups had decided to reduce external influences on the organization, functioning, and political orientation of the armed forces as much as possible.[11] The second factor had its roots in technical and administrative needs. All of those who took courses abroad now teach at military schools; they do not have field commands. Sending them to foreign schools was intended to cultivate military self-sufficiency by promoting constant interaction between instructors trained abroad and those trained locally.

Self-sufficiency in arms production has also been a long-standing goal of the Mexican military. In the 1950s and 1960s, Mexico produced the Vargas submachine gun and the Obregon automatic pistol. In the 1970s the manufacture of automatic assault rifles and Belgian gas-powered machine guns began. By 1985, Mexico made two more automatic rifles, the German G–3 and H-K, as well as H-K pistols, submachine guns, and light and heavy machine guns. In addition, Mexico now produces armored personnel carriers and reconnaissance weapons (DN-I, DN-IV, DN-V and SeDeNa–1000), as well as grenades, ordnance for mortars and howitzers, small arms munitions, and experimental rockets.[12]

The National Defense Secretariat procured arms and equipment for the army, navy, and air force from a number of sources. The more significant purchases include: 40 French-made Panhard armored personnel carriers and 27 Panhard armored reconnaissance cars; 35 M–3 antitank guns from the United States; 2 Gearing class destroyers, also from the United States; 6 Halcon Coast Guard cutters from Spain. Locally made weapons systems include 38 patrol boats of the Azteca class (Scottish patent), 6 Olmeca-class patrol boats, and 4 Aguila Coast Guard cutters. Also purchased from the United States were 5 Bell helicopters and 12 FSE jet aircraft, and 55 Pilatus airplanes were bought from Switzerland.[13] Moreover, according to the *Revista del Ejército y la Fuerza Aérea*, between 1971 and 1974 Mexico bought more airplanes and maintenance equipment than at any time since 1944.

THE MEXICAN ARMED FORCES: SIZE AND DISTRIBUTION

Between 1974 and 1984 the Mexican armed forces increased by one-third, from 80,000 to 120,000 persons. Of the latter, 94,500 are in the army; 5,500 are in the air force, and 20,000 are in the navy.[14] The army is distributed throughout Mexico's nine military regions and 36 military zones. Thirty-one of these zones correspond to individual Mexican states and the Federal District. Four states—Oaxaca, Veracruz, Guerrero, and Chiapas—are each divided into two military zones. The first three are the locus of frequent rural conflict. Chiapas was divided into two zones in 1984 when oil and gas production turned it into a region of strategic importance. Moreover, an influx of Guatemalan and Salvadoran refugees had increased tensions in Chiapas itself, and sparked a new conflict between Mexico and Guatemala. The Guatemalan government was convinced that Guatemalan guerrillas used Chiapas as a staging ground for their operations, and that the Mexican government deliberately turned a blind eye to this situation.

But what of the location of Mexico's air and naval bases? The air force has eight bases distributed—in ascending order of importance—in the following manner: Santa Lucia, Mexico; Ciudad Ixtepec, Oaxaca; El Cipres, Baja California Norte; Cozumel, Quintana Roo; Zapopan, Jalisco; Puebla, Puebla; Pie de la Cuesta, Guerrero; and Merida, Yucatan. The navy has 15 bases of which five are on the Atlantic: Veracruz, Veracruz; Tampico, Tamaulipas; Chetumal, Quintana Roo; Ciudad del Carmen, Campeche; Yucalpeten, Yucatan. The navy's Pacific bases include: Acapulco, Guerrero; Ensenada, Baja California Norte; La Paz, Baja California Sur; Puerto Cortes, Baja California Sur; Guaymas, Sonora; Mazatlan, Sinaloa; Manzanillo, Colima; Salina Cruz, Oaxaca; Puerto Madero, Chiapas; and Lazaro Cardenas, Michoacan.

This breakdown of the military's geographic distribution reflects strategic considerations of both an internal and an external nature. The heaviest concentrations occur in two types of regions: those that have a tradition of social conflict, and those with natural resource reserves, such as hydrocarbons, minerals, and seafood reserves.

MILITARY DOCTRINE

Mexico possesses a defensive military doctrine, although it has an offensive component at the tactical level—rapid counterattacks and then back to the main defensive strategy. Two factors have influenced Mexico's choice. The first factor is rooted in the country's international and domestic experience. With regard to the former, Mexico has absorbed the lessons of U.S. expansion (which led to the loss of almost half of Mexico's territory) and the French invasion (which subjected Mexico to six years of military occupation). Of course, Mexico has also learned the futility of initiating expansionist conflicts with the United States. These experiences led Mexico to develop three fundamental foreign policy norms—nonintervention, self-determination, and the peaceful settlement of international disputes. By the same token, the country's history of domestic upheaval has shown Mexicans the difficulties inherent in building a nation-state.

The second factor that led Mexico to adopt a defensive military strategy is rooted in political realism. On the one hand, Mexicans realize the pointlessnes of drawing plans to invade the United States, or of mounting a convention defense against a U.S. invasion. On the other hand, the possibility of a war w Guatemala seems outlandish. For one, Mexico's capabilities far exceed those Guatemala, thus precluding an invasion by the latter. By the same token, the principles that inform its security doctrine make it unlikely that Mexico would start an armed conflict with Guatemala.

Based on their defensive military doctrine, the Mexican armed forces have developed three major defense plans (*Planes de Defensa Nacional*, or DNs). In case of invasion, insurgency, or disaster, they would bring either DN–1, DN–2 or DN–3 to bear, respectively.[15] The underlying assumption of DN–1 is that a people's militia would join the army in repulsing an invasion. In this plan, the armed forces are responsible for meeting the first onslaught of the invading armies. They would then fall back and organize a people's militia that would take up a large share of the fighting. In short, regular and irregular forces would engage in extensive guerrilla warfare.[16]

The armed forces would turn to DN-2 plans in the event of internal disturbances caused by armed or unarmed political movements intent on undermining the constitution. In this sense "undermining the constitution" is defined as an attack on laws, institutions, or predominant property rights. The latter mainly refers to private property, although there is also communal, ejidal, social, and public ownership.

DN-2 charges the military with controlling two types of behavior. The first type consists of civil disturbances, such as demonstrations, strikes, and land invasions. The second type involves acts of violence, such as sabotage and guerrilla action. When disturbances occur, the plan directs the military to immediately control or repress those responsible. At the very least, the armed forces should isolate the problem and keep it from spreading.

DN-2 underscores the Mexican leaders' awareness of the disproportion between the size of a relatively small military, on one hand, and a large population in an extensive territory, on the other. DN-2 is also rooted in a thorough understanding of the nation's history of military and social rebellion. All of these factors highlight the need to control or isolate disturbances before they force the armed forces to overextend their scarce resources. At the national level, this strategy is similar to that of the Rapid Deployment Force developed by the United States to invade countries in the free world that are threatened by Communism. Such plans call on the armed forces to immediately saturate the conflict zone with elite troops and sophisticated equipment. Of course, such actions require the military to establish and maintain adequate logistical lines.

The Director Guardian plan is a good example of the DN-2 strategy. For example, one of its subplans (Guardian of the Valley of Mexico) is designed to protect the capital and its environs—an area that has a great concentration of people and economic production.

The third type of defense strategy, DN-3, offers citizens relief and protection in the event of disasters such as earthquakes, floods, epidemics, fires, droughts, and famines, or widespread crime and drug addiction. The underlying assumption is that this type of national emergency leaves the state vulnerable to either external or internal enemies. In other words, the military have to combat events or actions that weaken the physical and moral health of the people. After all, they are the source of the nation's line of defense—the "people's militia."

A number of permanent plans flesh out the DN-3 strategy. For example, the Aquarius plan directs the armed forces to distribute water free of charge to arid rural and semirural areas. Lefedar, short for *Ley Federal de Armas* (Federal Arms Control Law), is designed to control the illegal use of firearms and to promote their registration. There are also plans to protect cattle ranchers from rustlers and to promote forestry conservation.

The military have also carried out a number of civic action campaigns under the wing of the DN-3 strategy. They are generally undertaken as part of summer and winter general maneuvers. They provide medical, dental, and veterinarian services, and distribute material goods that help the population to meet its basic needs. The armed forces often dispense these services in regions with particularly acute political conflicts, in the hope of stifling their expansion.

In order to fight the international drug trade, the military has developed Canador, short for *Canabis Adormidera* or Dormative Cannabis. Canador consists of 12 regional subplans; for example, subplan Condor covers the mountains of the border states of Sinaoloa, Chihuahua, and Durango. Canador has absorbed the energies of up to 25,000 soldiers (15,000 in direct action), 1,225 officers, and 20 generals. Between January 1983 and February 1985 Canador operations had yielded the following statistics: the destruction of 137,000 plantings of poppies and 80,750 plots of marihuana, impeding the production of 118,300 kilograms of opium and 8,840,000 kilograms of marihuana. The military confiscated 640 vehicles, 14 airplanes, and 7,700 firearms, and arrested 10,200 Mexicans and 40 foreigners. Moreover, between March of 1984 and March of 1985 the armed forces also confiscated 716 kilograms of cocaine with a street value of up to two billion pesos. The army and the air force suffered 315 casualties during these operations.[17]

The Mexican government released these statistics to the media to counteract allegations raised by the Reagan administration that Mexico was not doing enough to halt crossborder drug traffic.[18] This issue came to a head with the murder of a Mexican aviator and a U.S. Drug Enforcement Agency operative in February 1985.

MILITARY INSTITUTIONALIZATION AND THE NATIONAL DEVELOPMENT PLAN, 1983–1988

Mexico's current National Development Plan establishes a number of principles designed to guide policy making. To begin with, it assumes that balanced development—that is, economic, political, cultural, and financial development—requires broad social support. The first policy guideline, then, is that the government consult its citizens before taking action, so as to assure citizen support. Second, policy should strive to build a more just, egalitarian, and democratic society. Third, policymakers must take the nation's history and traditions into account and seek to harmonize them with international market pressures.

With regard to the relationship between the armed forces and national security, the National Development Plan stated that the military play both a security and a development role in Mexican society by calling on the armed forces to "defend the country's borders, independence, and sovereignty" and by stipulating that "they have an important role to play in the nation's development by ministering to the needs of the nation's most depressed areas."[19] The latter required the military to supply water and to engage in literacy campaigns, reforestation, disaster relief, drug traffic interdiction, and the preservation and rational management of ocean resources. These security and developmental functions clearly relate to defense plans DN–1 and DN–3. An examination of the development plan's section on military doctrine, however, shows that it has also assigned the armed forces tasks that correspond to plan DN–2-type activities.

In general, the development plan stipulates that military doctrine is based on the underlying norms and principles that guide the armed forces' organization, education, training, outfitting, and action. The function of these norms and principles is to facilitate communication among the armed forces and to assure the efficient execution of orders.

The development plan stresses that the 1917 Constitution and the president of the republic determine the general character of Mexico's military doctrine. The president is the commander in chief of the armed forces, and as such he is empowered to use them as he sees fit to guarantee the nation's internal and external security. Of course, a number of other factors—such as the military virtues of valor, honor, loyalty, and patriotism, a flexible organizational structure, and a sense of vocation and professionalism among soldiers—also influence the military doctrine's content. Altogether, these factors, help to promote the type of coordinated effort that national development requires.

Furthermore, the National Development Plan offers a number of specific proposals designed to guarantee the military's contribution to national security. These are, of course, subject to modification by the President.

1. The General Plan for Education and Human Resource Development must be updated in order to assure high professional standards.

2. There is a need for continual revision of the norms and systems that affect the quality of communication among the armed forces, and hence, influence the efficiency with which orders are executed during joint maneuvers.

3. The military must protect strategic installations and natural resources, which requires creating more units to increase the armed forces' operational capabilities.

4. The military must defend and develop ocean-based resources, that is, it must patrol territorial waters and investigate their fishing and mineral resources.

5. The armed forces are also charged with defending the nation's airspace and communications systems. This requires airborne surveillance and logistical support services.

6. There is also a need to modernize the military's secondary education, especially with regard to the rules of discipline, promotions, and the general curriculum.

7. The government must support military industries in order to reduce external dependence. This is done by acquiring patents for weapons systems that complement the nation's industrial base and stimulate research and development.

8. There is a need to strengthen postgraduate professional training for military men, which can be achieved by developing new courses and schools and by sending soldiers to train abroad.

9. Soldiers also require better living standards, which they are entitled to under the Armed Forces' Social Security Law. This means increasing salaries, social services, housing, and special benefits.

The National Defense Plan concludes: "The modernization of the armed forces complements the nation's democratic development. As the state modernizes its political institutions it also promotes the development of military institutions in accord with the philosophical principles of our *National Project*, that is, the armed forces are *organically* integrated with Mexico's democratic institutions."[20] The previous government's development plan had expressed many of the same sentiments.[21] The armed forces are modernizing within the framework of a broader economic, social, and political project.

The discussion, so far, has highlighted three issues. First, it seems evident that Defense Plans 1, 2, and 3 rest on a foundation of principles and guidelines that have remained basically unchanged from government to government. Second, those who design national development plans assume that they are strengthening the link between social forces and the armed forces. On the one hand, they believe that the nation's *supposed* integrative political, economic, and cultural development nurtures a reserve army that the military can turn to in the event of external aggression (DN–1), insurgency (DN–2), and natural disaster or social disintegration (DN–3). On the other hand, they believe that a number of incentives will maintain the military's cohesion. These include: institutional material incentives, such as superior organizational resources, training, arms, and bases; individual material incentives, that is, better salaries, housing and benefits; and moral incentives, for example, public recognition, medals, and promotions. Third, all military plans emphasize that they are based on general guidelines issued by the president of the republic, who is the commander in chief of the armed forces, in accord with the articles of Mexico's 1917 Constitution.

Over the last 50 years the military has been subordinate to civilian political authorities and has seen its professional capabilities grow considerably, in terms of military arts and the general managerial and technical skills associated with civilian life. We may thus conclude that the armed forces are experiencing a process of integrative institutionalization along with a growing autonomy in professional matters. Nevertheless, the Mexican military is not immune to processes common to most of their Latin American counterparts. They, too, may develop their own interpretation of the constitution and of the legality of the president's actions. As a result, inventing descriptive labels for civil-military relations does not seem very useful. It may be more fruitful to analyze the concrete demands of society's fundamental classes, in order to expose their basic contradictions to the context of Mexico's current economic and political situation. We should then analyze the military's reaction to these social struggles.

CIVIL–MILITARY RELATIONS

Two methods stand out as the most fruitful ways of gathering data on the degree of control that civilian political authorities exercise over the military: first, one should study the formal legal and customary mechanisms that link them; second, analysis should focus on public statements about, and official evaluations of, the armed forces. We must limit ourselves to these sources, because the military themselves do not publicly express their private views on the political issues of the day. When they do make official pronouncements they always support the position adopted by the government. But this does not mean that the military refrain from privately conveying their position on a given issue to the president and his cabinet.

In any case, both the government and the military appear satisfied with each other. A 1983 government-ordered progress report on the National Development Plan stated that the military had revised all of their strategic plans and conducted maneuvers in each of the military zones. It also reported that the armed forces had implemented the Vital Installations Protection Plan and intensified their drug interdiction and arms control operations, along with other plans contemplated in DN–3. The report further said that the armed forces, in compliance with presidential directives, had proceeded with their professional modernization.[22] For their part, at public events the military customarily reaffirm their loyalty to the president and the political institutions established under the constitution.[23]

There are a number of additional indicators that measure degrees of civilian control over the armed forces. For example, promotions to the rank of general require presidential approval; the same applies to the appointment and removal of military zone commanders, the secretary and undersecretary of defense, the chairman and vice chairman of the general staff, and the inspector general. The president must also give his consent before any military plans may be implemented.

Another indicator of civilian control over the armed forces is the austere military budget, which requires a careful distribution of scarce resources among the three branches of the service. The government has imposed these spartan budgets over the military's frequent complaints that they are insufficient to meet the tasks assigned to them. But the armed forces are careful to add that they recognize that the state allocates a large share of the national budget to such worthy causes as education and social security.[24]

The military high command's support of government initiatives constitutes yet another example of the armed forces' subordination to civilian authorities. Recall the border problems with Guatemala and the tensions with the United States over crossborder drug traffic. In the latter case, after the United States implemented Operation Intercept, President Miguel de la Madrid reassigned the chairman of the chiefs of staff, General Vinicio Santoyo, to command the 15 and 5 military zones—key drug-producing regions. This change in command not only ratified the president's authority, it also demonstrated the high command's willingness to cooperate by giving the matter their full and prompt attention. In this case they did so with the full knoweldge that they were helping the president to ease strained relations between Mexico and the United States.

Although orders flow from civilian authorities to the military, the former are nevertheless well aware that if they want to keep the latter satisfied they have to offer them moral and material incentives. As a result, President de la Madrid has been careful to supplement moral incentives (promotions, honors) with material rewards, such as salary increases. The underlying assumption is that a well-organized, well-remunerated, and publicly recognized military will have little interest in plotting coups d'etat.

In general, it seems unlikely that the Mexican armed forces will attempt to shake off civilian control or become isolated from society in the near future, but some secondary factors that might push them in that direction bear mentioning. Military education and productive capacity are increasing the military's potential for autonomy: the training of military professionals, such as doctors, dentists, engineers, managers, and so forth, plus their capacity to supply basic goods, such as food, suggest that the armed forces may one day be able to function without input from civil society. The military's growing and diverse professional and technical capabilities have already led to the temporary substitution of civilian bureaucrats for military officers during emergency situations, such as national strikes. This development represents an evolution of the division of labor that exists between the police and the armed forces. Traditionally, the police kept order in the cities and the army in the countryside. During emergencies in urban areas, however, the army took over primary responsibility for maintaining the peace.[25]

But officers may have the capacity to begin taking management positions in state enterprises even under normal conditions. If they did so, it would constitute another indicator of the state of civil-military relations. More important, however, it would also be an indicator of the overall relation between civil society (not just the political authorities) and the armed forces. Thus, in the event of a Southern Cone-style coup d'etat the military might begin to carry out most government functions by themselves.[26] And, for reasons touched upon earlier, they might also drastically isolate themselves from civil society.

These issues have also captured the attention of U.S. scholars. They recognized that the Mexican armed forces were a potential power contender in that nation's politics and concluded that the military would probably intervene directly in politics if Mexico's current economic crisis precipitated a total breakdown of society. The U.S. scholars demonstrated an interest in four general topics: the Mexican military's readiness to confront social breakdown; their influence in domestic and foreign policy making; the social composition of the officer corps; and the military's ideosyncratic approach to national security, or, to put it as gently as possible, their unwillingness to "recognize the importance of the United States as a significant factor in [Mexico's] security."[27] But the central question was the issue of the likelihood of a coup d'etat in Mexico in the near future.

The divergence of opinion resulted from a variety of factors, including lack of agreement over what constituted "professionalization," the military's capabilities to actually take over the government, and lack of data and secondary sources on the subject.[28] This made it difficult to judge whether military professionalization and their actual or desired participation in politics were increasing, diminishing, or stable.

It was argued that the military's capacity to maintain social order depended on two variables. The first factor turned on the relationship between the capital and the provinces. The armed forces could maintain order in the capital to the degree that the provinces remained quiescent. Conversely, the military could control disturbances in the provinces to the degree that Mexico City was at peace. But the Mexican army does not have resources to handle disturbances in the capital and in the provinces simultaneously.

The second variable takes into account the relationship between elites and the masses. As long as the masses remain quiescent, elite splits will not destabilize Mexico. By the same token, occasional mass mobilization will not endanger political stability as long as elites remain cohesive. But the likelihood of a military intervention, perhaps in alliance with some social groups, increases to the degree that social mobilization and elite splits coincide. After all, DN–2 is designed as a defense against insurgency, and its planners are aware of the Mexican military's lack of resources to fight in several theaters of operation simultaneously. The basic goal of DN–3 is to counteract the conditions that might lead to insurgency. But the military's efforts to provide social services and to control crime and drug trafficking may prove ineffectual, which might lead to widespread political and social disaffection among the population.

If the situation did not get out of hand, however, it would be an indication of a more deep-seated problem—a serious erosion of political and social control mechanisms. Or, it would denote a collapse of the passive consent which sustains Mexico's ruling and governing classes. Elite–mass conflict in both the capital and the states would demonstrate that the government's *Partido Revolucionario Institucional* (PRI) was losing control and that the Mexican political system was about to crumble, thereby increasing the likelihood of revolution or a coup d'etat. But in the meantime, since widespread insurgency, mass mobilization, and anomie are not now in evidence, the military are more likely to continue supporting the government, interpreting their mission as one of helping civilian political authorities to control sporadic small-scale conflicts wherever they may arise.

POSTSCRIPT

I will begin by expanding the theme of civilian control over the armed forces. Besides the factors previously discussed, civilians have a number of additional mechanisms at their disposal to curb disgruntled soldiers. One tactic is to transfer them to isolated hardship posts, such as jungles or deserts. Relegating officers from troop command to desk jobs or to secondary posts constitutes another means of disarming potential troublemakers. It is rumored that officers who request permission to join a party other than the PRI are given an indefinite leave of absence, which virtually amounts to being discharged from the service. Rumor also has it that rebellious officers are denied credit for housing and other benefits.

In general, legislation designed to secure civilian control over the military is geared toward assuring the latter's loyalty to constitutionally established political institutions and Mexico's de facto single-party system. So far, these rules seem to have accomplished their goal. Since 1935 the Defense Ministry has not officially leveled a single criticism against the incumbent president or the ruling party. The same holds true for the officer corps after 1952, the year in which a military man was the presidential candidate of an opposition party.

Since 1952, then, officers have channeled their political ambitions through the ruling political party—the PRI. These officers, usually generals, act as liaisons between the Defense Ministry, the president, and the PRI. Their function is to articulate the military's socioeconomic demands. Ironically, though, it seems that in urban areas soldiers vote more for opposition parties of the Left and Right than for the PRI.

These reflections lead me to expand a related topic, the relationship between the military and politics in general (the ruling party and social struggles). How do the military participate in politics within this framework? Answering this question requires an analysis of two factors. First, one would need to look at internal changes in the military, tracing the political consequences of increases in their material benefits, in terms of salaries, benefits, and weapons systems, as well as their access to high-level elective office as PRI candidates. Second, one would need to ascertain the political significance of the fact that high-ranking officers have begun to secure important positions in the government bureaucracy. Because these appointments place them in sensitive administrative posts they are now in a position to participate in government policy making and to shape official ideology.

These developments notwithstanding, the following examples demonstrate that the armed forces are still subordinate to civilian political authorities. For the last 30 years, the armed forces have placed themselves at the government's disposal to help insure peaceful municipal, state, and federal elections. Thus, in most cases, the decision to carry out electoral fraud does not rest with the armed forces. The manner in which the military conducted themselves in counterinsurgency campaigns during the 1970s also demonstrates their subordination to civilian control. For example, in negotiations with terrorists the officers involved always obeyed the orders given by civilian authorities and never undertook independent action. Moreover, during counterinsurgency operations the military carried out their civil action campaigns in coordination with civilian authorities.

Another issue is the question of whether there is a relationship between the oil boom (1977–1981) and the modernization of the armed forces. If the analysis focuses on the fact that the oil boom led to the creation of new strategic zones and expensive installations that require protection, then there is a relationship. This new situation forced the military and the government to come up with plans for insuring their security. One result was the establishment of a new military zone in Southern Mexico, which required building more bases, expanding troop levels, and acquiring more weapons systems.

I have left the most provocative question for last.[29] Is a contradiction developing between the military's growing self-sufficiency and modernization on the one hand, and the doctrine of a "people's war" to defend Mexico in the event of an invasion, on the other? Before addressing this issue, however, some clarifications are in order. To begin with, Mexico's notion of what constitutes a people's war differs from that of Yugoslavia or Cuba.[30] The main reason for this is that Mexico's distinct form of socioeconomic and political organization outweighs the fact that these other nations have comparable types of geopolitical location and histories of foreign invasion. Nor is Mexico's security doctrine similar to Israel's conception of total war. Although Mexico's socioeconomic configuration resembles that of Israel, the latter occupies a very different position in terms of the alliance structure that sustains capitalist imperialism, its geopolitical location, and the length of time it has been a sovereign nation-state. In short, Mexico has a unique security doctrine. According to DN–1, fighting a people's war requires the strategic use of a people's militia to back-up regular units in the field. Without such support, Mexico would never be able to resist, much less defeat, an invader.

But the people's war defense strategy requires close coordination and identification between the "people" and the armed forces. The overall thrust of the military's modernization, however, has been to build its self-sufficiency, both in terms of food supplies and technical and professional personnel. Some analysts have emphasized that modernization is also giving the military a distinctive social status which tends to isolate soldiers from the rest of society. It does this by creating a centralized command structure, full-time soldiers, bureaucratization, specialized high esprit de corps, technical sophistication, a corporate identity, and professional responsibility.[31]

Modernization has also given soldiers a series of material benefits not available to the masses—housing, medical attention, loans—which reinforce their distinctive social status. As a result, their economic status is higher than that of urban laborers, and much higher than that of rural laborers and poor peasants. The current economic crisis tends to sharpen the economic differences between the military and most of the laboring classes as mass unemployment, high inflation, and cutbacks in social services and public sector employment afflict the rest of the population.

Other scholars, however, insist that the problem lies elsewhere. They argue that professionalization may lead to strain in civil-military relations because of rising esprit de corps, a sense of belonging to a caste, growing sophistication in adapting social science to military doctrine, and the consequences that might have in the face of rising levels of social conflict.[32]

In my view, the economic crisis undoubtedly increases the differential in the standard of living between military personnel and most Mexican workers, although the distance has not become critical. But esprit de corps is inherent in all military institutions and becomes dangerous only when soldiers begin to think of themselves as a caste, which in my opinion is not yet the case in Mexico. Nevertheless, they might begin to do so if their material well-being continues while that of the bulk of the population continues to decline.

Although politically and economically the military are distancing themselves from the masses, I do not wish to adopt a fatalist-voluntarist or an economic-determinist stance. I think that the nation's capacity to defeat an invasion depends on other factors.[33] First, it depends on the ability of independent democratic and revolutionary organizations to revitalize the Mexican people's anti-imperialist historical memory. The second factor relates to the attitude of a number of key actors, such as the various factions of the dominant economic class, and of the pro-imperialist and nationalist factions of the dominant political class. Third, one must consider the dominant faction within the military itself. Fourth, one cannot ignore the international dimension, that is, the reaction of either capitalist or socialist great powers, as well as that of other Third World nations, particularly Latin American states.

This is not to suggest, however, that the relationship betwen the military and civil society plays no role in Mexico's, or any other state's, ability to win a war. An analysis of civil-military relations, then, should focus on the power relations between political-military and political-ideological forces. Methodologies based on this general approach can help scholars to uncover general trends in civil–military relations. They also generate expectations as to how the state of those relations might affect Mexico's chances of defending itself against invading armies. Attempts to predict what the military might or might not do based on a different set of variables essentially constitutes a retreat into scientism—an illusion.

NOTES

1. I have not included a discussion of the navy because of the dearth of adequate sources, and because it does not play a very important role in the military's overall power configuration. Hence, the navy has little impact on Mexico's power structure.

2. As I see it, the military's level of professionalization depends on three factors. The first one is the organizational-educational nexus. Its development requires the creation of new schools and military curricula based on modern technical-humanistic teaching methods; a restructuring of military institutions, e.g., rules of discipline, promotions, and administration; and an increase in the military budget for education. The second factor is the material-logistical nexus. Its modernization demands an infusion of new weapons and support systems, as well as new bases. The third factor is the political-ideological nexus. It entails cultivating a military doctrine that encourages institutional over personal loyalties—that is, loyalty to the president, the nation, the flag, and the constitution, among others, over loyalty to particular generals and other strongmen. For

an elaboration of this subject, see José Luis Piñeyro, *Ejército y Sociedad en México: Pasado y Presente* (Puebla: Universidad Autónoma Metropolitana and Universidad Autónoma de Puebla, forthcoming).

3. For the professionalization of the Mexican military, see José Luis Piñeyro, "El Profesional Ejército Mexicano y la Asistencia Militar de Estados Unidos: 1965–1975" (Master's thesis, Center of International Studies, El Colegio de México, México, D.F., 1976), especially 118–205.

4. Piñeyro, *Ejército y Sociedad*, 50–85.

5. Ibid., 180–85.

6. Piñeyro, "El Profesional Ejército Mexicano," 86–87.

7. These data are taken from an anonymous article, "Tiendas y Granjas Agropecuarias SeDeNa," *Revista del Ejército y la Fuerza Aérea*, July 1982: 31.

8. Quoted from an anonymous article, "La Educación Militar," *Revista del Ejército y la Fuerza Aérea*, July 1982: 33.

9. Ibid., 29–40; and Gloria Fuentes, *El Ejército Mexicano* (México: Editorial Grijalbo, 1983, 159–65).

10. For an elaboration of the relationships among military professionalization, social struggles, and U.S. military training programs see Piñeyro, *Ejército y Sociedad*, 120–34.

11. José Luis Piñeyro, "Las Relaciones Militares México–Estados Unidos: Ayer y Hoy," *Nexos*, March 1985.

12. Gloria Fuentes, *El Ejército Mexicano*, 219.

13. Piñeyro, "El Profesional Ejército Mexico," 176–80; and the International Institute for Strategic Studies, *The Military Balance: 1984–1985* (London, 1985), 122.

14. Ibid., 184.

15. These data are from: Raúl Benítez Manaut, "La Realidad Geopolítica de México, la Seguridad Nacional y la Intervención de Estados Unidos en Centroamérica" (Paper presented at the XV Congreso Latinoamericano de Sociologia, Managua, Nicaragua, October 1985), 8–10; Anonymous, "Aplicación Reciente de el Plan DN–3," *Revista del Ejército y de la Fuerza Aérea*, October 1984; Anonymous, "El Combate al Cultivo y Tráfico de Drogas," *El Día*, 24 February 1985; Piñeyro, "El Profesional Ejército Mexicano," 70–95; and various issues of *Revista de Ejército y la Fuerza Aérea*, 1958–1976 and 1980–1984.

16. Those familiar with the Goblin plan will recognize it as a DN–1-type strategy. In a speech delivered at the Military College in July 1970, Defense Secretary General Marcelino García Barragan said that there were three currents of thought among the highest command with respect to military strategy in the event of an invasion: one advocated sustaining a guerrilla war against the invader; another suggested that Mexico stay on the defensive and wait until international factors favored Mexico in its struggle; a third stressed the adoption of a defensive strategy punctuated by occasional offensive tactics. See *Revista del Ejército*, July 1970: 8–10.

17. *El Día*, 24 February 1985, 6–7; *Excelsior*, 26 March 1985.

18. Among other factors, the United States considers that drug production in the Third World constitutes a threat to its national security. U.S. officials never seem to take into account the fact that the drug traffic is just as much a problem of demand as it is of supply. Unfortunately for the United States, it is not only the largest potential market for drugs, it also has the largest demand for controlled substances.

19. Poder Ejecutivo Federal, *Plan Nacional de Desarrollo: 1983–1988* (México: Talleres Gráficos de la Nación, 1983), 63.

20. Ibid., emphasis mine.

21. Poder Ejecutivo Federal, *Plan Nacional de Desarrollo: 1980–1982* (México: Talleres Gráficos de la Nación, 1980), 132–37.

22. Poder Ejecutivo Federal, *Informe de Ejecución, 1983, Plan Nacional de Desarrollo* (México: Talleres Gráficos de la Nación, 1984), 29–31.

23. Anonymous, *Revista del Ejército y la Fuerza Aérea*, February 1985: 22–24.

24. *Excelsior*, 13 March 1985.

25. The division of labor between the police and the armed forces has its roots in an uneven process of professionalization that took place between 1920 and 1968. During that period, the introduction of modern educational and administrative methods and a restructuring of the political-ideological nexus were not accompanied by a corresponding modernization of weapons and support systems. The government distributed the few modern weapons and support systems that it did buy among elite units. These units were charged with controlling any disturbances that the police forces could not contain.

26. A Southern Cone-style coup d'etat is one in which the armed forces remain in power for a substantial period of time, attempt to implement a national project, and have a social basis of support.

27. Sergio Aguayo, "La Seguridad Nacional: Omnipresencia no Significa Omnipotencia," *La Jornada*, 15 March 1985: 16.

28. David Ronfeldt, "The Modern Mexican Military: An Overview," in *The Modern Mexican Military: A Reassessment*, ed. David Ronfeldt (San Diego, Calif.: Center for U.S.-Mexican Studies, University of California, San Diego, 1984), 17.

29. Seminario Internacional "Autonomización Castrense y Democracia: Dinámica del Armamentismo y del Militarismo en América Latina," Santiago de Chile, May 23–25, 1985.

30. For the Yugoslav case, see Nikola Lujubcic, "La Estrategia Militar de Tito y la Defensa Omnipopular," *Cuestiones Actuales del Socialismo*, nos. 7–8 (July–August 1980); Nikola Lujubcic, "La Defensa Popular Generalizada" and "Estrategia de Paz," *Biblioteca Cuestiones Actuales del Socialismo* (Belgrade: CAS, 1977); for the Cuban case, see, in this volume, Raúl Benítez Manaut, Lucrecia Lozano, Ricardo Córdova, and Antonio Cavalla, "Armed Forces, Society, and the People: Cuba and Nicaragua."

31. Virgilio Beltrán, et al., *El Papel Político y Social de las Fuerzas Armadas en América Latina* (Caracas: Monte Avila Editores, 1970), 37–38; and Virgilio Beltrán, *Las Fuerzas Armadas Hablan* (Buenos Aires: Paidos, 1968), 19–20.

32. Manfred Kossok, "Potencialidades y Limitaciones en el Cambio de la Función Política y Social de las Fuerzas Armadas en los Países en Desarrollo: El Caso de América Latina," *Revista Latinoamerica de Sociología*, nos. 2–3 (July–August 1971).

33. This holds true for both the invasion itself and the subsequent occupation, two moments that must be held distinct.

9 ARMED FORCES, SOCIETY, AND THE PEOPLE: CUBA AND NICARAGUA

Raúl Benítez Manaut, Lucrecia Lozano,
Ricardo Córdova and Antonio Cavalla

This chapter offers a sociological analysis of the Cuban and Nicaraguan armed forces and places their main characteristics in a historical and sociopolitical context. It will show that both the politicization of the Cuban and Nicaraguan armed forces and their intimate ties to the people constitute their core organizing principles.

The fact that Cuba and Nicaragua have experienced social revolutions sets their military institutions apart from those of the rest of the region. First, the Cuban and Nicaraguan armed forces had their genesis in victorious armed struggles against dictatorships. Second, they are people's armies, and thus they are committed to the sociopolitical processes that resulted from their revolutions. The commitment is the central organizing theme of the Cuban and Nicaraguan military. Third, military build-ups in these countries mainly responded to an international factor, the very real threat of invasion by the United States or its allies. This brings us to the fourth major distinction between the Cuban and Nicaraguan armed forces and those of the rest of the region—their military doctrine. At the heart of the relationships among the state, the military, and political system, and the citizenry lies a defense strategy that commits these countries to wage a "people's war" against invading forces. As a result, the Cuban and Nicaraguan armed forces should be understood through analyzing their political systems. In fact this novel relationship between the people and the state—which turns on creating people's militias to defend the nation—has given birth to a new way of conceptualizing democracy.

Thus, the Cuban and Nicaraguan armed forces did not become autonomous institutions in spite of their large military establishments—measured by their proportion to total population and in terms of their share of government spending.[1]

Nor have these countries experienced a separation between state and society. Actually, the reverse has taken place. Because the threat was external in nature it united the people in defense of the nation's sovereignty.

The following analyses represent an effort to fill a gap in the literature on postrevolutionary Cuban and Nicaraguan society. Most studies on this subject do not understand the Cuban and Nicaraguan military for two reasons. First, most specialists either passionately oppose or support these revolutions. The former refuse to consider that they may have had some positive effects, while the latter consistently turn a blind eye to their problems. Second, it seems that the military is a taboo subject for most sociologists. For these reasons, the genesis and consolidation of the Cuban and Nicaraguan armed forces cry out for more attention.

THE CUBAN REVOLUTIONARY ARMED FORCES, 1960–1984

The armed insurrectional movement that triumphed in Cuba at the beginning of 1959 swept away an entire neocolonial, pro-imperialist, dependent, or simply underdeveloped socioeconomic structure of domination. While this structure is common to virtually all Latin American societies, in the Cuban case two features stand out in sharper relief. First, Cuba's very close ties to the United States meant that it was a very weak nation-state. Second, the military coup d'etat of 1952, which resulted in the personal dictatorship of Fulgencio Batista, eliminated all mediation between the state and civil society.[2]

Given the characteristics of Batista's dictatorship, the leaders of the victorious "July 26 Movement" knew that they had to construct an entirely new state, as well as a new political system. As in other countries where armed revolution has triumphed, at the moment of victory the Cuban revolutionary army was the strongest institution in the nation. As such, it became the foundation upon which the structures of the new regime were built. And, as with all successful revolutions that enjoy the unconditional support of the vast majority of the population, the first task consisted of defending the new order.

The Cuban experience had yet another feature in common with other revolutions. Its leaders had to bring together disparate nationalist and anti-United States political forces. As a result, the history of the Cuban revolution is the story of the installation and consolidation of Cuba's present political system.

Any analysis of Cuban civil–military relations has to keep in mind that, beginning with the guerrilla war (especially between 1957–1958), the revolutionary leaders organized their armed forces according to principles that were the antithesis of those favored by the dictatorship. In other words, the revolutionary army's most important enduring characteristic is that its structure is radically different from that of the armed forces that Fulgencio Batista commanded between 1952 and 1958.

Another important feature of the Cuban armed forces, their defensive character, took shape during the first years of the revolutionary government. In essence, they are organized to counter U.S. military, diplomatic, political, or economic aggression. The key to that organization lies in the social and political thrust of Cuba's defensive military doctrine.[3]

When the Cuban revolutionary army first developed its military doctrine it relied heavily on a classical military doctrine that stressed the importance of morale: the more the general population willingly participated in the armed forces, the higher the morale. In the Cuban case that eventually included the entire population. The development and acceptance of this strategy had their roots in the revolutionary experiences of Fidel Castro and his followers in the July 26 Movement. (We have found, in fact, that the various stages of the insurgency—guerrilla warfare, followed by larger troop concentrations, and ending in a war of position with the occupation of territory—heavily influenced Cuba's current "people's defense" strategy.[4] We will expand on this point later.)

The core concept of Cuba's security doctrine is the notion that a people under arms constitutes the principle means of defense. Thus, the ways in which the people participate in the nation's defense and the form of the corresponding military–political structures may change over time, but their guiding principle does not.[5]

The Evolution of the Cuban Armed Forces, 1960–1980

Postrevolutionary Cuba established its main military and political institutions during the 1960s. As pointed out, the former actually originated during the insurgency against Batista and were consolidated before the political institutions. In any case, on October 16, 1959, the revolutionary leaders abolished the Defense Ministry and created the Ministry of the Revolutionary Armed Forces (MIN-RAF). A few days later (October 26), they formed the so-called National Revolutionary Militias (NRMs), which had already appeared in embryonic form in August with the organization of a small militia unit known as *Los Malagones*.

Throughout the first years of the revolution, the Revolutionary Armed Forces (RAF) had a structure that defined them as "irregular" forces. During this period, the RAF and the militias coordinated their operations with those of the Revolutionary Police. Cuba began to form regular divisions after these forces defeated the U.S.-backed invasion at *Playa Girón*, also known as the Bay of Pigs, in April 1961.[6] In response to this heightened security threat, Cuban leaders initiated a dual process of change in the organization of their military forces. They instituted a crash program of military professionalism, and increased the level of civilian participation in the armed forces.

Given this sequence of events, it seems that both the Cuban military's professionalization and the increase in civilian participation had their origin in what military theorists call the action–reaction principle. In other words, *the present structure of the Cuban armed forces is the direct result of U.S. military aggression and economic harassment*. The same holds true for the development of Cuba's political system. The threat of external aggression led to great national unity. Both of these factors probably influenced Cuba's decision to officially embrace socialism on the eve of the Playa Girón invasion.

The first half of the 1960s witnessed a rapid professionalization of the Cuban military and an accelerated integration of the general population in the nation's defense planning. In 1961 Cuban leaders created the so-called People's Defense units. "Their mission [was] to increase the technical and fighting capabilities of the people's militias."[7] These units remained active until July 11, 1966, and they were replaced by the Civil Defense (created by law no. 1194) once the last strongholds of the counterrevolution had been destroyed. Moreover, in July 1962, the authorities formed the Bandit Strike Force (BSF) arm of the NRM. The BSF bore the brunt of the fighting against U.S.-backed counterrevolutionary forces operating mainly in the Sierra del Escombray.[8]

However, the Committees for the Defense of the Revolution (CDRs), formed in September 1960, undoubtedly constitute the most important link between the people and the political system. They were also the most important civilian defense unit. The main difference between the CDRs and the NRMs is precisely the fact that the former are civilian defense units operating in cities and key economic centers. The NRMs were militarized forces that had active combat roles against counterrevolutionaries operating mostly in rural areas.

But the CDRs not only organized block-by-block defense, they also structured day-to-day life. For example, they coordinated vaccination drives, promoted cultural events, discussed government legislation, and so forth. Given the breadth of their activities and the fact that they became the most widespread Cuban mass organization, the CDRs developed into one of the principal channels of citizen participation in Cuba's people's democracy. In the 1970s they also provided the base for the People's Power groups, which complemented the activities of the CDRs.

Cuba instituted mandatory military service (MMS) in November 1963. Under this system, all 16-year-olds had to register and were called to service between the ages of 17 and 27 according to the military's manpower needs. Between active service and the reserve forces the MMS involved the entire population between 17 and 45 years of age in the nation's defense.[9]

In August 1973 Cuban leaders carried out two important reforms. Because they needed to make recruitment and admissions practices compatible with the military's general modernization, they replaced the MMS with the general military service law (GMS). They also formed the Youth Labor Army (YLA), which took over the military's economic and civic action role, thereby reducing the state's military spending for a time.[10] Table 3 gives an idea of what it costs Cuban society to maintain its armed forces.[11]

Between 1959 and 1980, the Cuban armed forces experienced constant development, which may be divided into five phases. The first phase involved the transformation of the insurgent's forces into the Revolutionary Armed Forces in 1959. During the second phase, the civilian population was incorporated into the nation's defense planning, in order to repulse U.S. invasion attempts and to

Table 3
Cuban Military Spending as a Percentage of GDP (in millions of Cuban Pesos, current prices)

Year	Total Military Spending*	% of GDP
1961	--	7.6
1962	--	8.0
1963	213	5.6
1964	223	5.2
1965	214	4.4
1966	--	4.5
1967	--	4.8
1968	--	5.8
1969	--	4.5
1970	--	5.1
1971	--	5.2
1972	365	5.1
1973	--	---
1974	282	3.6
1975	(326)**	(3.7)
1976	--	---
1977	700	7.3
1978	784	7.6
1979	841	7.8
1980	811	7.2
1981	842	7.5
1982	924	8.0
1983	1,126	---

* The value of the Cuban peso parallels that of the U.S. dollar; toward the end of the 1970s the Cuban peso was valued about 5 or 8% above the dollar.
** () = estimate.

Source: Figures for the 1958-1972 period are from Domínguez, Cuba, Order and Revolution, p. 347. Those for period between 1974 and 1983 are from Stockholm International Peace Research Institute, World Armaments and Disarmament, SIPRI Yearbook, 1984 (London: Taylor and Francis, 1984, pp. 126 and 129.

fight the U.S.-backed counterrevolutionaries. This period lasted from 1960 to 1966. After the defeat of the counterrevolution, the third phase, which lasted until the end of 1972, witnessed a push to professionalize the military. In the fourth phase, Cuba demilitarized a significant proportion of the civilian population in order to free them for economically productive activities. This civilian demilitarization paralleled the Cuban government's efforts to modernize the military, roughly until 1980; moreover, beginning in 1975 the U.S.S.R. greatly stepped up economic and military assistance programs to Cuba. The formation of the Territorial Militias in May 1980 marks the beginning of the fifth phase. We shall elaborate on this period later on.

The development of professional standards in the Cuban armed forces turns on the military and academic training of their officers. Cadets, who must be high school graduates, receive their military training at one of eight military academies: the RAF's General Antonio Maceo Interservice Academy, the General

José Maceo Interservice Academy at Santiago de Cuba, the Comandante Camilo Cienfuegos Artillery School, the General Carlos Roloff Communications and Chemical Warfare School, the Revolutionary Navy's Military Technical Institute, and the air force's Technical Academy and Flight Academy. High-ranking officers attend the RAF's General Máximo Gómez Superior War College.[12]

After the victory at Playa Girón, two additional events marked watersheds in the development of the RAF and their link to the civilian population. The first one consisted of Cuba's prior political and ideological commitment to revolutionary movements in Latin America.[13] But this factor is related to the action–reaction principle we alluded to earlier. In other words, Cuba's internationalism was a defensive reaction against the United States' unflagging hostility, which led to Cuba's virtual isolation in the region. (For a time, Mexico was the only Latin American state that maintained diplomatic relations with Cuba.) Cuban leaders concluded that these circumstances relieved them of any obligations toward these states.[14]

A similar set of conditions led to Cuba's intervention in Angola toward the end of 1975, which marked the second watershed in the history of the RAF. Cuba sent roughly 16,000 troops to Angola in response to a request for assistance issued by the recently installed government of Agostinho Neto. Cuba dispatched those soldiers only after the United States had overtly begun to support Zaire and South Africa in their efforts to thwart the Angolan revolution.[15]

The Cuban participation in Angola proved the quality of Cuba's elite troops in the field, as well as the Interior Ministry's capacity to conduct both conventional and counterinsurgency warfare. After the Cubans defeated the South African forces, even observers who had no sympathy for Cuba—and who insist on analyzing every event in terms of East/West confrontation—have grudgingly admitted that the introduction of Cuban combat troops in Angola and Ethiopia has radically changed the correlation of forces in Africa.[16] For their part, the Cubans have repeatedly asserted their willingness to bring their troops home on two conditions: first, that the South Africans withdraw from Namibia and guarantee the independence of Angola; and second, a guarantee that the United States and its allies will also refrain from attacking or harassing Angola.[17]

The actual size of the Cuban armed forces depends on international political factors, that is, on the magnitude of the perceived U.S. threat. For example, between 1960 and 1963 they numbered 300,000 persons. In 1970 that figure dropped to 250,000, and it reached a low of 100,000 in 1974 (although the YLA counted with another 100,000 men and women).[18] Meanwhile, the navy had about 6,000 sailors in 1970 and 7,500 in 1975, and the air force commanded 12,000 people in 1970 and 20,000 in 1975. These figures do not include approximately 500,000 reservists upon whom the government can immediately draw on in an emergency.[19]

According to the London-based International Institute of Strategic Studies (IISS), the Cuban armed forces numbered 227,000 persons in 1981 and 153,000 in 1984. These figures do not include paramilitary organizations, which in light of the Cuban military's reorganization probably accounts for the surprising drop in personnel. The IISS estimated the troop strength for paramilitary forces as follows. In 1981, the Interior Ministry had 150,000 people working for the internal security department, the border patrol numbered 3,000, and the YLA had 100,000 people. In 1985, the security department and the YLA maintained the same personnel levels, while that of the border guards increased to 3,500. In 1985, the IISS counted two more categories: the civil defense forces, which added 100,000 persons; and the Territorial Militias, which contributed another 530,000 people to the island's defense.[20]

The RAF began to modernize shortly after the fall of Batista when the Soviet Union started sending military aid. An attractive feature of the Soviet's military aid program was that they did not tack the cost of that assistance onto Cuba's trade balance. The Soviet military aid program changed qualitatively in 1968 with the delivery of 300 light tanks, anti-aircraft batteries, small submarines, and patrol boats.

In 1968, the air force had 24 batallions divided into 144 units. It had 600 missiles, and most of its aircraft were MIG–15s and MIG–17s. In the 1970s these were replaced by MIG–19s and MIG–21s. (The latter are supersonic jets that arrived in 1975.) This modernization represented a significant change, because it substituted new fighter-bombers for the old interceptors. Moreover, in 1975 the Soviets also gave the Cubans 15 T–62 tanks.[21] The U.S. Defense Department and the CIA maintain that 1975 marked the beginning of a massive increase in Soviet military aid to Cuba. They calculated such aid at 10,000 metric tons in 1974, 15,000 in 1975, and 20,000 in 1980.[22]

But there was disagreement over this assessment. A private study commissioned by the Defense Department in 1983, which was leaked to the *Miami Herald* in April 1984 without eliciting any denials, estimated that the Cuban armed forces had a total of 25 divisions, 950 tanks, more than 270 jet fighters, 209 boats equipped with surface-to-air missiles, and three submarines.[23] According to this study, the Soviet Union supplied most of this military hardware to the tune of 34,000 metric tons per year beginning with the Cuban Missile Crisis in 1961. The study also calculated that Soviet military aid between 1980 and 1983 totalled U.S.$1.7 billion. The study concluded that the air force alone had about 200 airplanes and emphasized their offensive capabilities. These aircraft included an indeterminate number of MIG–23 and MIG–21 fighters, Antonov AN–24, AN–26, and Ilyushin LL–12 transport planes. The *Miami Herald* story emphasized that the MIG–23 had sufficient range to attack the southeastern U.S. seaboard, most of Central America and many of the Caribbean nations. By the same token, although the Soviet AN–26 was a short-range transport, the study nevertheless argued that it had the capability to supply almost any Central American country, including Nicaragua.[24]

We have shown elsewhere that these assessments are incorrect. Neither the MIG–23 nor the AN–26 transports have the range to fly round-trip missions to Central America when they are fully armed and loaded. And none of these airplanes could ever constitute a threat to U.S. security given the quality and quantity of U.S. air defenses, not to mention the enormous risks that such actions have for world peace.

A *Miami Herald* report in late 1982, citing Pentagon sources, claimed that the Cuban navy's steady build-up had given it the capability to conduct limited interdiction operations against shipping in the Caribbean. To support this assertion, the report offered details on the deployment of the Cuban navy. It is said that the Cuban navy had 92 Soviet-built combat ships and 32 auxiliary vessels, including 50 high-speed patrol boats, two modern Foxtrot-class attack submarines, one Whiskey-class submarine, two Koni-type modern frigates, hydrofoil torpedo boats, and minesweepers. In addition to this adjective-laden information, the *Miami Herald* story also informed its readers that the Soviet-built and subsidized Cuban navy had developed into the most serious potential military threat to the United States in the region. In the event of a superpower conflict elsewhere, the U.S. navy would have to divert scarce resources to counter a possible Cuban–Soviet threat to vital sea-lanes in the Gulf of Mexico, the Florida Straits, and Windward Pass.[25]

In terms of the Cuban military's foreign commitments we have found the following, although unfortunately data from Western sources is not very reliable. In March 1984 *Latin American Weekly Reports* estimated that Cuba had about 22,000 troops in Angola alone. The story reported that the RAF also had troops stationed in Ethiopia (16,500), Mozambique (300), and the Congo. But the RAF had set up training camps in Algeria, Equatorial Guinea, Libya, Madagascar, and Zambia.[26] As usual, the report does not cite any sources for this information.

Most U.S. officials and press treat Soviet military aid as if it were some sort of covert action. But that is not the case, Cuban officials readily recognize their desire for such aid in speeches and press releases. For example, Carlos Rafael Rodríguez, the vice president of the Council of State, said in an interview that Cuba "was pressing the Soviet Union to deliver in two years the amount of weapons that had been planned for five."[27] Moreover, it is interesting to note that until 1980 most Soviet military aid came in the form of heavy materiel. But with the creation of the Territorial Militias, the Soviets now send small arms as well.

The Political System and the Politicization of the RAF

After the fall of Batista, the need to defend the revolution led to a more rapid development of Cuba's military institutions than of its political institutions. As a result of this process, the form of political participation for the average citizen took on a sui generis character. That is, the general population's political activities were channeled through the Committees for the Defense of the Revolution, or took place fighting against counterrevolutionaries. Furthermore, the political institutions emerged after the revolution had found its ideological orientation. Cuban leaders declared their revolution socialist in 1961, but the Cuban Communist Party (CCP) was not created until 1965. A substantial number of junior and senior officers, cadets, and regular soldiers belong to either the Communist Party or the Communist Youth.[28]

The institutionalization of Cuba's political system developed in two major phases. The first one involved the installation and consolidation of the CCP, which was formed in 1965 and held its first congress in 1975. The second phase consisted of the leaders' efforts to build the organizational foundations of what they called "people's power." This process essentially took place in the first half of the 1970s.

Currently, the Communist Party is Cuba's central political institution. The rest of the nation's political, mass, and military institutions are structured around it. Cuba's constitution defines the CCP as the organized vanguard of the Cuban working class. The Party's congresses, held every five years since 1975, constitute Cuba's most important political event. At these meetings Cuba's political leaders approve five year socioeconomic plans and the general guidelines for the nation's foreign policy. At the time of this writing, within the framework of the Third Congress, the Cuban people were debating a draft of the Party's next program, to be approved in December 1986. The plan also contains a new military strategy—the "Total People's War" (*Guerra de Todo el Pueblo*). This plan is a blueprint for the organization of Cuban society to maximize security during peacetime and war, as well as in the event of a partial occupation of the island by foreign troops.[29]

At the state level, the National Assembly of People's Power is Cuba's legislative body and as such is the nation's highest governing body.[30] Its deputies are elected by municipal assemblies throughout the land. The National Assembly appoints the Council of State, including its president, and the Council of Ministers—Cuba's executive branch. From time to time, the deputies must give a public accounting of their activities to their constituents.

A number of representative associations also form part of the political system. These associations, which represent social, professional, and economic groups, include such diverse organizations as the National Association of Small Agriculturalists, Student Federations, the Pioneer's Union, and the Cuban Women's Federation.

With respect to citizen participation, communications do not just flow from the top down in the form of party or state decisions and directives. Communications also flow from the bottom up. As a result, the citizenry participates in the CCP's policy-making process and negotiates, directly with the state. The channels of access to governing bodies are not static or defined simply from above, according to their needs, the people themselves demand changes in the way they are structured.

In order to understand Cuba's sui generis democracy we need to link citizen political participation to two factors, economic production and defense. All citizens take part in these activities, and society evaluates a person's politics on the basis of his or her contribution to the nation's wealth and security. With respect to the nation's defense, Cuba has placed special emphasis on universal military training and on disseminating knowledge of current military doctrine. In the second half of the 1970s, these principles became law. (For example, the Civil Defense Act makes Cubans aware of the nation's defense doctrine to the degree that it involves all citizens in some kind of defense activity, including disaster relief.)[31] Cuban authorities also passed legislation that required primary and secondary school curricula, as well as those of higher education, to include courses on military subjects. The Cuban authorities had concluded that the growing technical sophistication of modern warfare compelled them to introduce this requirement.[32] Moreover, the general modernization of the RAF forced the authorities to revise existing legislation concerning military service. (It is interesting to note that the Ministry of Education, the State Labor and Social Security Committee, and the Central Planning Board participated in drawing up the new legislation.)[33]

The Cuban Military in the 1980s: The Territorial Militias and Total People's War

The formation of the Cuban Territorial Militias in 1980 constituted a virtual revolution in Latin American military organization by giving a large sector of the population that had formerly served auxiliary or support functions an active role to play in the nation's defense system.

The Territorial Militias were a direct response to an increase in the perceived threat to Cuba's security that resulted from a reinvigorated display of hostility on the part of the United States and its allies.[34] The late 1970s witnessed a resurgence of anti-Cuban discourse in the United States, the downing of a *Cubana de Aviación* aircraft in Barbados, the sinking of two fishing boats by the Peruvian navy, and U.S. maneuvers in the Caribbean, designed to train U.S. forces for action against Cuba.

Another important development in the United States that influenced the Cuban leaders' decision to form the Territorial Militias was the creation of the Rapid Deployment Force (RDF) toward the end of 1979. After all, the RDF's central purpose was to intervene in conflicts quickly and with sufficient force to ensure victory in a short period of time. U.S. strategists believed that in this manner they could overcome the main error committed in Viet Nam—gradual escalation.

The defense strategy of which the Territorial Militia is a part also includes plans for coping with a partial occupation of Cuba. In such an event, the Cuban armed forces would wage both conventional and guerrilla warfare. In other words, the strategy calls for a deconcentration of Cuban military forces. The guiding principle behind this deconcentration is the Clausewitzean concept of total war, that is, to engage the enemy at all levels of struggle—economic, political, ideological, military, cultural, diplomatic, and so forth. The government's ability to mobilize the Cuban masses makes credible the threat of a "total people's war'' in the event of an invasion; for example, five million people (half the population) attended rallies designed to publicize the new defense strategy.[35]

The decentralization of the Cuban armed forces has also given rise to new ways of organizing them territorially. These include the division of Cuba into a number of defense zones defended by medium and small units of the Territorial Militia. A close look at the size of the combat units and the type of training that they receive demonstrates that these forces are strictly defensive in nature.

Along with the formation of the Territorial Militias, the Cubans also developed the concept of the total people's war, which represents a significant evolution in Cuban military thought. It explictly recognizes that Cuba had unfortunately strayed from its original conceptions of defense, and the nation had come to rely more and more on the regular troops of the RAF for its security. Thus, the new doctrine reversed that trend by territorially decentralizing the armed forces and by once again involving the bulk of the population by the nation's defense.[36]

The Second Congress of the CCP addressed these issues head on. It debated the need for a new recruitment policy. Party leaders also expressed a desire to raise the cultural and technical levels of newly commissioned officers, in order to insure the flexibility of the Territorial Militia's command structure.[37]

Within two years of the creation of the Territorial Militia, the Cuban armed forces had received a substantial boost in personnel. Cuban military institutions trained 40,000 officers and formed 200 regiments consisting of 1,000 battalions, which brought the Territorial Militia's manpower to 500,000 troops. Each militiaman or woman received 40 hours of military training per year, and participated in a 10-day military exercise at least once every five years.[38]

Cuba also substantially upgraded its physical defenses during those two years. Cuban authorities designated a permanent workforce of 18,000 workers, 3,000 machines and 15 percent of the nation's cement production to strengthen the island's fortifications against a U.S. attack.[39] Meanwhile, Cuban leaders proclaimed the need to build the Territorial Militia's troop levels to 1 or 1.5 million persons.[40] This represents a formidable deterrent, especially since Cuba has the capacity to arm each and every one of them.[41]

The high level of political awareness among the Cuban population imbues the Territorial Militia with very good morale. Since the CCP is largely responsible for the population's political sophistication, one may conclude that its ideological work has a strategic value. Although Cuba is a militarized society, that militarization does not have its roots in a clash between the interests of the state and society, which is the case in many Latin American countries. According to the CCP, Cuba's militarization is sustained by the conscious and active participation of the entire citizenry.[42]

The U.S. invasion of Grenada in October 1983 stimulated a number of changes in the structure of the RAF and its subordinate relationship to the CCP. Cuban leaders also increased their efforts to strengthen the relationship between the military and the civilian population.[43] Thus, in the event of an attack on Cuba, the first line of defense, naturally, consists of the regular forces of the RAF.

But in each defense zone, the Territorial Militia units assigned to it, under the command of the senior local CCP official, will also engage the enemy. The militia have also concluded a series of maneuvers designed to test their decentralized structure and the troops' readiness. Of course, the amount of training that the Territorial Militia receives has increased.[44] So has the publicity surrounding Cuban defense capabilities.[45]

The Cuban military's size and the proven ability of its combat troops in Angola (where approximately 120,000 soldiers have had a tour of duty) are constantly cited by the United States as evidence of Cuban expansionism.[46] In order to contain the export of the Cuban Revolution, the United States devised the national security doctrine, with its well-known counterinsurgency tactics.[47] Important U.S. strategists have also started talking about the Cuban factor within the framework of the North Atlantic Treaty Organization (NATO). They explictly argue that Cuba has a specific strategic role to play in the East/West conflict. Cuba's military might ostensibly leaves NATO's Western Hemispheric flank (the Caribbean Basin) vulnerable to the enemy.[48] The bulk of the evidence leads us to conclude that the Cuban armed forces are essentially a defensive force. If any of its branches have been highly developed, for example, the air force and the army, it is because Cuba needs a strong deterrent in the face of unrelenting U.S. hostility.

NICARAGUA'S SANDINISTA PEOPLE'S ARMY, 1979–1985

On July 19, 1979 the Nicaraguan people, through their participation in a broad-based insurrectional movement led by the Sandinista National Liberation Front (*Frente Sandinista de Liberación Nacional*—FSLN), put an end to 45 years of Somoza family rule.

Two factors contributed to national unity in Nicaragua, expressed in the creation of the National Patriotic Front (NPF) in February 1979. The first factor was the Sandinistas' alliance strategy during the final offensive against the Somoza dictatorship. The second factor turned on the sharp contradictions that arose between the regime and important factions of the Nicaraguan bourgeoisie during the final years of the dictatorship. As a result, the NPF represented a coalition of heterogeneous political and social forces that joined in the revolutionary struggle against Somoza and accepted the FSLN's general platform and political project.

The dictatorship had closed off any possibility of peaceful change through a combination of nonviolence and elections. The Somoza regime had routinely violated human rights and democratic practices and guarantees. The murder of opposition leader Pedro Joaquín Chamorro in January 1978 served as the catalyst that transformed an acute political crisis, which had begun in 1977, into an armed insurrection.

Understanding this phase in the armed struggle against Somoza is important for two reasons: first, it tells us why the FSLN's broad-front strategy won out over that of rival groups; second, the experiences of that period shaped the way in which the revolutionary regime developed Nicaragua's political, economic, social, and military institutions.[49]

No doubt, Anastasio Somoza's intransigence greatly contributed to the failure of the bourgeois opposition's attempts to liberalize the dictatorship through peaceful means. Somoza refused to democratize Nicaragua—a key demand of the bourgeoisie and of the people who pressed their point by staging mass demonstrations. Instead of negotiating, Somoza resorted to the use of indiscriminate violence to overcome his regime's political crisis. When the bourgeois opposition's attempt to change Nicaragua failed, the people embraced the FSLN's project.

These events shaped the composition of the two main political forces in Nicaragua today. On the one hand, we find the bourgeoisie, organized in the Broad Opposition Front (BOF). On the other, we have the grass-roots movement led by the FSLN, whose various organizations are aggregated in the United People's Movement and the National Patriotic Front.

During the dictatorship's final crisis, the Sandinistas characterized the BOF efforts at political change as "somocismo without Somoza." True, the BOF wanted to abolish the dictatorship and democratize Nicaraguan political and social life through peaceful reforms. But as the Sandinistas pointed out, the BOF wanted to retain full control of this process, and to use it in order to contain social conflict, thus limiting the gains of most Nicaraguans. The BOF also wanted to keep the National Guard intact and agreed that the Somoza family should retain its economic wealth. The Sandinistas, however, advocated the violent overthrow of the Somoza regime, and won support for a mass uprising by promising to install a people's democracy.[50]

The Nicaraguan people developed three forms of struggle against the Somoza dictatorship between 1977 and 1979. They staged an uprising in every major city. The FSLN waged an armed struggle throughout Nicaragua—including conventional combat in which they attacked enemy garrisons in the cities and also conducted a war of position in the countryside.[51] And, during the final phase of Somoza's overthrow, the people organized a general strike beginning on June 4, 1979.

Beginning in 1978, but particularly during the general insurrections in September of that year and in June–July 1979, the active participation of the masses in the armed struggle laid the foundation upon which the Sandinista regime later built the people's militias. From the start, the Sandinista government considered the militias to be a fundamental component of the country's defense system, as well as a means of incorporating the people in that task. Meanwhile, the FSLN's guerrilla fighters became the nucleus of the Sandinista People's Army, which was officially created in November 1979.

The general strikes that accompanied the urban insurrections of 1978 and 1979 gave birth to self-defense organizations called the Civil Defense Committees

(CDCs). After the victory of the revolution in July 1979, the CDCs became the Sandinista Defense Committees, which were responsible for carrying out community work (e.g., health and education) and maintaining public safety.

When Somoza collapsed so did the two pillars that sustained the order he had created. One of those pillars was the National Guard, initially formed by the United States in 1927 during one of the U.S. occupations of Nicaragua. The other one crumbled when the new government destroyed the economic empires of the Somoza family and their associates. The Sandinista government expropriated their assets on July 20, 1979—the day after the Sandinista victory. Decree no. 3 placed important productive assets under public ownership, the so-called People's Property Area (*Area de Propiedad del Pueblo*, or APP). The APP had holdings in the agro-export (about 20 percent of cultivated land), financial, and import/export commercial sectors. Observers estimated that in 1982 the APP's economic activities amounted to 39 percent of GNP. Besides the APP, Nicaragua's mixed economy has a sizeable private sector that includes large, medium, and small property owners. There are also a number of joint ventures between the public and private sectors.

The National Guard collapsed during the climax of the July insurrection, when Anastasio Somoza fled the country on July 17, 1979. The National Guard had always been Somoza's creature, and when he abandoned it the guard's command structure disintegrated, along with the morale of the troops. But U.S. action had also weakened the National Guard: in February 1979, in the face of massive human rights violations in Nicaragua, the Carter administration cut off all economic and military aid and withdrew the U.S. military mission, along with 50 percent of its diplomatic mission.[52]

The Nicaraguan Political System

About a month before the fall of the Somoza dictatorship, on June 18, 1979, as the insurrection gained momentum, the leaders of the revolution formed the Junta of the National Reconstruction Government.[53] Its five members represented the broad spectrum of the political and social forces involved in the struggle, and thus symbolized national unity in the Sandinista-led fight against Somoza.[54]

After the fall of Somoza, the Junta of National Reconstruction became the executive branch, nominated a cabinet, and began to implement the governmental program announced on July 9, 1979. Since it was first formed, however, the composition of the junta has changed, reflecting fluctuations in the power of Nicaragua's social and political forces and the development of new alliances as the Sandinista regime began to consolidate.

The National Reconstruction government's platform embodied the spirit of the program enunciated by the FSLN in 1978, which, in turn, reaffirmed the demands the FSLN had made when it was formed in 1961. Those demands included the dismantling of the National Guard, the expropriation of the Somoza family's and the Somoza economic group's assets, and the implementation of sweeping agrarian reform.

Moreover, working within the bounds of the compromise that made national unity possible, the National Reconstruction government's platform called for the creation of a mixed economy. The government also formulated a series of programs designed to meet immediate needs. These programs included a national Emergency Plan, which addressed the basic needs of a war-ravaged population, and an Immediate Economic Recovery Program "intended to trigger economic stabilization and reactivation."[55] In addition to these projects, the government developed an ambitious medium-range program, the "Plan for Reconstruction, Transformation, and Socioeconomic Development."[56]

Politically, the revolutionary government's program guaranteed the full observance of basic human rights and liberties. To that end, it abolished repressive laws and institutions, such as the National Security Agency and the Military Intelligence Service, and made it clear that these institutions had mainly been used to "repress the people and their organizations."[57]

Since the fall of Somoza, the revolutionary leaders have installed a political system composed of four major institutions. We have already introduced the first one, the Junta of the National Reconstruction Government, which is the executive branch and shares legislative functions with the Council of State. Initially, it was composed of five members, but that number was reduced to three in 1980.[58] Second, on May 4, 1980, the Council of State became the legislative branch of the new Nicaraguan state. It was replaced by the National Constituent Assembly on January 9, 1985.[59] The third major political institution, the Supreme Court, is charged with interpreting the law of the land. Finally, in April 1984, the government created the Supreme Electoral Council, designed to organize, regulate and supervise elections in Nicaragua. Moreover, with an eye toward streamlining its decentralized administration, the revolutionary government reorganized the country's political divisions in 1982. The 16 provinces or departments were reduced to six regions and three special zones, each with its own local government and ministerial office.[60]

Of course, one of the central concerns of the FSLN's government has been to broaden, deepen, and consolidate Nicaragua's mass organizations and to guarantee the defense of the revolution.[61] The dictatorship had stifled the independent organization of labor. Thus, many of the groups that played an important political role in the final offensive were quite new, having formed in the heat of battle between 1977 and 1979; for example, the Agricultural Workers Association (AWA) was founded in 1978, the Association of Women Concerned with the National Question in 1977, and Nicaraguan Revolutionary Youth in 1977.

With the triumph of the revolution, labor organization experienced dramatic changes. For example, in July 1979 the government formed the most important labor organization in Nicaragua, the Sandinista Workers Central, which had 111,498 members in 1983. The year 1981 saw the creation of the National Union of [Small] Cattlemen and Farmers (NUCF), which eventually absorbed the AWA; in 1983, between small- and medium-sized producers, it had 75,228 members. Through the Production Council, NUCF union delegates, like those of the AWA before them, directly participated in the management of state-owned agricultural units.[62]

In August 1983 the Council of State passed the Political Parties Law, which legalized all of the political forces of the nation, both those that had representation on the Council of State and those that did not. By 1984, Nicaragua had a multiparty system with as many as 12 political parties. These parties represented the full gamut of political positions in the country, from a radical left that considers the Sandinistas to be merely reformist and pro-capitalist at heart, to a pro-United States right that accuses the Sandinistas of having transformed Nicaragua into a totalitarian state.

Of the parties of the right and the left that oppose the Sandinistas' program, some have sought to form broad-based alliances and others have not. Those that did find themselves to the right of the spectrum—the Social Christian Party (SCP), the Social Democratic Party (SDP), and the Liberal Constitutionalist Party (LCP)—founded the Nicaraguan Democratic Coordinating Committee (*Coordinadora Democrática Nicaragüense*, also known as the Coordinadora). The Coordinadora, through the SPC, has links to the Nicaraguan Workers Union, and the SDP ties it to the Confederation of Trade Union Unity (two non-Sandinista Labor organizations). Other opposition parties to the right of the Sandinistas include the Independent Liberal Party (which abandoned the Patriotic Front of the Revolution in 1984), the Democratic Conservative Party, and the Popular Social-Christian Party. Meanwhile, the Marxist-Leninist Popular Action Movement, the Nicaraguan Communist Party, and the Revolutionary Marxist League stand to the left of the Sandinistas.

With respect to the role of the armed forces in the revolutionary process, title 4, article 23 of the Statutes of the Republic decreed the replacement of the National Guard with:

a new patriotic National Army dedicated to the defense of democratic processes, national sovereignty, independence, and territorial integrity. The National Army will include FSLN combatants; former National Guard officers and soldiers who conducted themselves with patriotic honesty in the face of the dictatorship's widespread corruption, repression, and denationalization, as well as those who joined the struggle against the Somoza regime; all persons who fought for national liberation and want to join; and any other citizen who wishes to enlist. But soldiers who are corrupt and guilty of crimes against the people are ineligible for service in the National Army.[63]

The Military Doctrine of the Sandinista People's Revolution

The first major characteristic that stands out in the Sandinistas' military doctrine is its commitment to the people. This commitment has had its roots in the historical and strategic goals of the Sandinista revolution.[64]

Nicaragua's current military doctrine has its roots in the FSLN's struggle for national liberation, which began in the 1960s and was inspired by the anti-interventionist battles of Sandino and other Nicaraguan patriots during the 1920s. It reflects the outcome of heated debates over how to make the transition from triumphant irregular combat forces to a modern professional army. Those who favored the view that the military doctrine's central tenet should be the defense of the revolution won out, for the Sandinista government has attempted to actively involve as much of the population as possible in civil defense activities. The war deeply influenced the development of the first two fundamental principles of the revolutionary Nicaragua's military doctrine: the link between the people and the army, and its defensive character. The deployment of the Nicaraguan armed forces supports the claim that they are not intended for offensive use.[65]

The massive participation of the people in the nation's defense acts as a deterrent against invasion. Invading forces would not only face regular troops in well-established defensive positions, but they would confront a large sector of the population. This presents potential invaders with the unpleasant problem of getting bogged down in a long and costly war. The threat of invasion, which has greatly contributed to political unity among Nicaraguans, has given birth to the People's Army—the regular troops supported by widespread citizen participation in the nation's defense.

A third fundamental principle of Nicaragua's military doctrine is its emphasis on balance. It takes into consideration the military's relationship to the nation's productive, political, and diplomatic structure. Of these elements the state of the economy is probably the most important because of the close link between economic well-being and national security. Thus, U.S. aggression confronts Nicaraguan leaders with the dilemma of having to divert scarce resources to the war efforts, resources which they would rather channel into productive economic activity. As a result, the standard of living in Nicaragua has declined, and the state has had to cut back on a wide gamut of social services established after the fall of Somoza.

Another fundamental characteristic of Nicaragua's military doctrine is its strictly defensive nature, which is expressed in four directives. The first directive instructs the authorities to negotiate a permanent peace settlement compatible with the nation's right to self-determination. It underscores Nicaragua's commitment to the Contadora and the Esquipulas II processes and to reopening a dialogue with the United States, which the latter unilaterally broke off at Manzanillo.[66]

The second directive instructs Nicaragua to maintain a nonaligned position in international politics. Nicaragua thus steadfastly refuses to align itself with either the Eastern or the Western bloc, preferring to advance its foreign policy in the Nonaligned Movement and other Third World forums. Politically, Nicaragua is close to the Socialist International, the Cuban government, and maintains close relations with a number of Latin American governments as well as with nations of the so-called socialist bloc.

A third directive, the regime's concern for human rights, has heavily influenced the content of Nicaragua's State of National Emergency. Consequently, it does not resemble the "states of siege," which characterize those South American regimes that have embraced the doctrine of national security.[67] The fourth directive ensures that weapons procurements stay in line with the need to arm a people's army (light weapons) and, in general, lean heavily toward the purchase of defensive weapons systems. We will expand this topic in the following sections.[68]

The Sandinista People's Army

The structure and organization of Nicaragua's armed forces is heavily influenced by the capabilities and actions of its enemies, the terrain, and the level of support they enjoy among the general population. The armed forces as such consist of the Sandinista People's Army (SPA), the air force and antiaircraft defense, and the navy. Given the counterrevolutionary war and the defensive and mass orientation of Nicaragua's military doctrine, the army has always dominated the other branches of the service.

The Sandinista People's Army has three levels of organization. The first level consists of the permanent troops. These regular, full-time soldiers constitute but a small portion of the total number of men and women that the Sandinistas are capable of mobilizing. The other two levels are the reserve brigades and the Sandinista People's Militias. According to knowledgeable sources, in 1985 Nicaragua had 61,800 soldiers distributed in the following manner: 44,000 in the regular army, 1,500 in the air force, 300 in the navy, 12,000 on active reserve duty, and 4,000 border guards.[69]

The Sandinista People's Army has five basic types of units: armored, artillery, antiaircraft, infantry, and border guards. The armored units are the Nicaraguan army's main shock force, while the artillery provides the heavy firepower. The army has also recently developed light infantry units—the Chasseur Battalions— to engage the contras. The men and women who participate in the reserves are people who have received military instruction but who normally either work or study. They are organized into a number of infantry reserve battalions.

The Sandinista People's Militia also fields a large number of troops. They represent the incorporation of a significant proportion of the civilian population into the nation's defense forces. Observers estimate that in 1985 they and other civil defense organizations enlisted the services of between 30,000 and 60,000 volunteers.[70] The militias perform a variety of functions. Initially, their most adept members went into the army reserves; currently, they are on active duty and operate along Nicaragua's frontiers. The militias are organized territorially according to the residence of their troops. In the combat zones they have acquitted themselves effectively in support of regular and reserve units.

The Military Service Law (MSL) of October 1983 regulates citizen participation in the defense of the nation.[71] MSL made military service, which had been voluntary, mandatory for two years for all males between the ages of 18 and 40. For women, military service remained voluntary. The MSL also made an important distinction between active and reserve duty. It defined active duty as full-time service in any of the permanent units or dependencies under the direction of the Defense Ministry. Reserve duty applied to the part-time military instruction of students and working people.

Civil–Military Defense Structures

The Nicaraguan people participate in the nation's defense in four types of organization. The Defense and Production Cooperatives, also known as self-defense cooperatives, have their origin in the peasants' response to contra aggression. As their name implies, these cooperatives bring their organization of production and defense under one roof. So far, the border region cooperatives have been consolidated, and the system is expanding toward the mountains. The northern First (Esteli, Madriz, and Nueva Segovia) and Sixth Regions (Jinotega and Matagalpa) have the most cooperatives—73 each in 1985, with a total membership of 2,215 and 2,955 persons respectively.[72]

The Sandinista Defense Committees (SDCs) are the largest mass organizations in Nicaragua, in terms of membership, the number of functions they have, and the territory they cover.[73] The SDCs emerged during the insurrections of September 1978 as support combat units to the FSLN. At that time they were called Civil Defense Committees in some places and Neighborhood Sandinista Committees in others. Their functions included keeping watch over their territory, running messages, supplying FSLN combatants and the general population with medical stocks, and disseminating information about the Sandinista program.

After the fall of Somoza, the SDCs consolidated themselves into block organizations. As of this writing the SDCs are not militarized units, nor do their members bear arms. They are essentially responsible for curbing counterrevolutionary activities. Other functions include ministering to the general needs of the population under their jurisdiction and transmitting the citizen's demands to higher authority. Their expressly political function is to serve as the FSLN's main link to the people. By the end of 1983 there were approximately 15,000 SDC block organizations with almost 600,000 members of all social classes, ages, and sexes throughout Nicaragua. Of these, about 300,000 belonged to the so-called Revolutionary Guard.

The Civil Defense Committees (CDCs) were organized to assure the safety of the general population in the event of an enemy attack. The Ministry of Defense coordinates the CDCs, which link the Sandinista Defense Committees with other mass organizations, such as unions, within the framework of a Civil Defense (CD) network.[74] Civil Defense units have many functions, including the construction of antiaircraft bunkers and the stockpiling of food and water. In case of an attack, it is their job to supply the general population with basic necessities, help rescue the wounded, transport the seriously wounded to hospitals and bury the dead, as well as to take charge of children, senior citizens, pregnant women, and other noncombatants. Other tasks include fighting fires, clearing away debris, and keeping lines of communication open.

The Civil Defense Committees do not have a complicated organizational structure. At their base, they are block organizations led by resident delegates. At the next level, these block committees form neighborhood committees, which are charged with preparing the neighborhood to meet an attack, and organizing the population in order to reduce their exposure to danger during an assault. In other words, Nicaragua's civil defense units have the following broadly defined functions: to organize the people in such a way that at all times and under any circumstances they will know what to do; to protect the population and the economy; and to either neutralize or reduce the consequences of an enemy attack.

Civil defense units are usually organized as task-specific brigades. These include a brigade in charge of the security, care, and feeding of children; a rubble brigade, whose task it is to either clear or deliberately plant rubble depending on whether Nicaraguan or enemy forces are advancing; a fire brigade, which works closely with the fire department; a first-aid brigade; and a sanitary brigade.

Nicaragua also has a voluntary police force in which workers and students receive basic training in law enforcement. The voluntary force was created in 1980 as a supplement to the regular police forces and to develop civic awareness. Volunteers are on duty 24 hours every day of the week and they may arrest suspects and control traffic even in the most heavily populated districts. However, they almost exclusively serve in areas that the regular police (for lack of resources) cannot attend to.

The establishment of a voluntary police force is an important political accomplishment, for the volunteers constitute a significant instance of citizens dedicating themselves to the task of overcoming the corruption that characterized the police force under Somoza. A 50 percent drop in reported crimes between 1982 and 1983 stands as a testimony to their effectiveness.

In general, Nicaraguan youths participate more actively in the nation's defense than any other segment of the population. About 30,000 (54% men, 46% women) belong to the 19 July Sandinista Youth. Of these 30,000, 53 percent take active part in the regular army, militias, army reserves, and defense committees, among other organizations.[75]

The Militarization of the Economy

Nicaragua's defense minister, Humberto Ortega, has characterized the Reagan administration's military, political, diplomatic, and economic hostility as a "multiple-siege" strategy. Most of the Nicaraguan and the international media have concentrated on the military aspects of U.S. aggression. But U.S. economic aggression is no less important. This is especially true if one adds to the United States' efforts to destabilize the Nicaraguan economy the effects of the international economic crisis. The latter has depressed the world prices of the commodities that Nicaragua depends on for foreign exchange (coffee, cotton, sugar cane, and cattle products), with the consequent negative effect on its trade balance. Nicaragua has in effect maintained a large deficit in its balance of payments since 1980.[76] But Nicaragua's balance of payments deficit is not only due to U.S. aggression and international economic crisis; it is also affected by decapitalization and the general destruction of Nicaragua's economic infrastructure that occurred during the war for national liberation.

The Nicaraguan economy grew significantly during the first two years of revolutionary government.[77] Beginning in 1982, however, the rate of GDP growth began to slow down and soon registered a net decrease. Nicaragua's economic decline was the direct consequence of a failing international economy and stepped-up U.S. hostilities, which led to the closure of important sources of international finance. In 1983, for example, Nicaragua did not receive loans that it sought from the World Bank, the Special Operations Fund of the Inter-American Development Bank, and official sources of U.S. financial aid.[78] Moreover, in May 1985, the Reagan administration decreed a commercial embargo against Nicaragua, which by the end of 1985 had cost it U.S.$50 million in foreign exchange, and severely affected Nicaragua's supply of raw materials, replacement parts, and accessories for its largely U.S.-made industrial infrastructure.

The war has forced the Nicaraguan government to increase its defense spending and cut back funding to stimulate economic growth. As a percentage of total government spending, state investment in economic infrastructure and production fell from 34 percent in 1983 to 16.3 percent in 1985. Meanwhile, expenditures for defense and public order during the same period soared from 18 percent to 38 percent.[79] Redoubled U.S. efforts to topple the Sandinistas in 1986 have led observers to estimate that the Nicaraguan government will be forced to dedicate fully half of its budget to security-related items, thus bleeding the treasury dry of funds earmarked for economic development and social welfare.

Nicaragua's 1985 "defense economy" budget gave priority to the war zones in the provision of social services, infrastructure construction, and the supply of utilities. It also characterized the Pacific zone as a rear guard area. This meant that the government "[would] not build new schools, hospitals, housing, streets, electricity, or water networks" in that region.[80]

War damage to the Nicaraguan economy increased sharply after 1981, when it totalled U.S.$2.7 million. In 1982 that figure jumped to U.S.$9 million, and then skyrocketed to U.S.$102 million in 1983. War-related economic losses added up to U.S.$171.4 million in 1984.[81]

Observers have also predicted a number of medium-term effects as a consequence of the unrelenting aggression that afflicts Nicaragua. The most important of these is the war's negative impact on Nicaragua's human capital formation. In 1985, fully 20 percent of the labor force—about 50,000 persons—dedicated themselves to the nation's defense. This meant that these people (adults as well as the young) were forced to interrupt their education and acquisition of job-related skills. According to Managua, "the explicit goal of [U.S.] aggression is to wear down the economy and to undermine the social bases of the revolution."[82] As a result, Nicaragua has developed a security doctrine rooted in a conception of total war, where virtually all of the country's economic, political, human, and cultural resources are dedicated to the nation's defense.

Nicaragua and the Regional Military Balance

The Reagan administration has used Nicaragua's rapid build-up in defense capabilities to justify its support for the contras, military maneuvers in Honduras, and military and economic aggression against Nicaragua. The United States argues that Nicaragua has upset the regional military balance of power, and thus poses a threat to the security of Honduras, El Salvador, and Costa Rica. However, the United States is largely responsible for upsetting the regional balance of power. As part of a general strategy of Communist containment, the Reagan administration created an entire army, the contras, and introduced its own troops in the region, principally in Honduras.[83] Observers estimate that between 1981 and 1985 approximately 90,000 U.S. soldiers have participated in military training exercises in Honduras. Moreover, the United States has about 1,000 men on permanent duty in that country who are assigned to various U.S. military installations.[84] Without a doubt, these troops possess the most sophisticated equipment and the greatest firepower of any in the region.[85]

The best way to compare Nicaragua's military capabilities with those of its neighbors is to look at the strength of their respective armies and air forces. The navy is not really relevant because it has not experienced significant qualitative or quantitative changes in any of these countries.[86] By contrast, the air force has experienced changes and because it is essentially an offensive tool it has a great impact on the regional balance of power. The countries in which the air force has grown the most are Guatemala, El Salvador, and Honduras. Of course, the United States keeps pointing out that Nicaragua has obtained 25 MI–18 and 12 MI–24 helicopter gunships (used to fight the contras).[87] These helicopters, however, cannot be considered offensive weapons, particularly since the United States has equipped the contras with modern antiaircraft armaments, such as Soviet-made SAM–7 missiles. By the same token, since El Salvador's air force is also mainly employed against guerrillas it too may be classified as a defensive force. But the same cannot be said for Honduras's air force. Table 4 provides a more detailed comparison of their respective air strength.

The United States government has also argued that the Nicaraguan army's armored divisions have given it an offensive capability. But Nicaragua's tanks (T–54 and T–55) are designed to be used as armored support units for infantry in defensive positions. They have been deployed in defensive emplacements in the interior to provide backing for the soldiers charged with defending Nicaragua from invading forces.[88] Nicaragua's artillery is also mainly defensive in character;

Table 4
Military Balance in Central America: Mechanized Warfare Capabilities, 1980 and 1985

	GUATEMALA		HONDURAS		EL SALVADOR		NICARAGUA	
	1980	1985	1980	1985	1980	1985	1980	1985
Tanks	--	33	--	17	12	25	2	63
Armored carriers	15	--	--	27	--	18	45	20
Trop carriers	--	--	--	--	20	30	3	80
Armed carriers	26	38	--	15	--	--	--	32
Artillery pieces	36	84	24	54	30	50	24	144
Combat aircraft	10	16	24	38	17	36	--	--
Attack helicopters	8	29	3	15	2	19	1	--
Reconnaissance airplanes	7	--	--	--	8	4	--	--
Counterinsurgency airplanes	10	16	6	14	17	32	3	12
Transport airplanes	19	22	11	23	19	14	4	6
Counterinsurgency helicopters	--	--	--	--	3	25	--	6
Training airplanes	9	42	38	19	3	25	1	--

Source: International Institute for Strategic Studies, Military Balance 1980-1981 and Military Balance 1984-1985 (London: IISS, 1980 and 1985). For 1985 figures we also drew on, NARMIC, La Guerra en Centroamérica. Guía a la Escalación Militar de los Estados Unidos (USA: American Friends Service Committee, 1983); and Caribbean Basin Information Project, On a Short Fuse: Militarization in Central America (San Francisco: n.p., 1985).

most of the guns are antiaircraft. Nicaragua has invested heavily in this type of weapon in order to defend against aerial bombardment and deter the landing of airborne troops.

The United States' Central American allies have repeatedly argued that Nicaragua's rapid military build-up makes it impossible for them to accept the Contadora group's proposals for a regional peace settlement.[89] True, Nicaragua has the largest military establishment, but it is not that much larger than that of El Salvador or Guatemala (see Table 5). Moreover, the size of Nicaragua's army is influenced by the magnitude of the threat posed by the counterrevolutionaries (which is why most of these troops are armed only with light weapons).

Any regional conflict would polarize the conflicting forces: Nicaragua on one side; and on the other, Guatemala, El Salvador, Honduras, and Costa Rica, who would count with the full support of the United States. A quick glance at Table 4 shows that even though Nicaragua has the largest army in Central America, in the event of a regional conflict it would be outgunned. That is why Nicaragua argues that prior to sealing any peace treaty the countries involved in the conflict

Table 5
Military Balance in Central America: Troop Strength in 1977, 1980, 1985

	1977	1980	1985	% increase 1977 - 85
Guatemala	14,300	14,900	51,600	360%
Nicaragua	7,100	------(c)	61,800	870%
Honduras	14,200	11,300	23,000	160%
El Salvador	7,130	7,250	51,150	717%
Costa Rica	5,000(a)	5,000(b)	19,800(d)	396%

(a) Paramilitary forces, according to Military Balance 1977-1978, p. 74.

(b) Paramilitary forces, according to Military Balance 1980-1982, p. 86.

(c) Military Balance 1980-1981 (p. 86) only notes the dissolution of the National Guard. It does not take the FSLN's armed force into account.

(d) The sum of regular troops and paramilitary forces.

Sources: International Institute for Strategic Studies, The Military Balance, 1977-1978 and The Military Balance 1980-1981 (London: IISS, 1977 and 1980). Troop strength for 1985 was calculated by the authors from Central American and U.S. official sources, and from figures provided by U.S. research institutions.

have to define what constitutes defensive versus offensive force. The Nicaraguans maintain that this is the only way to realistically assess the regional military balance of power. As a first step, the Nicaraguans propose that defensive forces should be defined as those that a country estimates it requires to defend itself against external aggression. Consequently, negotiations should turn on arriving at an agreement as to what those levels are, and then proceed to set limits and controls on the number and type of offensive forces.[90]

CONCLUSIONS

The analysis of the Cuban and Nicaraguan armed forces demonstrates that in order to understand a nation's armed forces one must also look at the history of its social formation and its position in the international state system. It simply does not suffice to limit analysis to the internal dynamics of the military, its organizational process, military ideology, arms acquisitions, or local geography. Most of these either directly or indirectly depend on socioeconomic, political, and diplomatic conditions that have their roots in the country's social processes.

Consequently, the military establishments of Cuba and Nicaragua owe their distinctive characteristics to the nature of the struggle that culminated in the formation of "people's armies" that staged mass insurrections and vanquished the regular army both militarily and politically. The regular army disbanded, as a result of its military defeat and because its political defeat led to dismemberment when the high command fled and the troops deserted. In other words, the armed forces of the new order represent the continuation of guerrilla forces that have their roots in the people. These forces replace the army that propped up the dictatorships.

The Cuban armed forces experienced significant changes in the first half of the 1980s, but those innovations did not represent a break with their previous organization and doctrine. As a result, Cuban military institutions have not shown any tendency toward autonomy or professionalization, in the sense of taking over managerial tasks usually performed by civilians. On the contrary, Cuba's defense became deconcentrated, and encouraged widespread citizen participation within the framework of a doctrine that stressed total war and scorched-earth tactics in the event of an invasion. Because this is a markedly defensive strategy that calls for the involvement of an entire population in the nation's defense, it clearly minimizes the possibility for the Cuban military's professionalization and autonomy.

A similar process took place in Nicaragua from the very beginning. Nicaragua also has a military doctrine rooted in the concept of total people's war. And, although Nicaragua's doctrine is less developed, its military organization less complex, and the general population less involved than in Cuba, it has no equal in the rest of Latin America.

It seems clear that Cuba and Nicaragua formulated their military doctrines in response to the United States' development of a new strategy for military intervention—rapid deployment combined with a saturation of the theater of operations.[91] In effect, the United States' Rapid Deployment Force, and the military doctrine that spawned it, made Cuba's old defense strategy obsolete. It has been based on the timely deployment of a well-equipped professional army in a territory that the Cubans assumed would not be saturated with enemy troops. Army reserves, territorial militias, and a noncombatant civil defense force would supplement the regular armed forces' efforts to repulse the invaders. But Cuba's new defense strategy permanently saturates any theater of operations. It forces the enemy to fight for every inch of land, thus impeding the rapid deployment of invading forces and engulfing them in a "people's war" that would cost them dearly both in terms of lives and materiel. The Nicaraguan case is similar to the Cuban. In response to contra aggression and the ever-present threat of direct intervention, the Nicaraguans also developed a defense strategy based on the concept of total war and involved large sectors of the population in the country's defense.

In light of the magnitude of the security threat that these two countries face, it seems that their defense strategies have proven highly efficacious. Both the Cubans and the Nicaraguans have deterred the United States from undertaking serious preparations for direct intervention, at least in the medium term. They have probably managed to do so because their defense strategy has made the cost of such intervention too high in terms of maintaining U.S. domestic and international support for a protracted people's war that would be very costly in lives and materiel. Nicaragua, however, unlike Cuba, has been forced to dedicate increasingly larger shares of its scarce resources to fight counterrevolutionaries. Thus, given unrelenting U.S. maneuvering to hinder the consolidation of their revolutions, it seems clear that Cuba and Nicaragua will maintain these broad-based defensive systems in order to exercise their rights of sovereignty and self-determination.

NOTES

1. See August Varas's introductory chapter in this volume, "Military Autonomy and Democracy in Latin America."

2. See Francisco López Segrera, *Cuba: Capitalismo Dependiente y Subdesarrollo, 1510–1959* (La Habana: Casa de las Américas, 1972); and Julio Le Riverand, *Historia Económica de Cuba* (La Habana: Editorial Nacional de Cuba, 1965).

3. For an elaboration of this theme, see Ernesto Che Guevera, "Proyecciones Sociales de Ejército Rebelde," vol. 1, in *Obras Completas* (Buenos Aires: Ediciones Argentinas, 1973), 266–67.

4. Lieutenant Colonel Jose Ramon Herrera Medina et al., "Estudio del Pensamiento Militar de Fidel," in *Historia Militar, El Oficial*, no. 4 (1982).

5. For details, see Ernesto Che Guevara, "Proyecciones Sociales del Ejército Rebelde," vol. 1, 266–67.

6. The beachheads at Playa Girón and Playa Larga were bombarded on April 15, 1961, in an effort to soften them up for the approximately 1,300 Cuban exiles who landed on April 17. Two days later the invaders were defeated. See First Lieutenant Marta Borrayo Morales, "Las Milicias Nacionales Revolucionarias," *El Oficial*, no. 2 (1982). (*El Oficial* is the journal of the Revolutionary Armed Forces and specializes in publishing theoretical debates and general information.)

7. Ibid., 6.

8. For details, see *Verde Olivo*, no. 6 (1979): 43.The intelligence services, under the direction of the Interior Ministry, also played an important role in the war against the counterrevolutionaries. This ministry is organized along military lines and commands elite troops. In fact, one of its units was the first military contingent that Cuba sent to Angola to defend that country against South African aggression. The Interior Ministry is also responsible for maintaining law and order, traffic control, and keeping watch over the so-called antisocials. See Fidel Castro, "Acto Conmemorativo del Décimo Aniversario de la Creación de Ministerio and del Interior, 6 de junio de 1971," in *Discursos*, vol. 1 (La Habana: Editorial Ciencias Sociales, Instituto Cubano del Libro, 1976), 162–63.

9. For details, see "Ley no. 1129, del 26 de noviembre de 1963. Defensa Nacional. Ley de Servicio Militar Obligatorio," in *Leyes del Gobierno Revolucionario de Cuba* (La Habana: Editorial Finanzas al Dia, 1963). Article 11 states that the reserves will join active-duty forces depending on need.

10. For more details, see "Resumen del Segundo Congreso del Partido," December 17–20, 1980, in *Juventud Rebelde*, special issue (December 1984).

11. A quick look at the numbers reveals that Cuba's defense spending rises and falls

according to the perceived severity of threat that the United States poses. During the 1960s the highest budgets occurred during the Cuban Missile Crisis; during the 1970s they declined significantly and then increased sharply when the Reagan administration took office, after which the Cubans formed the Territorial Militias.

12. From "Convocatoria para ser Oficial de las Fuerzas Armadas Revolucionarias," *Granma*, 5 October 1984: 2. Cuba restructured its ranking system in 1973 and 1976 to bring it into conformity with those of the rest of the world. In 1976 Fidel Castro was nominated commander in chief of the Revolutionary Armed Forces. That same year, Raúl Castro became a general in the RAF; he also holds the position of minister of the RAF. The designation commander in chief dies with Castro and in its place, the armed forces will be headed by the commander of the army (*General de Cuerpo de Ejército*). Naturally this post is vacant for the time being. From there, in descending order of rank, the command structure is as follows: a División General heads each one of Cuba's three armies (these armies defend the oriental, central, and western sections of the island); after these come the ranks of Brigadier General, Colonel, Lieutenant Colonel, Major, Captain, First Lieutenant, Lieutenant, Second Lieutenant, Sergeant Major, 1st, 2nd, and 3rd Sergeant, and Soldier. A military career spans 25 years of service. Promotions take the following course: soldiers are promoted to various grades of noncommissioned officer every six months. Sergeant majors may apply for the rank of second lieutenant after one year. Second lieutenants may be promoted to lieutenant after two years, and from there to first lieutenant takes at least another three years. Promotion for each grade between first lieutenant and lieutenant colonel takes four years, and after that advancement depends on the will of the high command.

13. For more details, see "Declaración del Comité Central del Partido Comunista de Cuba ante la Nueva Amenaza de Agresión Imperialista, 17 de mayo de 1967," *Política Internacional*, no. 18 (1967): 242–43. This journal is published by the Instituto de Política Internacional del Ministerio de Relaciones Exteriores, La Habana.

14. See "Discurso del Comandante Raúl Castro en el Acto de Graduación de la Escuela Básica Superior General Máximo Gómez, 22 de julio de 1967," *El Oreintador Revolucionario*, no. 17 (1967): 301. As far as Cuba's support for Latin American revolutionary movements was concerned, Fidel and Raúl Castro believed that they might succeed in four countries: Guatemala, Colombia, Venezuela, and Bolivia. See "Discurso del Comandante Fidel Castro en la Velada Commemorativa de la Derrota del Imperialismo Yanqui en Playa Giron, 19 de abril de 1967," *Política Internacional*, no. 18 (1967): 186.

15. See Gino Lofredo, "Las Relaciones Cuba–Estados Unidos, 1968–1980. De Nixon a Carter," *El Día* (Mexico), 14 February 1985. Wayne Smith originated this thesis that Lofredo advanced in "Dateline Havana: Myopic Diplomacy," *Foreign Policy*.

16. See Alberto Miguez, "Les Cubains en Afrique: Mercenaires ou Missionaires?" *Politique Internationale*, no. 25 (1984): 101. For a negotiated withdrawal from Angola, see "Carta de José Eduardo Dos Santos, President de Angola, al Secretario General de la ONU, Pérez de Cuellar," *Granma*, 2 (December 1984).

17. *The Washington Post*, 6 October 1984.

18. Domínguez, *Cuba, Order and Revolution*, 347. Domínguez got his data from speeches delivered by Fidel and Raúl Castro.

19. Ibid., 348–49.

20. The International Institute for Strategic Studies, *The Military Balance 1981–1982* (London: IISS, 1981), 96; and *The Military Balance 1984–1985* (London: IISS, 1984), 119–120.

21. Domínguez, *Cuba, Order and Revolution*, 349.

22. U.S. Defense Department–CIA, *La Fuerzas Armadas Cubanas y la Presencia Militar Soviética*, n.d., 7.

23. *Miami Herald*, 29 April 1984.

24. David Thomas, "Cuba's Military Machine," *Miami Herald*, 29 April 1984.

25. Ibid.

26. *Latin America Weekly Report*, 16 March 1984.

27. "New Weapons from Soviets Bolster Cuba," *Miami Herald*, 27 January 1984.

28. Marta Harnecker, *Cuba ¿Dictadura o Democracia?* (Mexico: Siglo XXI, 1984), 236.

29. Fidel Castro, "Informe Central al Tercer Congreso del Partido Comunista de Cuba," *Bohemia* 78, no. 7 (1986); and "Proyecto de Programa del Partido Comunista de Cuba," *Bohemia* 78, nos. 20–21 (1986).

30. People's Power consists of three basic organizations: the Municipal Assemblies of People's Power, the Provincial Assemblies of People's Power, and the National Assembly of People's Power. Both the Council of State and the Council of Ministers give an accounting of their activities to the National Assembly. However, the Council of State represents the Cuban state and has the power to remove ministers from their posts. When the National Assembly is in recess, or if it cannot meet in a timely and secure manner, the Council of State assumes the power to decree general mobilization, declare war, and sign treaties. For details on this subject, see Asamblea Nacional del Poder Popular, *Organos del Poder Popular* (La Habana: Unión de Empresas de Medios de Propaganda, DOR del CC del PCC, 1979): 37–38. For a breakdown of the formal powers of the People's Assembly, see "Reglamento de la Asamblea Nacional del Poder Popular," *Gaceta Oficial de la República de Cuba*, 20 July 1977. Section 5 of this document does the same for the Council of State.

31. Captain José Martinez Colón, "La Evacuación de la Población Civil," *El Oficial*, no. 4 (1982): 90.

32. For a characterization of civil defense see, "Reglamento de los Organos Locales de Dirección Militar," *Gaceta Oficial de la República de Cuba*, 25 November 1977. For defense subjects in school curricula, see "Código de la Niñez y la Juventud," *Gaceta Oficial de la República de Cuba*, 30 June 1978, 241; and "Decreto no. 24 del Consejo de Ministros," *Gaceta Oficial de la República de Cuba*, 14 July 1978.

33. "Decreto no. 37 del Consejo de Ministros," *Gaceta Oficial de la República de Cuba*, 21 December 1978.

34. "Entrevista a Fidel Castro Realizada por Periodistas de *The Washington Post*," *El Día* (Mexico) 11 March 1985, 12.

35. "Discurso Pronunciado por el Comandante en Jefe Fidel Castro Ruz, Primer Secretario del Comité Central del Partido Comunista de Cuba y Presidente del Consejo de Estado y del Consejo de Ministros de la República de Cuba, en el Acto Conmemorativo del Primero de Mayo efectuado en la Plaza de la Revolución José Martí el Primero de Mayo de 1980," *Juventud Rebelde*, 4 May 1980; and *Manual Básico del Miliciano de Tropas Territoriales* (La Habana: Editorial ORBE, 1981, especially 7.) This manual introduces the militiaman and woman to a wide range of military, political, and economic defensive tactics, from bombardment to the use of chemical weapons in the conduct of guerrilla warfare should the island suffer a partial occupation. The manual also specifies how the militia should be deployed (deconcentration) as well as the order of rank:

Militiaman, Militiaman first class, first-, second-, and third-class Sergeants, Sergeant Major, Second Lieutenant, Lieutenant, First Lieutenant, Captain, Major, and Colonel.

36. Fidel Castro, "Esta Tiene que ser la Guerra Económica de Todo el Pueblo," *Granma*, 5 January 1985. Also see *Manual Básico*, 9.

37. IISS, *The Military: Balance 1984–1985*; and "Resumen del Segundo Congreso del Partido efectuado del 17 an 20 de diciembre de 1980 en el Palacio de Convenciones, el Teatro Karl Marx y la Plaza de la Revolución," *Juventud Rebelde*, special issue, December 1980.

38. Fidel Castro, "Discurso con motivo del XXVI Aniversario del Desembarco del Granma y de la Fundación de las FAR, 11 de diciembre de 1982," *Granma*, 13 December 1982.

39. Manuel Somoza, "Cuba. Defensa. Tarea de Todos," *Prisma Latinoamericano* 10, no. 146 (1984).

40. "Todo lo que hacemos es para evitar le guerra," *Verde Olivo*, no. 15 (1984), 16.

41. Fidel Castro, *Granma*, 13 December 1982.

42. Tenth Plenum of the Central Committee of the Cuban Communist Party, "Acerca del Trabajo Político Ideológico para la defensa del País," *Granma*, 4 February 1985.

43. ANSA cable, 16 November 1983.

44. *Latin American Weekly Report*, 6 July 1984, 6–7.

45. Editorial, *Granma*, 24 May 1983.

46. IISS, *The Military Balance 1984–1985*, 120. This source cites the following international troop deployments for Cuba: 19,000 in Angola; 750 in the Congo; 3,000 in Ethiopia; 750 in Mozambique; 2,000 in Iran; 3,000 in Libya; 300 in South Yemen; 3,000 in Nicaragua; 500 in Afghanistan; and another 500 in various African countries. But these figures are not entirely reliable. For example, in 1983 Cuba insisted that it only had 200 advisors in Nicaragua; see Fidel Castro, "Conversación de Fidel Castro con Periodistas Estadounidenses," *El Día* (Mexico), 25 August 1983. In the first half of 1986, on the eve of a breakthrough in the *Contadora* negotiations, Carlos Rafael Rodríguez, vice president of the Council of State, said that the Cuban military mission in Nicaragua had 800 soldiers; see *La Jornada* (Mexico), 24 May 1986.

47. The best works on this subject include Roger Fontaine, Cleto di Giovanni, and Alexander Kruger, "Castro's Specter," *The Washington Quarterly* 3, no. 4 (1980); Carmelo Meza-Lago and June S. Belken, eds., *Cuba in Africa* (Pittsburgh: Center for Latin American Studies, University of Pittsburgh, 1982); Informe del Comité de Santa Fe, "Las Relaciones Inter-Americanas: Escudo de Seguridad del Nuevo Mundo y Espana de la Proyección del Poder Global de Estados Unidos," *Cuadernos Semestrales*, no. 9, CIDE, (México); and Mark Falcoff, "Thinking about Cuba," *The Washington Quarterly*, no. 2 (1983).

48. Admiral Wesley McDonald, U.S. Commander in Chief, Atlantic, "Atlantic Security—the Cuban Factor," *Jane's Defence Weekly*, 22 December 1984.

49. See Marta Harnecker's interview with Humberto Ortega in "Augusto C. Sandino, Carlos Fonseca, FSLN," in *Nicaragua: La Estrategia de la Victoria* (México: Nuestro Tiempo, 1980), 11–57.

50. From the outset, in 1961, the FSLN argued that armed struggle was the only path capable of toppling the dictatorship and initiating the Nicaraguan revolution. See Carlos Fonseca, *Bajo la Bandera del Sandinismo—Textos Políticos* (Managua: Editorial Nueva Nicaragua, 1981), especially 209. The idea of staging a mass armed insurrection began to take shape in 1975–76, when the FSLN split into three tendencies—Proletarian FSLN,

People's War FSLN and Third Line or Insurrectional FSLN. Armed struggle became the dominant form of resistance to the dictatorship between 1978 and 1979, in the wake of the insurrectional experience of the Indian neighborhood of Monimbo Masaya in February 1978 and the general uprising of September 1978.

51. During the final offensive the FSLN organized seven fronts: the *Carlos Fonseca Northern Front*, which conducted operations in the departments of Nueva Segovia, Madriz, Esteli, Jinotega, and Matagalpa; the *Rigoberto López Pérez Western Front*, with operations in Chinandego and Leon; the *Camilo Ortega Saavedra Central Front*, with operations in Managua, Masaya, Carazo, and Granada; the *Benjamín Zeledon Southern Front*, with operations in Rivas; the *New Guinea Front*, which never really got started because the FSLN unit that was charged with opening a front in the southeastern department of Zelaya and from there linking up with the Camilo Ortega Front to the west was decimated by the National Guard; the *Roberto Huembes Eastern Front*, with operations in central Zelaya; and the *Pablo Ubeda North Eastern Front*, with operations in northern Zelaya.

52. Lucrecia Lozano, *De Sandino al Triunfo de la Revolución* (Mexico: Siglo XXI, 1985), 243.

53. The first governmental junta was composed of: Daniel Ortega, a member of the FSLN's National Directorate; Moises Hassan, a leader of the United People's Movement and of the National Patriotic Front; Alfonso Robelo, president of the Nicaraguan Democratic Movement and a leader of the Opposition Broad Front; Sergio Ramirez, a member of the Group of Twelve; and Violeta Barrios de Chamorro, widow of Pedro Joaquín Chamorro, one of the leaders of Democratic Union for Liberation and president of *La Prensa*. (He was assassinated by the dictatorship on January 10, 1978.)

54. The creation of the Patriotic Revolutionary Front (PRF) in July 1980 had its origins in a number of factors. These included the need to set up a political base that would permit the consolidation of the revolution, and the need to maintain the national unity that had materialized during the struggle to overthrow the dictatorship (expressed in the National Patriotic Front) and to adapt it to new circumstances. The PRF backed the revolutionary government's policies and counted with the participation of the FSLN, the Popular Social-Christian Party, the Nicaraguan Socialist Part, and the Liberal Independent Party. The latter withdrew from the alliance in 1984.

55. Programa de Gobierno de Reconstrucción Nacional, *Cuadernos de Marcha* 1, no. 5 (1980): 107–16.

56. Ibid., 110.

57. Ibid., 109.

58. Alfonso Robelo and Violeta de Chamorro left the governing junta in April 1980 due to irreconcilable policy disagreements. They were replaced by Rafael Cordova and Arturo Cruz, who were members of the Democratic Conservative Party. Cruz left the government in 1981.

59. All of Nicaragua's political and social forces have the right to representation in the Council of State. In 1984, 52 delegates of 31 political, mass, business, and labor organizations represented a broad spectrum of Nicaraguan society. In the course of five legislative periods (one per year), the Council of State has labored to pass laws designed to create a legal framework for the Sandinista revolution—that is, in line with interests of the people, and in accord with the profound political, economic, social, and cultural transformations that Nicaragua has experienced. So far, the Council of State has passed 319 laws. Of these, the governing junta initiated 151 and the Council of State initiated

168. Moreover, 109 are of a political nature, 65 administrative, 56 social, 36 economic, 34 cultural, 10 judicial, and 9 are military in character. See Lucrecia Lozano, *De Sandino al Triunfo de la Revolución*, 302.

60. *Region 1* consists of the northern departments of Esteli, Madrid, and Nueva Segovia, with 21 municipalities and an estimated population of 290,000 people (1984). The capital is Estili. *Region 2* consists of the western-Pacific departments of Leon and Chinandega, with 490,000 inhabitants and 23 municipalities. The capital is Leon. *Region 3* consists of Managua. *Region 4* includes the eastern-Pacific departments of Granada, Masaya, Carazo, and Rivas, with 31 municipalities and a population of 480,000 people. The capital is Granada. *Region 5* includes the central departments of Boaco and Chontales, with 260,000 people and 19 municipalities. The capital is Boaco. *Region 6* consists of the northern-central departments of Jinotega and Matagalpa, with 15 municipalities and 360,000 inhabitants. The capital is Matagalpa. *Special Zone 1* consists of Northern Zelaya (also known as the Atlantic Coast), with six municipalities and 80,000 inhabitants. The capital is Ciudad Rosita. *Special Zone 2* includes Southern Zelaya, with 3 municipalities and 60,000 inhabitants. The capital is Bluefields. *Special Zone 3* consists of the department of Rio San Juan on the border with Costa Rica. It has 30,000 inhabitants and its capital is San Carlos.

61. Lozano, *De Sandino al Triunfo de la Revolución*, 293.

62. For an analysis of the Nicaraguan labor movement, see Lozaro, *De Sandino al Triunfo de la Revolución*, 297–300.

63. Estatuto Fundamental de la República, *1979–1984. Principales Leyes Aprobados por el Gobierno de Reconstrucción Nacional* (Managua: Consejo de Estado, 1984).

64. FSLN, Departmento de Propagando y Educación Política, "El Ejército Popular Sandinista y la Participación de las Masas en la Defensa de la Soberanía," (Managua, 1984, Mimeographed) especially 8–10.

65. Humberto Ortega, "El Carácter Defensivo del Ejército Popular Sandinista," *Excelsior* (Mexico), 12 and 13 April 1985.

66. "Propuesta Oficial de Nicaragua para el Proceso de Negociación de Contadora," *El Día* (Mexico), 18 May 1986.

67. The government decreed a state of emergency on May 15, 1982. Since then, the decree has been ratified and modified according to the nation's security needs. For example, in July and August of 1984, in order to ensure open and fair elections, the government reinstated the rights of free association, movement, and expression, as well as the right to strike and to seek asylum; however, it continued to censure information regarding security and military affairs. On October 15, 1985, stepped up contra attacks forced the government to once again suspend those rights.

68. FSLN, Departmento de Propaganda y Educación Política, *El EPS y la Participación de las Masas en la Defensa de la Soberanía*, 24.

69, Council of Hemispheric Affairs, *An Analysis and Critical Evaluation of Administrative Claims* (Washington, D.C., n.p., 1985); and IISS, *The Military Balance 1984–1985*.

70. Ibid.

71. "Ley del Servicio Militar Patriótico," decree no. 1,327, of October 6, 1983, issued by the Junta de Gobierno de Reconstrucción Nacional, in *1979–1984. Principales Leyes Aprobadas por el Gobierno de Reconstrucción Nacional*, 97–115.

72. Centro de Investigaciones y Estudios de la Reforma Agraria, *La Democracia Participativa en Nicaragua* (Managua: CIERA, n.d.), 52–53.

73. Ibid., 55–57; Lozano, *De Sandino al Triunfo de la Revolución*, 207–11; and Carlos Vilas, *Perfiles de la Revolución Sandinista* (La Habana: Casa de las Américas, 1984), 169–89.

74. CIERA, 72.

75. Ibid., 71–72.

76. See statements of Defense Minister Humberto Ortega in *Barricada* (Managua), 15 and 16 May 1986.

77. GDP growth rates for 1980 and 1981 were 10 percent and 8.5 percent, respectively.

78. International loans to Nicaragua totalled U.S. $682 million in 1981 and dropped to U.S.$270 million in 1982. See CEPAL, *Notas para el Estudio Económico de América Latina: Nicaragua* (Mexico: CEPAL-Mex, 1981–1985).

79. CEPAL, *Notas para el Estudio de América Latina y El Caribe, 1985* (Mexico: CEPAL-Mex, 1986).

80. Infopress Centroamericana, "Efectos Económicos de la Guerra en Nicaragua," *Informa Especial*, no. 681 (1986).

81. Gobierno de Nicaragua, *La Derrota de la Contrarevolución* (Managua: 1984).

82. Ibid.

83. The idea of Communist containment in Central America, which implies action against Nicaragua, is clearly articulated in the Kissinger Report, especially chapter 6, which is on security. See *Comisión Kissinger, Informe de la Comisión Bipartista sobre Centroamérica* (Mexico: Editorial Diana, 1984).

84. Since January 1983 the United States has maintained a permanent mission of over 1,000 men in Honduras. The troops on maneuvers have oscillated between a low of 800 in March–April 1984 and a high of 5,500 in August–December 1983. The permanent mission consisted of about 100 men in 1980–1982, 346 in 1983, and 2,000 in 1984. Most of these men are stationed at the U.S. Headquarters in Palmerola. For more details, see Council of Hemispheric Affairs, *The Military Balance in Central America*.

85. "Extractos de las Declaraciones del Comandante Humberto Ortega, Ministro de Defensa, a la Prensa Nacional y Extranjera," *Barricada*, 15 May 1986.

86. Between 1981 and 1985 only Guatemala increased the number of its assault vehicles. It purchased twelve. Meanwhile Honduras increased the number of its patrol boats from five to nine, while Nicaragua acquired four more patrol boats, bringing its total up to 14. See IISS, *The Military Balance, 1980–1981* and *The Military Balance, 1984–1985*.

87. *The Los Angeles Times*, 26 June 1986.

88. Humberto Ortega, "El Carácter Defensivo del Ejército Popular Sandinista."

89. "Texto Integro de la Versión Definitiva del Acta de Paz. Evitar la Guerra, lo logrado por Contadora," *Excelsior* (Mexico), 9 June 1986.

90. "Propuesta Oficial de Nicaragua para el Proceso de Negociación de Contadora," *El Día* (Mexico), 18 May 1986.

91. See Lilia Bermudez and Antonio Cavalla, *Estrategia de Reagan hacia la Revolución Centroamericana* (México: Editorial Nuestro Tiempo, 1982); and Antonio Cavalla and Ricardo Córdova, "Las Fuerzas de Despliegue Rápido: ¿Nueva Guerra de los EE.UU. en el Tercer Mundo?" *Andes*, no. 2 (1985): 89–107.

10 THE DEVELOPMENT OF MILITARY AUTONOMY AND CORPORATENESS IN CENTRAL AMERICA

Gabriel Aguilera

This chapter uses a conjunctural approach to analyze the armed forces of Costa Rica, El Salvador, Guatemala, and Honduras. It outlines their major characteristics, examines their relationship to society, and inquires into their role in the Central American crisis. While focussing on a five-year period that begins in 1979 and ends in 1983, brief synopses of the political history of these countries provide a framework within which to understand the present functions of their military and security forces. Each country case looks at the forces of order from three angles: their relationship to the state; their performance in the military, social, and economic arenas; and their international connections.

GUATEMALA

Background

General Jorge Ubico, the last of the traditional oligarchic dictators, fell in 1944. Army officers of middle rank played an important role in his downfall. The decade that followed, known as the "October Revolution," witnessed a vigorous attempt to reform and democratize Guatemalan society. For the most part, the military, which came to be known as the army of the revolution, supported the changes. Once again, army officers played important roles in Guatemalan politics, but this time they supported progressive policies. The army continued to professionalize by forcing officers who had not attended the military academy to retire. The military also democratized the command structure by creating the Superior Council—an elected collegiate body. Survey studies conducted during this period revealed that most officers had middle-class backgrounds, which partially explains their support for the social and political forces that directed the "October Revolution." In any case, most military writings of the time had a populist flavor to them. This so-called revolutionary period ended with the invasion of a U.S.-sponsored expeditionary army in 1954.

After the fall of Arbenz, efforts to professionalize the Guatemalan army intensified under the guidance of U.S. advisers, who brought with them a polarized vision of the world and disseminated their anticommunist discourse among Guatemalan military men. But not all of them accepted the new doctrine. Resistance was especially strong among officers who still held populist views. This friction led 40 percent of the officer corps to rebel against the dominant faction in the military on November 13, 1960.

In 1961, the Guatemalan political regime took on a closed, authoritarian character. This authoritarian regime evolved gradually in a process that was full of contradictions, and it influenced the rise of armed people's movements.[1] The emergence of the guerrilla war had important consequences for the subsequent development of the armed forces. In 1963, heightened social struggle and insurgency, coupled with the constitutional government's inability to curb them, led to a coup d'etat staged by the military qua institution. The former defense minister became the new head of state.

Although the military stayed in office for only three years, in that time they restructured Guatemalan politics, thus demonstrating that they had achieved a high degree of autonomy. They had won more than their autonomy, however; the armed forces had also gained hegemony over other state institutions. For example, in 1966 the military high command forced the new civilian president to sign a secret agreement with them before they allowed him to take office.[2]

During the second half of the 1960s the guerrilla war and the use of modern counterinsurgency tactics, including the systematic application of state terror, had a twofold effect on the Guatemalan military.[3] On the one hand, the armed forces became experienced at fighting a protracted internal war. On the other, they developed policies that routinely violated human rights.

An increase in the autonomy and corporateness of the Guatemalan military during the 1970s was another consequence of the guerrilla war. For example, after 1970 all Guatemalan presidents were high-ranking military officers, many of whom followed the same career path: from chief of staff, to defense minister, to president of the republic.[4] Starting with the presidency of General Carlos Arana Osorio, the tendency for high-ranking officers to establish lucrative businesses and thus become members of the dominant class has accelerated. This trend holds true for high-ranking officers, although the most recent survey (1972) shows that most officers were still middle-class.

The most salient characteristic of the regime established in 1970 was its lack of legitimacy, the legacy of systematic electoral fraud, and repression of social demands. Toward the end of the 1970s, the relative success of the guerrillas weakened the political system. The guerrillas had become strong, in part, because the government's repression of social groups demanding democratization and social change left people with no other recourse for action. In March 1982, a military coup d'etat overthrew the government of General Romeo Lucas García. The new government initiated a series of reforms that culminated in the elections of 1984 and 1985. These elections were free and clean, and they ushered in a civilian government that enjoyed a high degree of legitimacy. Nevertheless, the guerrilla war makes it highly likely that the military will continue to play an important role in Guatemalan politics.

Guatemala's Military Institutions

Unlike their counterparts in the region, the Guatemalan armed forces have been fighting a guerrilla war for the last 20 years. It waxes and wanes, but its uninterrupted character has deeply affected the military's structure, ideology, and relationship to society.

Guatemala's troop strength stands at about 40,000 men. This figure seems low, given that the military has both an external and an internal function. But the Guatemalan armed forces themselves are largely responsible for their slow expansion; although Guatemala has a universal conscription law, usually only peasants are inducted.

The Guatemalan military's structure, tactics, and weaponry reflect the needs of counterinsurgency combat. Of the three branches of the armed forces, the army and the air force are the most important. The navy, the youngest branch of the service, is the least developed, with only coast guard units. In the army, which has bases throughout the country, the infantry has pride of place. Armored units are relatively weak, because they are not very useful for guerrilla warfare. They mostly consist of armored personnel carriers, but they also have a few light tanks, some of which are obsolete. Although artillery is more useful than armor, the army does not have very many batteries.

The air force is also large, and is geared toward conducting guerrilla warfare. Its fighters are either subsonic jets or turboprop airplanes. Paradoxically, the air force does not have many helicopters. That is largely due to a U.S. military embargo imposed by the Carter administration, and to the fact that Guatemala does not have the resources to purchase many of them in international arms markets.

With respect to the quality of the troops, their morale, combat spirit, unity, and combat effectiveness is high. Many of the officers have combat experience, and its elite forces, the airborne units and the *kaibiles*–jungle warfare experts— are considered to be the best in the region. The army also has a solid base of experienced noncommissioned officers. Many of them are enlisted men, and therefore are professional soldiers.

The Guatemalan military's counterinsurgency strategy draws on direct field experience and borrows from international experience, especially that of the Israeli-Palestinian conflict. Guatemalan military strategy emphasizes measures designed to punish and control the civlian population that supports the guerrillas. It also prescribes taking action at the political, economic, and ideological level.

The Guatemalan Military and Their Relationship to Society

Since the October Revolution, high-ranking Guatemalan officers have exhibited a tendency to acquire ownership of the means of production. During the 1950s and 1960s this usually meant that they bought modest coffee and cotton farms. Upon retirement, some officers became small- and medium-sized merchants. During the 1970s civil–military interest groups took advantage of their control of the state to become large property owners in the agro-industrial and agricultural sectors. They did not, however, make deep inroads in the financial and industrial sectors.[5]

This relationship between the military and the dominant civilian elite applies only to high-ranking officers, mostly middle-aged generals. Institutionally, the Guatemalan armed forces maintain a high degree of internal social cohesion and differentiation with respect to civil society. This is largely due to the officer's socialization experience. Officers usually begin their careers during adolescence by enrolling in a military academy to complete their secondary education. After that, they attend the Politechnic, receiving a second lieutentant's commission upon graduation. At this point the soldier has two options. He may continue in active duty, in which case he will most likely be posted in the provinces, see action, and receive special services training. Promotions follow higher education studies at the Center for Military Studies. The most able, or those who play their politics right, reach the rank of general, which gives them the opportunity to attain political and economic power. Others retire after 25 or 30 years of service with the rank of colonel.

Politechnic school graduates, however, may also attend the university on an army scholarship, where they usually train for a technical profession. The young officers retain their rank and receive all promotions due to them while at the university. Once graduated they go into their chosen professions. But they are committed to taking a military refresher course once a year, and so maintain both a military and a civilian existence. During their careers, these men may occupy important positions in public administration or in institutions that are closely linked to the military. Some of them even become powerful politicians.

Officers tend to socialize among themselves. Consequently, in many marriages both partners come from military families. They have their own housing developments, clubs, leisure centers, hospitals, medical insurance, grocery stores, and specialty shops. Although officers do not mix frequently with civilians, they do come into contact with them more often as they rise in rank. (This observation, of course, does not hold for officers who have civilian careers.) By the same token, high-ranking officers (colonels and generals) have more contact with the civilian local and national elite. They frequent the same clubs, leisure centers, conferences, and the boardrooms of public and private institutions.

As a result of this socialization process, the military's mind-set tends to be somewhat unidimensional. They generally think that the role of the armed forces is to defend the nation against its enemies, namely, the "Communist" guerrillas, and see themselves as individuals guided by sentiments such as honor, sacrifice, and duty to the fatherland. Many officers, often due to their experiences in the provinces, agree that overcoming the ills of Guatemala's underdevelopment requires social change, but they want to achieve it through an authoritarian revolution from above without social upheaval. Overall, then, military thought in Guatemala loosely follows the basic principles of the Doctrine of National Security. But it is so weakly adapted to national conditions that it would be an exaggeration to speak of a Guatemalan military doctrine.

The Guatemalan Military and the Economy

Military spending as a proportion of GDP is the usual indicator by which one measures the armed forces' relationship to the economy. Unfortunately, the data for Guatemala are too spotty to draw any firm conclusions about that relationship. Official sources indicate that the appropriations for the Defense and Interior (Gobernación) Ministries amounted to 9.6 percent of GDP in 1979 and 14.6 percent of GDP in 1983. But other data suggest that expenditures for the military and security run higher than that. For example, security-related appropriations in other ministries are transferred to the Defense Ministry on a monthly basis. In addition to these factors, some of the security-related assets of ministries other than the Defense Ministry (vehicles, personnel, and so forth) are not taken into account. Unfortunately, the partial nature of the evidence makes it impossible to calculate spending in these areas.

The Guatemalan armed forces also receive income from other sources, such as their commercial, industrial, and financial enterprises. For example, the army owns a parking building in Guatemala City, the Banco del Ejército, a television station (channel 5), and factories that make military equipment. The army also has plans to build a cement factory (Guatotoya).[6] All of these businesses are administered by the Military Insurance Institute (Instituto de Previsión Militar). Current sources make it impossible to tell whether these are all the firms in which the military have an interest. The available data are also insufficient to calculate either the value of the firms we do know about or how well they are performing.

Some of the enterprises in which the army has an interest clearly have no bearing on the military's primary function—to safeguard the country's security. The fact that the armed forces are involved in nonmilitary commercial firms can only be explained as a consequence of the development of the state in relation to the political system and civil society.

The Guatemalan Military and the Political System

As I have indicated, the army is the most important and decisive political actor in Guatemala. The high command decides which forces may participate in the political system, and what the electoral system will be, and gets involved in the internal decision-making processes of political parties and candidacies for political office. Sometimes the high command makes these decisions after consulting with the rest of the officer corps. This suggests that some decisions reflect the balance of power within the army. Thus, although the army has a hierarchical command structure, upon occasion the high command seems compelled to forge a consensus around decisions that involve fundamental issues. This is particularly true when these consultations focus on the opinion of officers with troop commands.

In short, the army makes decisions with respect to long-term governmental policy and is involved in economic activities that are normally the purview of nonmilitary state or societal actors. This is a de facto situation, since the legal framework of Guatemala is supposedly based on a constitution that provides for the separation of powers and the military's subordination to the presidency. Civilian political actors, however, accept reality and behave accordingly, by limiting their actions to what they think the military will tolerate.

The constitution also stipulates the armed forces' normative guidelines, and these also reflect the military's political power, for those principles were taken from the army's own constitutive statutes. In the writing of Guatemala's constitutions (four in the last 30 years), the deputies of the constituent assemblies usually stayed within the bounds of what they knew the military would accept.

The external indicators of this situation are not always evident. The coups d'etat, the states of exception, the overthrow and substitution of constitutional government are conjunctural events that find their resolution in the emergence of a new legality. But these events do not play the same role that they do in other regions where they are the result of nationwide social struggles. For example, the coups d'etat of 1982 and 1983 were viewed as correctives to dysfunctional situations, but they never altered the fundamental bases of civil–military relations.

The intensity and form of military intervention in Guatemalan politics have varied over time. In the 1970s they resorted to systematic electoral fraud in order to assure the victory of their presidential candidates (who were all generals).[7] The military also spent an excessive amount of public funds on expanding their personnel. After the coup d'etat of the early 1980s, the army gave its highest priority to the counterinsurgency effort. This gave it a high degree of autonomy in Guatemalan politics because other political actors failed to challenge it. The armed forces also sought to implement a vast effort to reorganize society by creating a parallel system of public administration in 1982. This system, called the Inter-institutional Coordinator, was managed by the military commanders of Guatemala's provinces who had state revenue from internal and international development aid sources at their disposal.[8] The armed forces also enrolled one-seventh of the population in the so-called civilian patrols. Aside from their purely military function, the civilian patrols represented a novel form of peasant organization, especially among Indians.

The armed forces' penetration of Guatemalan social life owes much to their control of modern communications media, such as television, which enables them to broadcast military thought. Plans to open a military university may be interpreted in the same vein. The university will not be a center for advanced military studies. Its purpose is mainly to indoctrinate students in the military's conception of society. The army's various publications, released through its own publishing house (Editorial del Ejército), have much the same function.

The Guatemalan Military and Their International Connections

From the mid–1950s to the mid–1970s the Guatemalan armed forces turned to the United States for military assistance. Like other armies in Latin America, the Guatemalan military recived its arms, equipment, military doctrine, and strategies from the United States. Consequently, with the development of the guerrilla war Guatemala adopted U.S. counterinsurgency strategy and tactics. As an integral part of that strategy from the mid–1960s on, U.S. military advisers introduced the uses of terror to stifle the insurgency. But the United States' emphasis on internal war soon entered into contradiction with the long-standing desire of the Guatemalan dominant class—and of the military—to annex Belize. Guatemala's conflict with Great Britain over Belize brought the two countries to the brink of war on several occasions. Guatemala came close to invading Belize in 1976.

Guatemala's aggressive external military policy and its systematic violation of human rights led to increasing friction between it and the Carter administration. As a result, Guatemala renounced U.S. military assistance programs in 1976 and turned mainly to Israel for such help. From that date on, Israel provided Guatemala with most of its military hardware and counterinsurgency strategy, and even computerized its intelligence services. Other sources of military support included Argentina (intelligence and guerrilla warfare tactics), as well as Taiwan and South Korea (political aspects of war). Guatemala made up for whatever needs these countries would not or could not satisfy with purchases in the international arms market.

Another consequence of Guatemala's friction with the United States has been the increased self-sufficiency of its military establishment. For example, when Guatemalan soldiers could no longer train at the American School they established their own training program, the Kaibiles Commando School. The Guatemalan armed forces also built a munitions factory and an assembly plant for armored vehicles. This same situation has also given the Guatemalan state greater autonomy from the United States in dealing with the regional crisis. Nevertheless, the differences between the two countries are not as serious as they may seem at first glance. Throughout this period the United States did not cut off economic aid to Guatemala and the United States has established new ties with it. Direct U.S. military aid, however, has not been significant.

HONDURAS

Background

Honduras did not have a military academy dedicated to the training of professional officers until 1952. And even then, the Francisco Morazán Academy owed more to U.S. military assistance programs geared toward modernizing Latin American armed forces during the cold war than to any need of the Honduran state. But in the final years of the Juan Manuel Galvez adminstration (1950–1954) the U.S. military's interest in modernization coincided with a growing interest on the part of the Hondurans to modernize their state. That modernizing drive had its origins in the expansion of the Honduran capitalist economy in the post-war boom, the penetration of foreign capital in Central America, and, in the early 1960s, the formation of the Central American Common Market.

The modernization of the Honduran state also reflected changes in the country's ruling coalition. The rise of industrial social groups produced a contradiction in the traditional agrarian and commercial oligarchy. The armed forces, however, developed independently of elite social groups as these social and political changes unfolded. As a result, they quickly achieved a measure of relative autonomy that led them to stage the coups d'etat of 1963 and 1965, occasions on which civilian politicians had created power vacuums with their wrangling. These were traditional-style coups, meaning that shortly after their intervention the military convened elections and returned government to civilian forces.

In 1969, the conflicting interests of Honduras and El Salvador erupted into violence during the so-called hundred-hour war. War broke out as a result of the unequal benefits the two countries received from their participation in the Common Market, border disputes, and differences in their migration laws. The military confrontation left inconclusive results, although El Salvador managed to hang on to the disputed border territory.

The war shook the young Honduran army to its core. Honduran officers began to question their emphasis on counterinsurgency and the doctrine of national security, the result of U.S. military assistance programs which had left them ill-prepared and ill-equipped to fight a conventional war. These reflections led to a growth of nationalistic sentiment in the Honduran military and to a greater valuation of the role of the civilian population in the nation's defense.

After the war, the armed forces expanded in two directions. On the one hand, they began to prepare for a resumption of hostilities with El Salvador, which they believed was inevitable. On the other, they strengthened their autonomy from the ruling social coalition. The officer corps, observing developments in the rest of Latin America (Panama and Peru, for example) began to push for changes in their military institutions. This led to the development of a brand of military reformism in Honduras that saw the armed forces as a force for change along populist lines.

The military coup of 1972, directed by Colonel Oswaldo López Arellano and supported by middle-rank officers (lieutenant colonels), initiated a period of military reformism. The military ruled directly for several years and sought to bring about structural change in Honduran society by implementing an agrarian reform program that called for the transfer of 600,000 hectares to 120,000 families.

The Honduran military's reform project was quite similar to that of Guatemala during the 1944–1954 period. Like the Guatemalans, the Honduran armed forces proposed to democratize society. They hoped to accomplish this through the implementation of an extensive agrarian reform backed by an alliance between themselves and middle-class technocrats. Their goal was to increase the strength of the industrial bourgeoisie and to displace the traditional oligarchy and the political parties that served it. But if the conditions and the historical actors necessary to bring such a transformation about were absent in Guatemala two decades earlier, the possibility that they would emerge in the 1970s in Honduras was even more remote. The support for reformism with the military was by no means solid, and the progressive bourgeoisie on whose support reformists relied was small and possessed little autonomy from the ruling social coalition. More-over, the masses, although they enjoyed a relatively high level of organization, had by no means reached a consensus on the military's project.

Under these circumstances, the reformist project failed on two counts. First, it failed to gain sufficient momentum within the armed forces themselves. Superior officers (colonels and generals), in alliance with the oligarchy, foreign interests (the banana companies), and even some labor groups who were represented by white rural and urban trade unions, opposed the reforms. When President López Arellano and his cabinet were implicated in a U.S. brands bribery scandal (a sad commentary on the personal qualities of the professed reformists), their government was overthrown. Second, after the coup d'etat against López Arellano, subsequent military governments quietly dismantled the programs. By the time the masses realized what was happening it was too late for them to mount an effective defense.

The elections of 1981 that placed Roberto Suazo Córdova, a civilian, in the presidency, heralded a return to liberal democracy. The installation of a civilian government, however, coincided with a deepening of the Central American crisis and a U.S. administration that wanted Honduras to play a central role in its policy toward Nicaragua. The Honduran armed forces experienced an important change when General Gustavo Alvarez Martínez became commander in chief. With his South American military training, he systematized Honduras's national security doctrine, introduced repressive, authoritarian forms of action, and proved extremely pliable to U.S. interests. But the contradictions that his methods and policies produced within the armed forces led his peers to oust him in March 1985.

Honduras' Military Institutions

In terms of numbers, the Honduran armed forces are small, occupying a modest fourth place in the region, after the military establishments of Nicaragua, El Salvador, and Guatemala. But by the same token, they do not engage in active conflicts, which is one of the reasons the other countries keep their force levels so high. Instead, the growth of the Honduran military has primarily been a response to increased tensions with El Salvador and Nicaragua. Although it is true that small bands of guerrillas now operate in Honduras as well, they limit their activities to sabotage and armed propaganda. In 1983 the army easily crushed the only attempt by the guerrillas to build a real war front in Olancho. The fact that the Honduran army has deployed most of its force to secure the defense of its borders stands as a further testimony that the Hondurans mainly feel threatened by their neighbors, not internal war.

Since 1981, the United States has accelerated its training of Honduran soldiers, which has included their participation in U.S. military maneuvers. No one, however, really knows how well these troops would perform in combat. Their small, sporadic, and isolated confrontations with Salvadoran guerrillas and the Olancho incident do not offer enough data for firm conclusions. The same holds true for their elite battalions, such as the special forces trained for night and jungle fighting.

Increased U.S. military assistance has also resulted in an upgrading of the infantry's weaponry. The M–16 is now standard issue. Given the Honduran army's organization for external warfare, they have a higher ratio of armor and artillery to infantry than Guatemala does. The Hondurans have many artillery pieces and although they only have light tanks, they are all of the latest model (Scorpion).

The Honduran Air Force and Navy

Due to the peculiarities of the historical development of the Honduran armed forces, the air force is one of the oldest branches of the service. It already existed when the army began its first professionalization drive. During the short war with El Salvador in 1969, the air force acquitted itself better than any of the other branches. These factors explain why the Honduran air force has the best equipment of any in the region. Together with El Salvador, it is the only one to have supersonic jet fighters. They are neither the most modern (Super Mystere B–2), nor are they obsolete, due to Israeli reconstruction. The Hondurans have modern counterinsurgency airplanes and an adequate helicopter fleet.

The navy, by contrast, is comparatively young. Its main function is to conduct counterinsurgency maneuvers in coastal waters. For the most part, that means discovering and interdicting clandestine arms shipments in the Gulf of Fonseca. To that end, the Honduran navy is equipped with 25-foot Piranha-class and 60-foot Shark-class coast guard patrol boats.

The Honduran Military and Its Relationship to Society

Given the comparative youth of the Honduran military establishment, most of its officers are of middle-class extraction, although a few come from lower social strata. As in Guatemala, promotions bring social mobility. But high-ranking Honduran officers have not systematically become part of the country's socioeconomic elite. A few of them have amassed great wealth through corruption or drug trafficking, but these seem to be isolated cases.

Unlike in Guatemala, the socialization of officers has not given way to a process that isolates them from the rest of society. Although military academies at the secondary-school level exist, officers live among the general population, and the Honduran military is generally open to debates over the merits of competing social theories. Consequently, military thinking continues to exhibit populist and comparatively progressive traits. There seems to be a debate within the armed forces between officers who saw their ideas crystallize during the reformist era of López Arellano, and those who hold fast to the anticommunist line. The latter did not really gain ground until General Alvarez, who favored the Doctrine of National Security, became commander in chief. In keeping with that doctrine, he wanted to implement an authoritarian, repressive social project. He was also prepared to accommodate the Americans and place Honduras at the service of U.S. policy against Nicaragua. But his attempt to implement these projects was heavy-handed and artificial, and they were partially dismantled after his departure.

The Honduran Military and the Economy

Honduran military spending did not remain constant between 1980 and 1985. On the contrary, according to recent data, it grew from US$64 million in 1980 to US$116 million in 1985,[9] due to the ostensible expansion of the armed forces. For fiscal year 1984 official sources claimed that the government spent CA$54.9 million (9% of total government spending) on defense. But the daily *El Tiempo* calculated that the sum of CA$125 million, distributed in the following manner: $45 million as part of the overall budget, $50 million in U.S. military and economic aid, $17.5 million from the Communications Ministry, and $21.5 million from the executive branch. The CA$125 million represent 5.7 percent of GDP or 16 percent of total government spending.[10]

Aside from these characteristics, the Honduran military are not heavily involved in extra-military activities, which is quite unlike the situation in Guatemala. This is probably because the Honduran state is relatively less developed than the Guatemalan. However, the creation of the Bank of the Armed Forces indicates that such a process may be budding.

The Honduran Military and the Political System

Given the historically conditioned weakness of the Honduran state and dominant class, the armed forces have from their inception enjoyed a great deal of autonomy. They also retain final decision-making power in Honduran politics. The return to civilian government in 1981 has only nominally placed them in a subordinate political position. The commander in chief has the capacity to remove presidents at will. That holds true for the current commander in chief, General Walter López, as much as it did for Gustavo Alvarez.

There has always been a relationship between the armed forces and Honduras's two major political parties. In this respect, the National Party traditionally had an edge over the Liberal Party. But under the leadership of President Suazo Córdova, a member of the Liberal Party, the National Party is losing that margin. Some of the generals who occupied the presidency (Juan Albert Melgar Castro, for example) have also begun to play important roles within the political parties, but they have done so as private citizens. Institutionally, the armed forces arrive at fundamental decisions about politics through the development of an internal consensus.

The military builds consensus through a process of internal consultation within the Superior Council of the Armed Forces. This institution is similar to the Guatemalan Superior Council for National Defense that emerged during that country's reformist period. The Superior Council consists of the Honduran armed forces' high command. They are collectively responsible for deciding policy issues within the military.[11] Thus, the ouster of General Alvarez Martínez was also related to his attempt to cut back the council's jurisdiction and to reduce the number of officers who participated in it.

The Honduran Military and Their External Connections

The recent expansion of the Honduran military was mainly due to the regional crisis, and in particular, to the influence of U.S. geopolitical thinking and the role that it envisions for Honduras in the region. Accordingly, Honduras has received a massive infusion of U.S. military aid, which has reequipped, retrained, and reorganized the Honduran armed forces in order to help them prepare for an escalation of regional hostilities, especially in the event of a U.S. intervention in El Salvador or Nicaragua. U.S. military aid has taken several forms. In 1984, it allocated about $112 million for military and official security purposes.[12] Honduran troops have also participated in U.S. maneuvers since 1981. For example, 5,000 Honduran troops, about one-third of its active-duty personnel, took part in the Ahuas Tara II exercises between August 1983 and February 1984. Moreover, Honduran and Salvadoran troops began training at the Puerto

Castilla Regional Military Training Center.[13] It is difficult to calculate with any confidence how much the U.S. government has spent on the training of these soldiers.

In addition to these factors, the United States has built a military infrastructure in Honduras, including eleven military airports, a radar base, various hospitals, supply depots, roads, military bases, and antitank obstacles. The United States constructs these during the maneuvers but they are permanent structures, primarily for the use of U.S. forces in Honduras—around 2,000 men since August 1982. But after the exercise, the United States also leaves behind a significant quantity of weapons and material which are not included in the calculation of official aid. Much of this, however, is earmarked for the contras, who have their base camps in Honduras.

Nevertheless, as I have indicated, it is not at all clear whether this massive aid effort has turned the Honduran military into a more effective fighting machine. It seems that the contradictions within the Honduran armed forces have sharpened for reasons that are related to U.S. military assistance programs in Honduras. They have had their current geopolitical role thrust upon them, and they have to suffer the presence of 15,000 contras, which is a clear violation of Honduran sovereignty. Dissatisfaction stemming from these factors infuenced the officer corps' decision to oust General Alvarez.

EL SALVADOR

Background

The Salvadoran armed forces have been influenced by the character of the social struggles of the state building process in the 1930s. Officers not only came from middle-class backgrounds but from artisan families as well. Representatives of the masses carried out important political work within the military. Their organizing drives explain the closing of the National Polytechnic School in the wake of demonstrations staged by cadets from artisan backgrounds. It also explains the revolt of military units in San Salvador in support of the peasant insurrection of 1932.

Overall, however, the crisis of the 1930s demonstrated that the military's basic function was to maintain internal order. After the overthrow of President Arturo Araujo in December 1931 (less than a year after his election), and after the military had crushed the peasant insurrection, the Salvadoran armed forces began to directly administer the state. General Maximiliano Hernández Martínez became the first dictator, and ruled for 13 years until his forced resignation in 1944. He was followed by an uninterrupted string of military dictators and presidents up to 1979. This period of military rule had its roots in the bourgeoisie's need to consolidate social dominance in the wake of peasant insurrections; hence, it left the business of direct political rule to the armed forces. Nevertheless, the army found that it was not impervious to societal struggles. On a number of occasions some sectors within the military supported groups that were calling for democratization and social change. Such occasions included the so-called 1948 Revolution and the military uprising of 1972.

Overall, however, the army was used as a tool to repress social groups that demanded change. The Salvadoran armed forces, like their Guatemalan counterparts, demonstrated that they had a large measure of autonomy from the civilian elite, and even a certain amount of hegemony over them. Yet at the same time they also defended the interests of that elite. The military became so entrenched in government that they explicitly formed their own political party, the Party of National Conciliation, which remained El Salvador's ruling party for over a decade through the routine use of electoral fraud.

During the current century, the Salvadoran army did not engage in international warfare until 1969. In the aftermath of that confrontation, it refitted under the assumption that armed hostilities would inevitably resume. True, guerrilla bands began to operate in the early 1970s, but they did not constitute a serious threat. Consequently, the security forces, not the military, initially took charge of counterinsurgency action.

In 1979, the Salvadoran political regime found itself thoroughly delegitimized and assailed by a growing insurgency as a result of the military's long indirect political rule and the electoral fraud that perpetuated it. This situation provoked a military coup d'etat led by a circle of young officers. The civil–military junta that took over the government in 1979 sought to implement a project that would reform and democratize Salvadoran society. This project, however, failed because both the dominant class and the guerrillas opposed it.

Beginning in 1979, the insurgents' forces grew rapidly. By end–1980 the various guerrilla bands had consolidated into the Farabundo Martí Liberation Front (Frente Farabundo Martí de Liberación Nacional, FMLN). The FMLN had developed a force strong enough to mount attacks against army outposts and other fixed positions. Three years later, the guerrillas were conducting battalion-strength operations that occasionally even had heavy artillery support, and they were winning conventional-style battles. The military's counterinsurgency operations between 1980 and 1985 violently reconfirmed its repressive character and role in Salvadoran society.

El Salvador's Military Institutions

El Salvador's troop level is low, as far as its external war-fighting capacity is concerned. Increases in manpower have largely responded to increases in the number of guerrilla fighters. The Salvadoran army's goal is to reach a ten-to-one superiority over the insurgents, a figure derived from the experience of the British in Malaysia. The army, however, has had a difficult time increasing troop strength beyond 42,000 men because of its high casualty rate. For example, measured in terms of casualties the original army that began fighting in 1979 no longer existed in 1986.[14] Casualties among officers, including cadets from the military academy, have also been high. The army has had a difficult time finding enough recruits to replace casualties and increase overall troop levels at the same time. The army's recruitment problems stem from several factors: parts of El Salvador are no longer under government control; the general population has little enthusiasm for military service; and the morale of government troops seems quite low.

The Salvadoran military's weaponry, tactics, structure, and deployment are all conditioned by the civil war. In 1979, the Salvadoran army was prepared to meet both an external threat (Honduras) and an internal threat (insurgency). But the internal war has developed into conventional-style armed confrontations, to which the Salvadoran armed forces have tried to adapt as quickly as possible in order to gain the upper hand. They have not been entirely successful. True, foreign military assistance has allowed them to rearm quickly, to train new troops, and to make use of modern warfare techniques such as helicopter-transported troops. All of these were not available to the old army. Nevertheless, the insurgents have consistently managed to change and adapt their tactics and strategy more quickly than the army, thus frustrating the latter's attempts to gain the strategic offensive.

The situation of the air force is similar to that of army. For example, in one guerrilla commando raid in January 1982 the air force lost most of its operational fighters. (They were replaced almost immediately, however.) Because the air force does not have to contend with an enemy that has air power, it has favored arming its aircraft with air-to-ground weapons systems. El Salvador's counter-insurgency squadrons have relatively sophisticated airplanes, the AC–47 Spectre. The air force also has some supersonic fighters, but these are not very useful for guerrilla warfare. All in all, along with Honduras, El Salvador's air force is the largest in the region; ditto for its helicopter fleet.

By contrast, El Salvador's armed forces do not possess many armored vehicles, although they consistently replace the ones that they lose. This is probably due to the nature of the terrain in which they conduct their operations. They do have much modern artillery. Meanwhile, the navy is small and does not play an important role in the war.

In general, the morale of the Salvadoran armed forces is fragile, judging by the large numbers of deserters and by the amount of weaponry that the insurgents capture. By and large, until 1985, officers did not seem very persistent during operations, nor did they appear to be able commanders. Consequently, the army's rapid deployment and chasseur units, largely the product of U.S. military training, did not have much success in the field. At times, officers have had to accept the possibility of defeat. But massive U.S. efforts to turn the war around have slowly begun to bear results and the worst failings of the Salvadoran army appear to have been overcome.

El Salvador's military strategy essentially seeks to confront and destroy the insurgency's main forces and to regain control over territory and population. The Salvadorans have tried to implement counterinsurgency techniques borrowed

from Guatemala, including the organization of a militia called the Civil Defense.
But these efforts have not crystallized because the rebels control the strategic
offensive which tends to place government troops in the defensive.

The Salvadoran Military and Their Relationship to Society

El Salvador's officers, much like in the previous two cases, mainly come from
the middle class and ultimately become part of the more privileged classes when
they finally reach the higher ranks. In El Salvador high-ranking military men
usually join the oligarchy because they tend to acquire latifundia. The social
distance between junior and high-ranking officers partially explains the military
revolts of 1948, 1972, and 1979. On each of these occasions two conflicting
visions of society came to a head within the army. One faction had a traditional
conception of society that favored maintaining the status quo. The other faction,
conscious of the social problem, wanted to reform society.

Tensions between these two factions mounted in the months prior to the 1979
coup d'etat, and subsequent changes in the composition of the junta reflected
the ongoing struggle between them. In the end, the progressive faction lost
because the escalation of the civil war made reform from above impossible.
Nevertheless, the war also kept conservatives from establishing the type of regime
that had previously existed in El Salvador.

As a consequence of their experience in politics after 1979 and their involvement in a civil war in which they were not doing very well, the military began
to redefine their role in society. This redefinition owed much to the improvements
in the military capabilities of the officer corps. The old high command, based
on seniority, institutional hierarchy, and their connections to the dominant class,
confronted a new breed of officer, the combat-hardened commander. Many of
these, such as Colonel Domingo Monterrosa (now dead) and Colonel Sigfredo
Ochoa, rose rapidly through the ranks as a result of their combat abilities.
Meanwhile, old guard officers, such as former Defense Minister Humberto García, have lost their positions because of their inability to adapt to new military
strategies. The high casualty rate among officers also influenced the need to
promote rapidly.

The army has changed, then, as a result of its modernization and because, for
the first time in its recent history, it has had to fight a protracted internal war.
This does not mean that the Salvadoran army will democratize either itself or
society. On the contrary, the civil war has polarized Salvadoran society, and
since the army believes that its survival depends on the survival of the existing
social order, the war has tended to reinforce the army's desire to defend it.

The Salvadoran Military and the Political System

Until 1979, the armed forces enjoyed a high degree of autonomy from, and
even hegemony over, the civilian political forces. They wanted to rule and they

used electoral fraud and force to impose their will. But the civil war disrupted this state of affairs. The military's political role in Salvadoran society weakened when they found themselves on the brink of defeat, when they realized that they could not win the war by themselves and had to rely on U.S. military assistance.

Opening up political space for civilian political forces and assuring free and clean elections that result in the installation of constitutional civilian governments is a key component of the United States' strategy for Central America. The United States seeks to legitimize the political regimes of the region by establishing the rule of law, hoping that this will strengthen their ability to resist armed insurgency. Of course, the domestic politics of the United States also push the Reagan administration to espouse these goals. If it did not, it would probably not be able to get appropriations from Congress to aid countries such as El Salvador.

Because U.S. assistance is crucial for El Salvador, the United States has a great deal of influence in the political affairs of that country. Consequently, El Salvador experienced the inauguration of an electoral process that culminated with the installation of a civilian government in which the Christian Democrats became the ruling party. This has led to a change in the political role of the Salvadoran armed forces. The electoral process has not led to a consolidation of the new regime, however, because the insurgents continue to represent an alternative order to the degree that they control territory and have the sympathy of a sizeable amount of the population. Nevertheless, the armed forces no longer dominate Salvadoran politics as they did during the 1970s. Civilian political forces, represented by the Christian Democrats, have the capacity to exercise power over the army and, within limits, to subordinate it to their will. Of course, now more than ever, the army is the government's lifeline, and therefore it retains a substantial amount of political power. Although they are united in their struggle against the insurgents, a certain amount of tension permeates the relationship between civilian politicians and the military. For example, during the kidnapping of President Duarte's daughter the army strenuously objected to the way in which the government handled the negotiations with the insurgents.

The Salvadoran Military and the Economy

The budgets of the defense and security forces are normally reliable indicators of the military's impact on a given country's economy. But because El Salvador is at war this indicator gives us even less of the full picture than it did in the Guatemalan and Honduran cases. This is because the effects of the war on the economy transcend any budgetary calculations. To the appropriations for the forces of order one should at least add the cost of destroyed infrastructure and means of production, the disruption of the domestic market and production in general, as well as the lost labor of the men and women who joined the armed forces on both sides of the conflict.

The budget for the Defense and Interior Ministries (Defensa y Governación) amounted to CA$126.4 million in 1983, the equivalent of 15.3 percent of the state's budget—a modest 3.2 percent of GDP. U.S. military aid for fiscal year 1983–1984, however, climbed to U.S.$196 million. U.S. economic aid, most of which was earmarked for projects linked to the war effort, added another U.S.$231 million.[15] This brings government spending for defense to $553.4 million, or 14.2 percent of El Salvador's GDP. But even this figure does not give us the Salvadoran government's total spending on the war, because it does not include U.S. aid from other sources.

Calculating El Salvador's total defense spending faces a further difficulty which it shares with the preceding cases: budget allocations are manipulated to hide costs. Opposition sources figured that in 1985 the government spent roughly 50 percent of the national budget on the war effort, and that the security forces consumed another 30 percent.[16]

It is difficult to factor in the weight of grants and loans in the calculations of defense spending. But 1981 seems like a good year to attempt such an effort. In that year, U.S. economic and military assistance amounted to U.S.$149.1 million, aid from other countries (15 in all) reached U.S.$110.3 million, the World Bank and the Inter-American Development Bank provided U.S.$216.6 million, and the Venezuelan Investment Fund contributed U.S.$140.1 million. Since most of the government's economic programs are related to the war effort, total foreign aid for the war amounted to approximately U.S.$616.1 million.[17]

Unfortunately, reliable data on war damages do not exist. One U.S. source, however, estimated that in mid–1983 the economy had suffered a loss of U.S.$600 million in direct damage and another U.S.$400 million in indirect costs, such as falling production and increased insurance premiums.[18] Meanwhile, in order to compare spending with income, exports from El Salvador in that year totaled U.S.$880 million.

The Salvadoran Military and Their External Relations

In modern times, El Salvador's armed forces have mainly relied on the United States, and its military assistance programs heavily influenced their development prior to 1979. After 1979, the Salvadoran military drew even closer to the United States, once they realized that they could not hold their own against the insurgents. For its part, the United States progressively escalated its training programs, arms sales, weapon donations, and number of military advisers. Among other accomplishments, the United States trained four rapid deployment battalions, organized a number of chasseur units, and provided helicopters to transport them to combat zones. U.S. aid probably saved the Salvadoran army from defeat in the early years of the insurgency. It also transformed the Salvadoran military into a modern institution capable of fighting an extensive guerrilla war. As a result of this effort, U.S. officers now occupy important positions throughout the Salvadoran army's chain of command. They thus wield considerable influence in its decision-making processes, even at the middle levels of command. Moreover, as I pointed out before, the United States provides virtually all of the Salvadoran army's armaments, munitions, and equipment. This holds true both for the replacement of lost materiel and for efforts to expand El Salvador's armed forces. Although countries such as Argentina and Israel have also contributed to the Salvadoran government's war effort, the United States plays the decisive role.

The Salvadoran armed forces' dependence on U.S. assistance and advisers led to some friction between the two. The main conflict turned on U.S. attempts to limit the human rights abuses that the Salvadoran army regularly engaged in. In the U.S. Congress these violations became important issues in the deliberations over appropriations for El Salvador, especially in the wake of the highly publicized murders of U.S. agrarian reform advisers and nuns.

Currently, neither the Salvadoran state nor its military enjoy much autonomy from U.S. Central American policy. To the contrary, the United States plays a preponderant role in both. In fact, if the Salvadoran armed forces do not shape up, the United States has contingency plans ready to commit its ground troops to combat in El Salvador.

COSTA RICA

Background

Unlike its neighbors, after independence from Spain the province of Costa Rica was by and large spared the experience of violent civil wars.[19] This was due to several factors. The country was isolated and relatively poor in precious metals. Social inequities were not as pronounced in Costa Rica as they were in the rest of Central America, because it had neither gold nor Indians to exploit, which inhibited the emergence of latifundia. Instead, the colonists who arrived tended to be farmers, much like those who settled in the United States. Around 1800, the mean of Costa Rica's population consisted of independent, highly individualistic, conservative small farmers. The social structure did not require a well-developed military establishment to keep internal order.

Nevertheless, during the course of the nineteenth century Costa Rica became involved in a number of military conflicts with its neighbors. This motivated Costa Rica during the reform of 1850 to create a regular army, which became one of the most modern in the region and even established a military academy in 1852 (although it did not stay open very long). This explains how it came to pass that the Costa Ricans defeated the U.S. falange that occupied Nicaragua in 1856.

The military's expansion increased its influence in the state and society during the second half of the nineteenth century. That influence reached its zenith toward the end of that century, during the presidency of Tomás Guardia. Throughout this period, the Costa Rican armed forces staged numerous and riotous coups d'etat.

The Central American wars ended around the turn of this century. A period of liberal reformism set in, which, when coupled with the relative absence of social tension in Costa Rica, allowed a state dominated by agrarian interests to shift its resources from the military toward other societal needs. The military also began a slow, sustained mutation of its function from external to internal security. But given its low level of social conflict, Costa Rica did not develop sophisticated internal warfare capabilities. Eventually, the Costa Rican military became a hybrid institution—a cross between army and police force.

This process became more pronounced after 1923, when the Defense Ministry was transformed into the Ministry of Public Safety. During this process, however, these institutions did not expand their capabilities, not even in the depths of the Great Depression when revolutionary movements, such as the Communist Party, emerged and organized the banana workers' strike of 1934.

Within this framework, it becomes easier to understand the 1948 civil war and the subsequent abolition of the army. When the uprising began, the regular army (whose job it was to defend the government of President Teodoro Picado) was an army in name only—the former president later revealed that it had no more than 300 men.[20] This small force, supported by Communist militias, confronted the revolutionaries under the command of José Figueres. The latter, who emerged victorious, recast Costa Rica's political system in the Social Democratic mold that, to this day, has sustained the stability of Costa Rica's liberal democracy. The so-called Founding Junta of the Second Republic, which took over immediately after Picado's government fell, abolished the army and enshrined that principle in the new constitution. Of course, in reality the junta largely did away with a name and a concept, rather than a real entity. In any case, from that date on Costa Rica has had only public safety forces.

Costa Rica's Forces of Order as a Military Institution

The security apparatus of the Costa Rican state constists of two institutions: the Civil Guard watches over the borders and public safety in the cities, and is organized on paramilitary lines; the Rural Assistance guard, which is more like a police force, protects the countryside and small settlements. The Public Safety Ministry controls the former and the Interior Ministry is in charge of the latter.

Costa Rica does not have military academies, war schools, or recruitment services. And, although many of the officers who lead the guards have received training abroad, neither they nor the enlisted men are considered to be career soldiers. Instead, they are thought to be part of the civil service. Until recently, however, they did not have the same kind of job security that other branches of the civil service had. As a result, the turnover among guardsmen, especially officers, tended to be quite high. With each change in government came a change in the officer corps.

The guards mainly received police training at the Superior Institute for Police Studies, which was generally perceived as inadequate. Both officers and enlisted men supplemented such training by attending the Americas School in Panama, and more recently, the Regional Center for Military Studies at Puerto Castilla, Honduras. In 1985, the Civil Guard established its own training center at the El Murciélago hacienda in northern Costa Rica, where the guardsmen receive instruction from U.S. military advisers in infantry tactics. This second line of military instruction is generally regarded as more efficient than the first.

The Civil Guard's weapons are those of basic infantry units everywhere, modern light arms and supporting firepower. The Civil Guard does not have heavy artillery or armor. The air force consists of helicopters and light airplanes which apparently are not armed, and the navy is composed of patrol boats armed with machine guns.

Recently, Costa Rica has focused on Sandinista Nicaragua as a potential security threat. Tension between the two countries has escalated steadily since 1979, and there were even border skirmishes in 1984 and 1985. A great deal of the problem stems from the fact that contras use Costa Rica to build base camps from which they organize forays into southern Nicaragua. Deteriorating relations between Costa Rica and Nicaragua have led the former to refit its guards with more modern weaponry and to strengthen military training and organization.

The Costa Rican Military in Society, Politics, and the Economy

In the twentieth century, Costa Rican society has developed a strong anti-military bias. Costa Ricans generally do not value the military profession and have tended to resist attempts to expand or militarize existing public safety institutions. Since 1980, however, a change in views has occurred due to the influence of the Costa Rican media, which has adopted an uncompromising conservative position toward Nicaragua.

Although Costa Ricans may look down on the military, they are nevertheless familiar with firearms, a legacy of the 1948 revolution. Moreover, political parties and political movements often have their own armed bands. The militants of the large political parties who have military training usually become officers in the guards when their party is in power. As a result of increased tensions with Nicaragua, independent paramilitary groups have proliferated.[21]

The state's security forces have little if any influence in Costa Rican politics. There was some speculation in 1983, during the presidency of Luis Albert Monge, that political unrest in Costa Rica might induce conservative paramilitary groups to stage a coup d'etat.[22] But in moments of extreme tension such groups usually give way to the institutional rules of the game.

The state does not allocate a high proportion of its revenue to the security forces, not even now that political leaders have decided to expand them. The government has managed to keep the cost of expansion down by soliciting donations in the form of money and military hardware.

The Costa Rican Armed Forces and Their International Connections

Until the triumph of the Nicaraguan Revolution, Costa Rica's military and security forces were comparatively underdeveloped because they did not confront serious internal or external threats. But Costa Rica's close ties with the United States have induced Costa Rica to align its foreign policy goals with those of the United States. In other words, when U.S. policy toward revolutionary Nicaragua became hostile, so did Costa Rica's. Consequently, Costa Rica's diplomatic relations with Nicaragua deteriorated and Costa Rica began to upgrade the military training and equipment of its security forces. At some level, Costa Rica probably also recognizes that war with Nicaragua is a distinct possibility. Should Costa Rica continue to follow its present policy line it will no doubt further intensify the militarization of its security forces. However, it seems unlikely that Costa Rica will go so far as to create an army.

CONCLUSIONS

Before 1980, the armed forces of Guatemala, Honduras, and El Salvador exhibited high degrees of autonomy with respect to civil society. They were no longer praetorian armies, if by praetorian we mean that they essentially served the oligarchy and were not very sophisticated technologically and ideologically. On the contrary, they had attained a certain level of technical and military development, they were as institutionalized as any other state organ, and they demonstrated a tendency to overstep their institutional boundaries. This last characteristic led them to meddle in politics and society. The "extrainstitutional" activities of the Guatemalan and Salvadoran armed forces were the expression of fundamentally antidemocratic regimes. Subordinate social classes had no political or social channels through which to press their demands, and consequently expressed their grievances through demonstrations, organization, and revolutionary action. This brought them face to face with state repression. The need to repress the people placed the army and security forces in a privileged position within the state. Things took a different course in Honduras, however. The Honduran army's forays into politics and its social projects were related to the expansion of a comparatively more modern military establishment operating within the framework of a more underdeveloped state.

The armies of these three countries have also tended to reflect societal contradictions. At different times both the Guatemalan and Salvadoran armies had significant progressive factions. But the officers who favored democratization and social change failed to gain a hegemonic position within their respective military establishments, and thus their social projects failed.

Once again, the situation was somewhat different in Honduras. There, the progressive faction had a better hold over the army than in the other two cases. As a result, when they seized political power in the 1970s they managed to implement a series of partial reforms of Honduran society. This probably at least partially explains why social conflict is currently more muted in Honduras than in Guatemala and El Salvador.

The dynamic in Costa Rica differs sharply from that of the other cases. In this country, the armed forces are small, not very professional, and have over time slowly reverted to a paramilitary force that is totally subordinate to civilian political forces. In other words, it has no autonomy. The source of this rather extraordinary trajectory lies in the absence of severe internal social conflict or external threat.

In all four cases, the military and security forces have been reorganized and expanded since 1980 as a consequence of the regional conflict. Moreover, in Guatemala and El Salvador severe internal social conflict has exacerbated those trends. The forces of order in these four countries have acquired varying amounts of combat experience and have been restructured and refitted. In short, they have become more modern and better equipped than ever before, thanks to foreign assistance, without which they could never have achieved such a transformation.

By the same token, these countries' dependence on U.S. aid for the maintenance of the existing social order has altered the military's influence over, and control of, the state. In the Guatemalan, Salvadoran, and to a lesser extent in the Honduran cases, the army has become less autonomous. The political requirements of counterinsurgency warfare resulted in an opening of political space for civilian governments that were installed after the convocation of free and clean elections. These civilian governments now have more control and autonomy from the generals than at any other time in recent memory. Of course, this was not the case in Costa Rica, where the regional conflict has tended to weaken that nation's antimilitary tradition.

NOTES

1. The guerrillas have an umbrella organization called Guatemalan National Revolutionary Unity.

2. This pact was reproduced in full in the Guatemalan journal *Polémica*, nos. 14–15 (1984).

3. Examples of Guatemalan state terrorism carried out by the armed forces over the past 20 years include disappearances, execution of opposition leaders, and massacres. Reliable figures on the number of people who have lost their lives to these practices do not exist. Some sources estimate that as many as 100,000 persons may have been killed. See The Inter-American Commission on Human Rights, *Report on the Situation of Human Rights in the Republic of Guatemala* (Washington, D.C.: Organization of American States, 1983).

4. More recently the following presidents followed this career path: Eugenio Kjell (1974–1978), Romeo Lucas García (1978–1982), and the president-elect for the period 1982–1986 General Alfredo Guevara. The 1982 coup d'etat impeded General Guevara's ascent to the presidency.

5. During the 1970s, the generals who became president also owned substantial assets.

For example, General Carlos Arana was a financier, industrialist, and agro-exporter; General Eugenio Kjell was a financier who also invested heavily in real estate; General Romeo Lucas García was an agro-exporter who specialized in cardamom production.

6. This factory makes 5.56-caliber ammunition and replacement parts for the Galil rifle and assembles the 16-ton/12-man Armadillo model armored personel carrier, which comes equipped with a .30-caliber machine gun.

7. Electoral fraud was especially obvious in the 1974 and 1978 elections. General Efraín Ríos Montt and Colonel Enrique Peralta Azurdia, respectively, received the majority of the votes. But the government ignored the election results and elevated its own candidates, Generals Eugenio Kjell and Romeo Lucas, to the presidency.

8. These coordinating agencies operate at various levels of government: provincial, municipal, and even in smaller locales, where they are called Local Development Committees. The administrative agencies manage public funds and coordinate private efforts in health and education, as well as in public construction, mass organization, and religious services, to name but a few areas. These organizations are directed by army officers and are structured along counterinsurgency lines.

9. See Arms Control and Disarmament Agency (ACDA), *World Military Expenditures, 1987* (Washington, D.C.: Government Printing Office, 1988), 61. According to ACDA it is difficult to find reliable data on military budgets for Honduras in this period because it would exclude arms purchases and capital expenditures in acquisitions.

10. These data are from *El Tiempo* (Tegucigalpa), 3 November 1983.

11. The following officers participate in the council: the commander in chief of the armed forces; the chief of staff of the armed forces; the minister of defense and public safety; the general commanders of each branch of the service; brigade-level commanders; the chiefs of staff of each service branch; the chief of logistics; the commanders of air force bases; battalion-level commanders; the director of the National Defense School; the director of the Command and General Staff School; the inspector general of the armed forces; and the auditor general and comptroller general of the armed forces. See Leticia Salmon, "La Doctrina de Seguridad Nacional en Honduras," in *Boletín Informativo Honduras* (Tegucigalpas: CEDOH, 1984).

12. Caribbean Information Project, *On a Short Fuse: Militarization in Central America* (San Francisco: Public Media Center, 1985).

13. Since the proportion of trained troops favored El Salvador by two to one, after the fall of General Alvarez Martínez the Honduran government reconsidered its decision and will probably close that center.

14. In 1978, one year before the war started, the Salvadoran armed forces counted with 7,130 troops in addition to 3,000 public safety functionaries. From 1979 to 1985, the FMLN estimates that it has inflicted 20,000 casualties among government forces. Although the government's casualty figures are lower, they are nevertheless more than the number of troops it possessed at the start of the war. See The International Institute for Strategic Studies, *The Military Balance 1977–1978* (London: IISS, 1977); and El Salvador, Servicio de Informacíon y Análisis, *1984: FMLN–FDR Mantienen la Iniciativa Político-Militar* (San Salvador: CEL, 1984).

15. *Series Estadísticas Seleccionadas de Centroamérica* (SIECA), no. 19 (1984); and Infopress Centroamericana, January 1985.

16. Servicio de Información y Análisis, *1984: FMLN–FDR*.

17. Center for International Policy, *Central America: The Financial War* (Washington:

International Policy Report, 1983); and *AID Memo. Total Aid Package for El Salvador May Reach $523 Million* (Washington, D.C.: Center for International Policy, 1981).

18. Richard Alan White, *The Morass. U.S. Intervention in Central America* (New York: Harper and Colophon Books, 1984).

19. This historical background relies heavily on the work of Miguel A. Umaña, "Militares y Civiles en Costa Rica" (M.A. thesis, University of Costa Rica, 1978).

20. See Umaña, "Militares y Civiles."

21. In addition to the state's National Reserves, observers believe that there are at least 13 paramilitary groups in Costa Rica today. Most of these belong to the extreme Right. See Rodrigo Jauberth et al., "Para los Estudios de las Relaciones Estados Unidos–Costa Rica durante la Primera Administración Reagan," in *Costa Rica: Democracia y Soberanía Cuestionadas* (Mexico: CEDOCAC, 1985).

22. For the alleged militarization of Costa Rica and the problems that spring from it, see *Cronología de la Militarización*, Infopress Centroamericana, nos. 640 and 641 (1985).

11 THE ARMED FORCES AND DEMOCRATIZATION IN BOLIVIA, 1982–1986

Raúl Barrios

Bolivia's anguished return to formal political democracy in 1982 raises two important questions regarding the military's role in that society: How have the Bolivian armed forces accommodated the new political regime? What are the likely short- and medium-term consequences that follow from that new relationship?

Answering these questions requires an understanding of Bolivian history since the revolution of 1952. Two overlapping aspects of that history seem to be the most relevant. One angle involves the history of the Bolivian state since April 1952. Its authoritarian component gave it some elements of continuity. A second, and related angle, turns on the history of the military institution, a history which reflects the perennial problem of establishing hegemonic rule in Bolivia. The state's need to reproduce itself and to maintain social control shaped the armed forces' professional characteristics. In other words, particular correlations of social forces determined the various phases of the 1952 state, and these social coalitions affected the organization, role, and functions of the Bolivian military establishment. The types of relationships established between the military and society during that period heavily conditioned their present-day conflictual relationship, which has the quality of an ongoing duel between rapprochement and exclusion. This duel has its origins in the 1952 insurrection—when the military cooperated with social forces—and the subsequent organizational and doctrinal development of the armed forces in light of their social control function. A combination of social upheaval and periods in which the military achieved a measure of autonomy from the dominant social bloc gave rise to intermittent attempts at rapprochement. The armed forces, however, turned their backs on civil society when their role as guarantor of the state—their social control function—became a matter of primary concern.

The Bolivian military's power (troop and equipment levels) was inversely proportioned to the breakdown of social coalitions expressed in the state. The worker's withdrawal from the movement that led to the triumph of the National Revolution provoked such a breakdown. Internal disputes, however, limited the military's development. The military factions had their origins in periods of social upheaval that generated political solidarity in the corresponding generation or class of officers. Thus, for example, we may speak of the Chaco and the April 9, 1952 generations, or the class of 1957. These generations, classes, and even specialized contingents competed among each other for power within the armed forces.

In spite of its professional characteristics, then, societal conflicts replicated themselves within the military. Consequently, the Bolivian armed forces were wracked by ideological differences, with each faction using reason of state to justify its stance. This produced an asymmetrical, pendular, political motion in which the military not only took over direct rule from the dominant social classes, but gained a large measure of autonomy from them. The fact that the armed forces were receptive to changes in state forms and external societal influences explains how it was possible that they could support nationalization policies and efforts to create state capitalism on the one hand, and conservative economic projects on the other.[1]

In 1956, the expansion of the Bolivian military coincided with their first use of force to maintain social peace and order. This had two important effects: they regained their institutional identity; and mounting social conflict convinced them that they needed to get involved in national politics. This sense of political mission is one of the most important characteristics of the Bolivian military.[2]

The Bolivian armed forces owe much of their modernization to their involvement in the nation's social and political conflicts. That involvement fluctuates between acting as an arbiter and lending active support for particular forms of social order. The Bolivian military's distinctive trait, then, is that it measures its stagnation or modernization according to whether progressive or conservative forces dominate politics: the former produce stagnation, the latter facilitate expansion and upgrading.[3]

These characteristics suggest that the Bolivian military consolidated themselves as a consequence of the recurrent hegemonic crises of the Bolivian state. During each crisis the state found itself calling on the armed forces for protection. The latter, in turn, modernized in order to recast their relationship to civilians. The military wanted to show their dominance over civil society by changing the relationship that emerged between them after the triumph of the 1952 people's revolution. It is for these reasons that the armed forces place so much emphasis on internal security.

In summary, two factors best explain the Bolivian military's divergent actions since 1952. On the one hand, they feel that they are the sole repository of the general will which finds its expression in the state. On the other, civil society constantly calls their actions into question. As a result, the military's stance at any given moment depends on the state of their relationship to societal movements, that is, whether mass and labor movements are gaining or losing force. Consequently, in contemporary history the Bolivian armed forces strengthened their capacity to exercise social control whenever mass organizations fell prey to disarticulation, immobilism, and quiescence.[4]

As a first cut, then, two variables—state and societal factors—should help us to understand the military's behavior during the two phases of Bolivia's democratization process: the Siles Suazo regime and the subsequent neoliberal period. These two variables should also help us to understand why the military accepted or rejected particular sets of relationships among itself, civil society, and the government.

THE RETURN TO POLITICAL DEMOCRACY

The deterioration of dictatorial forms of political power in Bolivia has had a profound impact on the armed forces. Democratization implies overcoming a situation in which the military both governed and imposed their will on society. This is not an easy thing to do, which explains why the return to democracy— which began in 1978 with a political amnesty and a call for general elections— was slow, tortuous, and constantly menaced by backsliding on the part of the military.

Democratization took place within the general context of the unraveling of Hugo Banzer's political project (1971–1977). As a result, the transition to democracy did not lead to a long-term reordering of society. It did not engender a political pact among contending social forces that could serve as a framework for rule. Consequently, in July 1980 conservative hard-liners within the military used force to reverse the third consecutive electoral victory of the Democratic Popular Union (Union Democratica y Popular, UDP). This faction (dominated by criminal elements that supported García-Meza) recognized that the mass movement represented a potential danger to the prerogatives of power that they had become accustomed to over the years.

The former general had clearly erred in judgment when he declared that his national reconstruction program would last 20 years. The people may have been defeated militarily, but they were certain that in time political victory would be theirs. Thus, they devoted all of their energies toward promoting the fall of the dictatorship and a return to democratic forms of governance, concentrating their attack on the armed forces themselves. The debacle of García-Meza's regime (1980–1982) had two sources: on the one hand, it had to contend with constant civil disobedience because significant social groups rejected its project; on the other, the García-Meza regime suffered from deep divisions within the military itself, despite its best efforts to coopt the officer corps with sinecures and by cutting them into lucrative drug operations.

To their distress, the military found that the political issues they had hoped to stamp out by stifling public debate were reproducing themselves within their own institutions. Severe conflict wracked the armed forces shortly before the resignation of García-Meza.[5] Polarization within the military reached levels rarely seen in the past. For an instant, it seemed as though the armed forces' esprit de corps (their common sense of corporate identity) would not suffice either to hold the military establishment together, or to patch up their relations with civil society.

The governments of García-Meza, Torrelio, and Vildoso (lasting through October 1982) marked the limits of the Bolivian military's institutional crisis and its inability to govern. This period offers a good example of what happens when a repressive military establishment becomes extremely isolated from an ungovernable society. Nothing works to reestablish order, neither state terror nor quiescence and adherence to the rules of the game on the part of key social groups. This calamitous period witnessed the end of a precarious, or perhaps almost nonexistent, legitimacy for military government. Nevertheless, Vildoso displayed sufficient acumen to assure the survival of the military establishment. He had the presence of mind and political pragmatism to recognize that they could not contain social mobilization or stop Bolivia's eventual return to political democracy. Thus, the military's retreat from power under Vildoso responded to their need to maintain institutional cohesion. The armed forces temporarily abandoned a narrow goal—political rule—for the sake of a more general goal, institutional survival.

THE MILITARY DURING THE GOVERNMENT OF THE DEMOCRATIC POPULAR UNITY PARTY

The reintroduction of political democracy in Bolivia forced the military to give up direct rule. It also represented a victory of civil society over the armed forces, because society became engaged in an open-ended attempt to subordinate the military to it.

The Bolivian case suggests that as far as the military is concerned, two conditions are conducive to a successful transition to democracy. While they are in power, serious divisions must exist within the armed forces on how to overcome a pressing political crisis. Usually, one faction backs a return to democratic forms of government, even at the risk of damaging the military's institutional cohesion. Once political democracy is reestablished, the next step is to strengthen the dominance of the pro-democratic faction by punishing officers of the anti-democratic faction.

In Bolivia, that punishment mainly took the form of purges through forced retirement. Authorities based their judgments on moral and ethical grounds.[6] Meanwhile, the military had to accept their punishment in order to bolster the credibility of the claim that they intended to cooperate with the newly installed civilian authorities. The armed forces, after all, needed to rebuild their morale as well as the public's confidence in their institutions. Nevertheless, some quarters did not take their medicine lying down; they protested vigorously and supported their arguments by appealing to a virulent anticommunist discourse.[7]

In the main, however, the purges were an expression of civil society's victory over the military establishment. The degree of severity with which the punishment was meted out did not depend on external factors; it had more to do with internal conditions in the armed forces themselves. They accepted sanctions to the degree that they were necessary to restore a common corporate identity.

This suggests that the armed forces view democracy as a condition of societal hegemony, and hence under democratic rule they cannot help but feel unprotected, naked—like an army disarmed after a lost war. That is why their initial acceptance of political democracy hinges on the degree to which they need to restore institutional cohesion. This holds true especially when the armed forces' retreat from government results from a military defeat at the hands of a popular insurrection, for under those conditions the military's disarray is at its highest level.

Of course, Bolivia's return to democracy and the imposition of sanctions against certain officers would not have been possible without important changes in the composition of the military command structure. Among others, this recomposition affected the high command, troop commanders, and the general commitment to democratic processes. Moreover, they were not chosen at random, but represented attempts to consolidate factions within the military whose interests and positions complemented those of the civilian authorities. Thus, Generals Alfredo Villaroel Barja, Simon Sejas Tordoya, Muñoz Revollo, and Vice Admiral Wilfredo de la Barra became the commanders in chief of the armed forces, army, air force, and navy, respectively, and Lucio Añez was appointed chairman of the Joint Chiefs of Staff and the armed forces. These men shouldered the responsibility for leading the military in Bolivia's new political climate.

The military high command's restructuring, under the direction of Defense Minister José Ortiz Mercado, was part of the *Unidad Democratica y Popular*'s (UDP) military policy. Unfortunately, the UDP did not make full use of the opportunity that presented itself for initiating a thorough reform of the military's organization and doctrine. This was probably due, at least in part, to the government's indecisiveness regarding this matter, and because it did not fully comprehend the implications and possibilities of the situation. In short, the government regrettably never developed a coherent strategy for a serious overhaul of the Bolivian armed forces.

Thus, Defense Minister Ortiz's plans not only had to contend with resistance from the military but also came up against a government that did not understand what he was trying to do.[8] The government believed that the problem could be solved by installing a high command whose interests complemented those of the civilian leadership. But this strategy had a serious flaw: it left military organization and ideology intact. Thus, after a few months' respite, the armed forces managed to reproduce the same misguided conceptions that had led them to seek autonomy from civil society in the past. As usual, they held the mistaken belief that only they could resolve societal conflicts that the civilian leadership either fanned with inept policies or seemed incapable of tackling.

In other words, Bolivia's return to political democracy did not affect the military's disposition to mount coups d'etat. This continuity was due to the fact that the armed forces retained control over the restructuring of their image, while the civilians merely made some formal change. The military thus simply reproduced the basis for their antagonistic relationship with civil society.

Meanwhile, the government's ability to significantly reduce previously high levels of military spending, despite protests from the armed forces, stands as a testimony to the extent of their retreat.[9] The fate of the military budget serves as an indicator of the state of civil–military relations. For, aside from the military's ideology, decisions on appropriations reveal a lot about the degree of the armed forces' aquiescence to civilian leaders.

A new military discourse that professed unconditional support for the democratic regime accompanied the changes discussed so far—purges, promotions, and budget cuts. The armed forces hoped that this discourse would both make up for their past transgressions against democracy and society and underscore their repudiation of their dictatorial past. For example, General Villarroel stated that "the armed forces are dedicated to their specific tasks and support the democratic process as mandated by the state's political constitution." In the same declaration he also said that "the military's return to the barracks marks the beginning of their reencounter with their true profession."[10] General Sejas, for his part, indicated that "one of the main tasks of the army high command is to assure the depoliticization of the officer corps, so that officers may perfect their military capabilities, [furthermore], we owe our obedience to the Constitution, not to a political party." In short, these types of rationales flourished during the first phase of the military's retreat. Meanwhile, the civilian authorities attempted to recast civil–military relations by subordinating the armed forces to them.

In addition to rhetoric, the withdrawal of the Illimani regiment from the mining district of Catavi was an important symbolic act. The regiment's presence in that district over the past ten years had been an expression of the internal warfare function that the army had exercised since the 1960s.

Nevertheless, to the extent that the democratic regime proved incapable of restoring social peace and administrative regularity, the armed forces' belief in their tutelary role over civil society began to gain ground. The high command could not overlook the crisis of governability. The chairman of the Joint Chiefs of Staff voiced the military's concern regarding the political crisis. But he stressed that "[our concern] should not be interpreted as a political action; rather it stems from our preoccupation as Bolivians who see democracy endangered by these types of situations." He said that the military felt compelled to voice their worries because "the armed forces cannot be considered a passive entity; their sense of national duty with respect to the nation's development and defense impels them to take an active role in these matters; therefore, the military must take positions on decisions that affect society and the national interest.''[11]

During the UDP government, the military, without a doubt, took their cues from the deepening economic crisis and the high levels of social mobilization that accompanied it. It was, after all, true that state and societal initiatives to restore order had failed. Thus, the advent of democracy coincided with a period that witnessed an intensification of the dissolution of the 1952 state's hegemony— all this, despite a national consensus to overcome the problem. Under these circumstances, the "chaos and anarchy" that followed on the heels of heightened conflict between the Bolivian Worker's Central (BWC—the central labor confederation) and the government constitutes only the tip of the iceberg.

In any case, the conflict between these two actors deepened radically over the problem of featherbedding in public enterprises and the issue of a cogovernment between the BWC and the UDP. From the perspective of the workers and the people, positive movement on these matters symbolized imbuing democracy with a revolutionary orientation. The participants recalled the glory of April 9, 1952, and the experience of democracy as an expression of direct mass action. Rene Zavaleta correctly observed that democracy in Bolivia meant social mobilization and direct social action that were unmediated by quantitative mechanisms.[12] But the UDP did not accept the BWC's overtures for cogovernment, and thus precipitated the direct confrontation between labor and the government of Siles Suazo.

For their part, the military believed that labor union mobilization represented a repudiation of the existing order. For example, they declared: "The armed forces are concerned over the subjugation of legal power to sectors which, in an anarchical manner, refuse to respect the principle of authority or to obey the law. [But] as long as the armed forces command respect, civilian authorities can rest assured that the enemies of democracy and peace will not be able to achieve their illegal goals. Only respect for the military can guarantee democracy and peace in the nation.''[13]

The imagery and tone of this statement clearly reflect a preoccupation with maintaining the status quo and protecting the military establishment. Political democracy, moreover, existed at the pleasure of the armed forces. As a result, we see a shift from a conciliatory discourse to one that conveys a distinct threat: "The armed forces of the nation support and will continue to support democratic processes as long as they are in accord with the state's political constitution and the law of the land.''[14] Moreover, "the Bolivian Worker's Central has no place governing the nation because that would be unconstitutional.''[15]

The military expressed extreme concern over negotiations to form a cogovernment because if they succeeded it would transform formal political democracy into a system in which the people would enjoy direct participation in political decision making. The military made it clear that their tolerance for democracy stopped short of such participatory forms of government. They feared that they would be replaced as political actors by the organized people, and that would spell the end of the tutelary role over civil society. These transformations simply did not fit with the armed forces's conception of social reality. Communist party participation in the government coalition was as far as the military cared to go in their concessions to democracy.

The military, then, had ratified formal political democracy but the country found itself immersed in a deepening political crisis. Under these circumstances, relations between the armed forces and the Bolivian Worker's Central took on an increasingly hostile character. The BWC continually denounced the military's efforts to stymie democratic processes. The armed forces, for their part, launched a frontal attack against "external disorder." Over time, each side perceived the other to be the mortal enemy of democracy and thought of itself as the bulwark of democracy. At stake, of course, were two different conceptions of democracy. Each side defended the conception that best served its interests.

The military, however, gained the upper hand as the crisis deepened and the workers radicalized. Gradually, the armed forces' political positions took on an increasingly independent character. They were aided in their efforts to shake off civilian control by the fact that the defense minister was now a brother in arms—Colonel (ret.) Manuel Cardenas Mello. A series of events helped the military to involve a counterinsurgency discourse in order to justify their involvement in politics. Those events included the detention of irregular forces in Lirbay, reports of young Bolivians traveling to Cuba to receive guerrilla training, and the bombing of the Military Justice Tribunal.

As the political crisis deepened, the military issued a number of warnings that their tolerance had limits. For example, they declared that "the armed forces are disturbed about events that do nothing but promote anarchy in the nation."[16] They also stated that, "the BWC strike has failed," and, "the armed forces are very disturbed over the spate of illegal strikes and civil disorder."[17] The military drove their point home when the high command flatly said that they were the "guardians of the nation's internal security." These statements left no doubt that the military's posture and actions were a response to the goals of the Bolivian Worker's Central (cogovernment and higher wages and benefits). But the military's concern for internal security quickly transformed itself into an excuse to become directly involved in politics. They made their erstwhile unconditional support for political democracy conditional on the civilian authorities' ability to find political solutions to the crisis. Those solutions had to be capable of controlling the "licentious masses."

Siles began to meet more frequently with the high command. Meanwhile, politicians—who sensed the coming UDP debacle—secretly sidled up to various factions in the military. The conservative National Democratic Action party, however, openly proclaimed that "the day will come in which the armed forces will have to impose the rule of law and rechannel the democratic process."[18]

The first phase of Bolivia's return to democracy, then, was characterized by the military's attempts to make amends with civilian leaders, followed by threats, and then by their subsequent recourse to internal security rationales. Once they had resorted to the latter, the character of the civil-military relations in the fledgling democracy changed irrevocably. The main factor that led to this transformation was the social and political crisis that erupted during the UDP administration. Even those within the high command of the military who were most sympathetic to the government ultimately found that they agreed in principle with the position of their more conservative brothers in arms.

The military's turn to a more conservative stance responded to steady pressure from mid-ranking officers for changes in the high command. They concentrated their attack on General Sejas, whom the civilian leadership had successively appointed to the positions of commander of the army and commander of the armed forces. In a rebellious act of defiance, senior cadets at the military academy demanded his immediate removal. For its part, the Siles administration reiterated its support for General Seja because it was convinced that he could stave off coup d'etat attempts. The punishment meted out to the cadets for their seditious declarations, however, was never implemented. This fact underscored the rift between the high command—personified by General Sejas—and mid-ranking officers. It was also an indicator of the degree to which the armed forces were undergoing an internal recomposition.

The military's rapid about-face demonstrated the conjunctural and precarious nature of the officer corps' support for the UDP administration. In other words, there was not much room for "progressive" positions within the armed forces. Instead, the events in Bolivia highlighted the depth of the military's adherence to conservative doctrines. After all, officers believed that the well-being of their institution depended on those doctrines. Thus, the next commander in chief of the armed forces, General Oscar Villa Urioste, said, "the armed forces will not abandon the nation to the forces of anarchy, nor will they permit Bolivia to become another Central America."[19]

The conflict within the military between officers who supported the government and those with a more conservative bent, however, abated. The Catholic church managed to mediate a compromise between the government and the opposition which eased tensions within the armed forces. The military approved of a settlement which shortened Siles's term by a year and called for elections on July 14, 1985. Thus, the second internal rearrangement of the armed forces coincided with a reshuffling of social forces toward the right of the political spectrum.

The changes in the electoral schedule sealed the fate of the UDP's political project. Paradoxically, the UDP's social support had shrunk to the point where in the end its biggest detractor, the military, wound up assisting Siles in the final moments of his government. These events had their roots in a twofold process of change in the correlation of power among social forces. The political power of the Bolivian Worker's Central and the unions in general eroded on the one hand, while conservative social groups launched their counteroffensive on the other. From the military's point of view this represented the reestablishment of order and the principles of authority in Bolivian society.

NEOLIBERALISM AND THE BOLIVIAN ARMED FORCES

The armed forces supported the call for new elections because they believed that Bolivian politics had experienced a qualitative change. The rapid disintegration of the UDP and the union movement set the conditions for a return to conservative politics within the framework of political democracy. This reading of the situation kept the military from mounting a coup d'etat against the Siles government. The triumph of the conservative coalition (Nationalist Democratic Action–Nationalist Revolutionary Movement) on July 14, 1985, proved that the armed forces had interpreted the balance of political forces correctly and inaugurated a new period in Bolivian history. In any case, General Banzer's victory had important implications for the military establishment. He was, after all, a military man and former dictator. He represented the symbolic culmination of the military's recovery and the victory over the forces of "extremism and anarcho-syndicalism."

Banzer, however, did not win a clear-cut victory, failing to obtain sufficient votes to immediately take office. Congress had to chose among the top vote-getting presidential candidates. Under these circumstances, the forces of another conservative, Victor Paz Estenssoro, had a relatively good chance of forging a winning congressional coalition. In the face of this uncertainty, the armed forces—especially the mid-ranking officers—could not restrain themselves from openly siding with Bonzer. Thus, while the high command favored Estenssoro, the rest of the officer corps supported Banzer (who had gained a plurality of the vote). For example, a cable from the Eleventh Army Division in Oruro to the High Command in La Paz read: "The General Staff must exhort future parliamentarians to respect the victory of the candidate who received a plurality of the votes during the recent elections . . . these suggestions draw their inspiration from a desire to avoid the repetition of tragic days for our beloved country; but at the same time, they are a firm demand for the ratification of the will of the majority of the voters."[20]

Although it was clear that most of the officer corps favored Banzer, that support did not turn to violence when it seemed that Paz Estenssoro would most likely be the next president of Bolivia. Two days before Paz Estenssoro's election to the presidency by congressional vote, the Eleventh Division acknowledged that it would bow to discipline and obey the orders of the High Command.[21] Meanwhile, the latter underscored that the armed forces would ensure that the will of congress would prevail.[22]

During Siles's government, the military constituted a threat to Bolivia's fragile democracy. But Paz's relationship to the military had its foundations in his pragmatic desire to ensure the institutional consolidation of formal political democracy. Thus, the relationship between the new government and the armed forces took on a more harmonious character, especially after the government unveiled its national economic and political project in August 1985. The relationship between the military and the union movement also acquired new qualities. Two factors influenced the change: the recovery of the armed forces from the debacle of the early 1980s, and the erosion of the labor movement. It seemed as though the rearticulation of the former required the disarticulation of the latter. This did not, however, keep either side from verbally attacking the other under the guise of incipient tolerance. For example, the armed forces proclaimed that they had no quarrel with workers but that they objected to "anarcho-syndicalism." For their part, labor professed to make a distinction between "conservative, hard-line" and "progressive, democratic" soldiers.

The high command's official ratification of the new president was an expression of the military's recomposition during the Siles government. Thus, the new government did not have to immediately concern itself with purging it. That very high command had played an important role in negotiating the political solution that culminated in the election of Paz Estenssoro. Of course, some generals were not entirely happy with the new situation. For example, the commander of the Eighth Army Division, General Prado Salmon, declared that the military's ratification of the election constituted a "demonstration of respect for the legal order and a recognition that the military stood on the sidelines of the country's political changes."[23]

General Prado Salmon was mistaken in his appreciation of the situation. Yet it was true that the conservative coalition's approach to the military establishment was more subtle than that of the UDP. The latter had used promotions and appointments in a flagrantly political manner. By contrast, a certain harmony existed between the interests of the conservative politicians and the armed forces, so that the new administration could afford the luxury of leaving the military alone. The two actors saw eye to eye on the policies favored by Paz Estenssoro. I want to stress that I am not implying that the high command was apolitical, that is, that they did not have a place within Bolivia's power structure. Rather, the armed forces thought of the new government as the culmination of an institutional reordering which they favored. In other words, the military merely demonstrated respect for their "natural superiors."

When the National Revolutionary Movement took office, the party and the movement agreed on the character of their nascent conservative project. Thus, the new administration radiated a much more credible unity of purpose than the UDP had. It was on the basis of this foundation that the armed forces and the government built their fluid relations. A series of events cemented those loyalties. The most important involved the implementation of new economic policies (decree 21,060), designed to restructure Bolivia's economy, society, and politics according to neoliberal canons. This decree marked the end of the historical period that began with the 1952 revolution and the beginning of a new period.[24] The new policies sought to dismantle the state's participation in the economy and to deregulate private markets in order to expose them to the cleansing discipline of market forces. Politically, the policies aimed at atomizing civil society and isolating conflictive issues from each other. In short, the Bolivian state no longer concerned itself with economic development planning, but became a watchman state that policed the political arena.

At first, the labor movement's rejection of the neoconservative project impeded its implementation. The government, however, resorted to force in order to break labor and restore social peace—which the UDP had destroyed. The armed forces applauded the government's imposition of a state of siege, the imprisonment of labor leaders, and the military occupation of strategic industrial zones. From the perspective of the armed forces, these actions symbolized the reestablishment of respect for the principles of order and authority, as well as a reaffirmation of their tutelary role over civil society. This explains why the commander in chief of the armed forces urged Paz to insist on implementing his policies. On one occasion, in a clear reference to the Bolivian Worker's Central, he said that those policies "deterred the emergence of a dual power base that could threaten the nation's economic recovery." He concluded that "the unceasing efforts of extremists to destabilize the system still constituted a latent threat to democracy."[25]

The conservative's social project, then, found easy acceptance within the armed forces. The latter wholeheartedly supported the economic package unveiled on August 29, 1985, because "it [constituted] the only way out of the crisis."[26] Shortly afterward, the commander of the army, General Raul Lopez, made his support for the new measures known by repeating official statements practically word for word. He said that the government was engaged in "a tough battle against an economic crisis—fanned by the demagoguery of anarcho-synd- icalism—that weighed heavily on the nation's productive apparatus."[27] This quote implies that the military endorsed decree no. 21,060 because it promised to disarticulate the labor movement and to submit it to increasingly tighter restrictions. General Lopez later justified the armed forces' support for the neoliberal model during the anniversary celebration of the Special Forces Training Center. On that occasion he said: "We made our presence felt in the streets in order to safeguard principles of authority, an action that received applause both inside and outside of our borders, since we are the natural custodians of the nation's security and guarantors of internal order."[28]

Later, a political agreement, or democratic pact, between the two main political parties (National Revolutionary Movement and Nationalist Democratic Action) consolidated the reactionary solution to the protracted crisis of the Bolivian state. The high command of the armed forces repeatedly affirmed its support for this outcome. General Sejas summed it up nicely when he said that "the armed forces look upon the political accord between the NRM and the NDA with innermost satisfaction."[29]

In summary, three elements of the NRM's neoconservative project made it acceptable to the military. In the social arena it attacked and weakened organized labor, while restoring internal order and respect for authority. In the economic arena, the model managed to control hyperinflation. In the political arena, the neoconservatives forged a political pact designed to strengthen the new institutions of political democracy. In short, they managed to bring the worst excesses of the UDP's government under control.

The military, of course, gave their own interpretation to the neoliberal reordering of Bolivian society. As soon as the conservative government began to implement the new model, the armed forces started to emphasize their concern over the alleged existence of guerrilla groups in Bolivia. In other words, the military decided to play up their counterinsurgency role, a theme they had initially broached toward the end of the Siles administration. To this end, Defense Minister Fernando del Valle and the high command mounted a media blitz concerning the subversive threat. For example, del Valle declared that: "For the first time in the fifteen years since the last guerrilla *foco*, we have information suggesting that groups of irregulars have been detected in the southern part of the country; the military, at present, are evaluating this information."[30] Meanwhile, General Sejas assured the nation that "the armed forces are trained and willing to repress groups of irregulars wherever they may surface."[31]

The fact that it was later proved that such groups did not exist could not hide the intention behind the campaign. The military took that opportunity to warn potential insurgents of the likely consequences of their actions. They also urged it to reinforce their internal function, that is, the foundations of their professionalism. The neoconservative model allowed the military to recover their bipolar, anticommunist, and counterinsurgency vision of the world.

The military policy of the National Revolutionary Movement government sought to reconstruct civil-military relations within a neoconservative framework. Unlike the sad experience of the UDP, two factors favored this attempt. The military approved of the conservative government's social policies, which reestablished their tutelary role over society. The new government also resolved a series of adjustments that the armed forces had experienced during the transition to democracy and crystallized a conservative realignment in the military that reestablished a certain institutional harmony. The conservative realignment bridged the gulf between the high command and mid-ranking officers. Better still, the officer corps understood that under the guise of maintaining a strictly professional stance, the neoconservative project assured the military an important political role.

The neoconservatives, however, also had to satisfy the military's corporate interests—their economic and professional demands. Two tendencies prevailed. On the one hand, the armed forces received preferential treatment with regard to their economic interests. Clientelism and cooptation play a central role in this respect, and the military have come to expect these rewards. Satisfaction of economic demands, then, has become a central element of the military's esprit de corps. On the other hand, the neoconservatives have advanced the armed forces' professionalization by strengthening bilateral military ties with the United States.

In January 1986, the U.S. commander in chief of Southern Command, John

Galvin, visited Bolivia. During his trip, Bolivia ratified mutual military assistance treaties with the United States and agreed to engage in joint maneuvers with U.S. troops in the department of Cochabamba. These maneuvers bred such a "familiarity" among the troops of the two countries that the Bolivian military apparently voiced no concern over the fact that foreign forces were conducting operations on their soil. These factors suggest that the Bolivian armed forces embrace the neoconservative project as a means to consolidate themselves as a political actor with their own long-term project. They have already started, and nothing on the horizon suggests any fissures.

NOTES

1. The nationalist militarism of Generals Ovando and Torres (1969–1971) best exemplifies times in which the military attains autonomy from the dominant social bloc.

2. We refer to civic action and counterinsurgency plans developed by the Bolivian military in the early 1980s.

3. From this perspective, the most significant political-military processes were the coups d'etat of General Rene Berrientos in November 1964 and Colonel Hugo Banzer Suarez in August 1971.

4. For example, the army's shift in emphasis from production to counterinsurgency coincided with significant changes in the revolutionary process. By the same token, the military nationalism of Ovando and Torres, which sought to develop Bolivia's human and natural resources, was replaced by the doctrine of national security during the dictatorship of General Hugo Banzer Suárez.

5. During his short tenure, García-Meza faced continual military uprisings and pronouncements against him. The most significant of these forced him to renounce the presidency in August 1981.

6. The periodical purges of the Bolivian armed forces are significant because they expressed political realignments and changes in the internal correlation forces. They also reflect moments of international crisis. The most important purges occurred in 1952, 1971, 1974, and 1982–1983.

7. Officers who were forced to leave the military resisted their punishment by making anticommunist appeals in the press. They hoped that this well-worn ploy would galvanize heretofore missing support for their situation among their comrades in arms.

8. Ortiz Mercado had pointed out that "the constitutional government's policies with regard to national defense and the armed forces are not conjunctural in nature, they are planned" (*El Mundo*, 2 July 1983).

9. This is what prompted the military to oppose the practice of having a civilian defense minister. During its three years, the UDP administration had three defense ministers: Licenciado José Ortiz Mercado (October 1982 to August 1983); Colonel (r) Manuel Cardenas Mallo (August 1983 to December 1984); and General Elías Gutiérrez (December 1984 to August 1985). General Gutiérrez, however, was not as important a figure as the other two because he held the post during the terminal phase of the UDP's government.

10. *Presencia*, 21 January 1983.

11. *Presencia*, 11 January 1983.

12. Rene Zaveleta, *Las Masas en Noviembre* (La Paz: Editorial La Juventud, 1983).

13. *Presencia*, 26 May 1983.

14. *El Diario*, 8 August 1983.

15. *Presencia*, 17 August 1983.

16. *Presencia*, 6 December 1983.

17. *Hoy*, 17 May 1984.

18. *Hoy*, 23 May 1984.

19. *Presencia*, 5 December 1984.

20. *Presencia*, 3 August 1985.

21. *Presencia*, 4 August 1984.

22. *Presencia*, 3 August 1985.

23. *El Mundo*, 3 August 1985.

24. Gloria Ardaya and Horst Grebe, ''Elementos para el Estudio de la Crisis de Hegemonia y de las Opciones del Movimiento Popular,'' (*FLACSO*, Bolivia, 1986, Mimeographed).

25. *Presencia*, 31 August 1985.

26. *Presencia*, 23 August 1985.

27. *Presencia*, 19 September 1985.

28. *Presencia*, 30 September 1985.

29. *El Mundo*, 19 October 1985.

30. *El Mundo*, 2 October 1985.

31. *Presencia*, 3 October 1985.

BIBLIOGRAPHY

Albrecht, Ulrich. *The Current Warfare/Welfare Alternative*. Buenos Aires: EURAL, 1985.

Americas Watch Report. *The Central-Americanization of Colombia? Human Rights and the Peace Process*. New York, January 1986.

Ardaya, Gloria. "Ejército ¿Crísis para la Transición?" Ponencia presentada al Seminario: Automización Castrense y Democracia, Santiago, Chile, 1985.

Arriagada, Genaro. *El Pensamiento Político de los Militares*. Santiago, Chile: Editorial Aconcagua, 1981.

Atkins, Pope. *Arms and Politics in the Dominican Republic*. Boulder, Colo.: Westview Press, 1981.

Berghan, Volker. *Militarism: The History of an International Debate, 1861–1979*. New York: St. Martin's Press, 1982.

Bermúdez Rossi, Gonzalo. *El Poder Militar en Colombia*. Bogotá: Ediciones Expresión, 1982.

Black, Jan. "The Military and Political Decompression in Brazil." *Armed Forces and Society* (Summer 1980).

Booth, David, and Bernardo Sorj. *Military Reformism and the Social Classes: The Peruvian Experience*. New York: St. Martin's Press, 1983.

Brigagao, Clovis. "The Case of Brazil: Fortress or Paper Curtain?" *Impact*, no. 1 (January–March 1981).

———. *O Mercado de Segurança*. Rio de Janeiro: Editora Nova Fronteira, 1984.

Brogan, Christopher. "Military Higher Education and the Emergence of New Professionalism: Some Consequences for Civil–Military Relations in Latin America." *Army Review* (January 1962).

Bustamante, Fernando. "Los Paradigmas en el estudio del Militarismo en América Latina." Documento de Trabajo, no. 320. *Facultad Lationamericana de Ciencias Sociales* (FLACSO), 1986.

———. "Problemas y Dinámica de la Política Ecuatoriana Actual." Documento de Trabajo. Santiago: FLACSO, 1987.

————. "El Rol de los Términos de la Democratización Post-Militarista en la Evolución Democrática de los Países Andinos de Sud-América." Documento de Trabajo, no. 328. Santiago: FLACSO, January 1987.

Bustamante, Fernando, and Carlos Portales. "La Venta de Aviones F–16 a Venezuela. Un Caso de Transferencia de Tecnología Militar Avanzada." Documento de Trabajo, no. 361. Santiago: FLACSO, 1987.

Carranza, Mario E. "The Role of Military Expenditure in the Development Process: The Argentinian Case 1946–1980." *Nordic Journal of Latin American Studies*, nos. 1–2 (1983).

Child, John. *Unequal Alliance: The Interamerican Military System 1938–1978*. Boulder, Colo.: Westview Press, 1980.

Duvall, Raymond, and Bruce Russett. *From State Coercion to Insurgency and Back in Dependent Societies*. Rio de Janeiro: IPSA, 1982.

Encinas del Pando, José. "The Role of Military Expenditures in the Development Process, Perú: A Case Study 1950–1980." *Nordic Journal of Latin American Studies*, nos. 1–2 (1983).

Ewell, Judith. "The Development of Venezuela's Geopolitical Analysis." *Journal of Interamerican Studies and World Affairs* 24, no. 3 (August 1982).

FLACSO. *Militarización, Armamentismo y Desarrollo en el Tercer Mundo*. Santiago, 1982. Material Docente.

Frank, Rosa. "Argentina, Desmilitarización, Destape y Democracía." *Mensaje*, Santiago, Chile, no. 319 (June 1983).

Frühling, Hugo, Carlos Portales, and Augusto Varas. *Estado y Fuerzas Armadas*. Santiago, Chile: FLACSO, 1982.

Gallón Giraldo, Gustavo. *La República de las Armas: Relaciones entre las Fuerzas Armadas y Estado en Colombia, 1960–1980*. Bogotá: Centro de Investigación y Educación Popular, 1983.

García, Pío. "Notas Sobre Formas de Estado y Regímenes Militares en América Latina." *Revista Mexicana de Sociologia* (April–June, 1982).

Garretón, Manuel Antonio. "Evolución Política y Problemas de la Transición a la Democracia en el Régimen Militar Chileno." Documento de Trabajo, no. 148. Santiago: FLACSO, 1982.

————. "Proyecto, Trayectoria y Fracaso de los Regímenes Militares en el Cono Sur: Un Balance." *Alternativas* (Santiago, Chile). (January–April 1984).

————. *El Proceso Político Chileno*. Santiago: FLACSO, 1983.

Gaspar, Gabriel, comp. *La Militarización del Estado Latinoamericano, Algunas Interpretaciones*. Serie Cuadernos de Teoria y Sociedad. México: Universidad Autonoma, n.d.

Hartlyn, Jonathan. "Military Governments and the Transition to Civilian Rule." *Journal of Interamerican and World Affairs* (May 1984).

Jellinek, Sergio, and Luis Ledesma. "Uruguay: del Consenso Democrático a la Militarización Estatal." Research Papers Series, no. 27. Stockholm: Suecia, 1980.

Karl, Terry. "Petroleum and Political Pacts: The Transition to Democracy in Venezuela." *Wilson Center Working Papers*, no. 107. Washington, D.C.: Wilson Center, 1981.

Lechner, Norbert. *Estado y Política en América Latina*. México: Siglo XXI, 1981.

Maullin, Richard. *Soldiers, Guerrillas, and Politics in Colombia*. Santa Monica, Calif.: The Rand Corporation, 1980.

Needler, Martin. "The Military Withdrawal from Power in South America." *Armed Forces and Society* (Summer 1980).

Pease Garcia, Henry. "Perú: Del Reformismo Militar a la Democracia Tutelada." In *América Latina 80: Democracia y Movimiento Popular*. Lima: DESCO, 1981.

Portales, Carlos. "Militarization and Political Institutions in Chile." In *Global Militarization*, edited by Peter Wallensteen. Boulder, Colo.: Westview Press, 1985.

―――. "Vinculaciones Externas de las FFAA y Redemocratización del País." Documento de Trabajo, no. 242. Santiago: FLACSO, 1985.

Potash, Robert. *The Army and Politics in Argentina 1945–1962, Peron to Frondizi*. Stanford, Calif.: Stanford University Press, 1980.

Ronfeldt, David, ed. *The Modern Mexican Military: A Reassessment*. San Diego, Calif.: Center for U.S.–Mexican Studies, 1984.

Rouquié, Alain. "Demilitarization and the Institutionalization of Military-Dominated Politics in Latin America." Wilson Center Working Papers, no. 110. Washington, D.C.: Wilson Center, 1981.

―――. *L'Etat Militaire dans L'Amérique Latine*. Paris: Editions de Seuil, 1982.

Ruhl, Mark. "Civil–Military Relations in Colombia: A Societal Explanation." *Journal of Interamerican and World Affairs*, no. 2 (May 1981).

―――. "The Military." In *Politics of Compromise: Coalition Government in Colombia*, edited by Albert Berry, Robert Hellman, and Mauricio Solaún. New Brunswick, N.J.: 1980.

Schaposnick, Eduardo. *La Democratización de las Fuerzas Armadas Venezolanas*. Caracas, Venezuela: ILDIS, 1985.

Smith, Peter. "Argentina: The Uncertain Warriors." *Current History* (February 1980).

Varas, Augusto. "Democratización y Reforma Militar en Argentina." Documento de Trabajo, no. 251. Santiago: FLACSO, 1985.

―――. "Desmilitarización del Estado y Democratización Castrense: Una Política Militar Alternativa." Documento de Trabajo, no. 233. Santiago: FLACSO, 1984.

―――. "Estado y Fuerzas Armadas en América Latina. Economia y Política de la Militarización y el Armamentismo." Documento de Trabajo, no. 140. Santiago: FLACSO, 1982.

―――. "Las FFAA en la Sociedad Chilena." In *Primer Congreso Chileno de Sociologia*. Santiago: Colegio de Sociologos de Chile. Santiago: 1985.

―――. "Foreign Policy and National Security Doctrines." Documento de Trabajo, no. 100. Santiago: FLACSO, 1980.

―――. "Fuerzas Armadas y Gobierno Militar: Corporativización y Politización Castrense en Chile." Material de Discusión, no. 21. Santiago: FLACSO, 1981.

―――. *Los Militares en el Poder: Régimen y Gobierno Militar en Chile, 1973–1986*. Santiago: Pehuen-FLACSO, 1987.

―――. *Militarization and the International Arms Race in Latin America*. Boulder, Colo.: Westview Press, 1985.

―――. *La Política de las Armas en América Latina* (Santiago: FLACSO, 1988).

―――. "Las Relaciones Militares Internacionales de América Latina: Evolución y Perspectivas." In *Las Relaciones Entre América Latina, Estados Unidos y Europa Occidental*, edited by Lagos Gustavo. Santiago: Editorial Universitaria, 1980.

―――. "Seis Consideraciones sobre Armamentismo, Militarismo y Conflicto Social en América Latina." Documento de Trabajo, no. 290. Santiago: FLACSO, 1986.

Varas, Augusto, Felipe Agüero, Fernando Bustamente. *Chile, Democracia y Fuerzas Armadas*. Santiago: FLACSO, 1980.

INDEX

ABOUT THE CONTRIBUTORS

FELIPE AGÜERO, Chilean sociologist and political scientist (Duke University); assistant professor at the Department of Political Science, Ohio State University; co-author of *Chile, Democracia y Fuerzas Armadas* (1980), and *El Proyecto Político Militar* (1983).

GABRIEL AGUILERA, Guatemalan sociologist, former director of ICADIS in San José, Costa Rica; currently working as senior researcher at FLACSO (Guatemala); author of "Los Conflictos en América Latina," in Agustín Silva Michelena, ed., *Paz, Seguridad y Desarrollo en América Latina* (1987).

RAÚL BARRIOS, Bolivian sociologist and international relations researcher at FLACSO (La Paz); author of *Fuerzas Armadas y Revolución Nacional: La Intervención Militar Norteamericana (1952–1964)* (1985).

RAÚL BENÍTEZ MANAUT, Mexican political scientist, and co-author of *Viejos Desafíos, Nuevas Perspectivas: México, Estados Unidos y América Latina* (1988).

FERNANDO BUSTAMANTE, Ecuadorian sociologist and associate researcher at FLACSO (Chile); co-author of *Chile, Democracia y Fuerzas Armadas* (1980) and *El Proyecto Político Militar* (1983).

ANTONIO CAVALLA, Chilean political scientist, former director of the Centro de Estudios Latinoamericanos at the Universidad Nacional Autónoma de México; author of *Geopolitica y Seguridad Nacional en América* (1979).

RICARDO CÓRDOVA, Salvadorean sociologist and international relations analyst; author of *Evaluación de las Maniobras Militares de los Estados Unidos en América Central (1983–1985)* (1986).

LUCRECIA LOZANO, Mexican political scientist and director of studies at the Centro de Estudios Latinoamericanos, Universidad Nacional Autónoma de México.

JOSÉ LUIS PIÑEYRO, Mexican sociologist (University of Rome); researcher and professor of sociology at the Universidad Autónoma Metropolitana–Azcapotzalco, México; author of *Estado y Sociedad en Mexico: Pasado y Presente* (1985).

JUAN RIAL, Uruguayan historian, researcher and director of PEITHO (Sociedad de Análisis Político); author of *Partidos Políticos, Democracia y Autoritarismo* (1984).

ELIÉZER RIZZO DE OLIVEIRA, Brazilian political scientist, researcher and director of the Nucleo de Estudos Estrategicos, Universidad de Campinas, Brasil; author of *Militares: Pensamento e Acao Política* (1987).

MARCIAL RUBIO CORREA, Peruvian lawyer, professor at the Universidad Católica del Perú and researcher at the Centro de Estudios y Promoción del Desarrollo (DESCO), Lima, Perú.

AUGUSTO VARAS, Chilean political sociologist and international relations analyst at the Facultad Latinoamericana de Ciencias Sociales (FLACSO) in Santiago, Chile. He is director of the Latin American Center for Defense and Disarmament (CLADDE), and author of *Militarization and the International Arms Race in Latin America* (1985) and *Soviet-Latin American Relations in the 1980s* (1987).